INTRODUCING SYSTEMATIC SIMPLI
TO MANAGE DECISIO...

G000136782

How a Systematic Simplicity Approach Builds
Clarity about Opportunity, Risk and Uncertainty
Essential to All Best Practice Decision Making

CHRIS CHAPMAN

Emeritus Professor of Management Science
Southampton Business School
University of Southampton
Southampton SO17 1BJ
UK

First published in Great Britain in 2021
Copyright © Chris Chapman

Editing, Design, typesetting and publishing by UK Book Publishing
www.ukbookpublishing.com
ISBN: 978-1-914195-45-7

Contents

Dedication

This book is dedicated to everyone who is interested in user-friendly approaches to keeping it simple in a well-grounded and defensible best practice sense when making any kinds of decisions that really matter as well as other more routine decisions that may not matter very much.

Foreword by Stephen Ward

Whatever your background education and experience or areas of current primary interest, this book can change your view of what 'to manage decisions' ought to involve, and introduce you to valuable practical tools.

Most important decisions with significant consequences are not simple to make. Often the nature and consequences of potential decision options are very complex, and significant uncertainty about possible trade-offs between various performance criteria is involved. In such cases keeping things simple is an attractive proposition. But simplification which obscures important considerations and misrepresents key interactions and trade-offs can be seriously misleading and counterproductive.

When illustrating the systematic simplicity approach, Chris Chapman explains how to pursue the right kind of simplifications – those that facilitate insightful analysis of key issues and lead to better decisions. A central feature of the approach is effective and efficient deconstruction of key factors in ways that maximise clarity for a given level of effort.

Part 1 examples drawn from decades of consulting work and reflection initiate illustration of what is involved. Key concepts are demonstrated in a recommended approach to achieving unbiased estimates, meaningful target setting, and making choices based on efficient trade-offs between all relevant aspects of performance together with associated risk. Part 2 outlines how systematic simplicity can be applied in corporate, project and operations management contexts, discussing the processes underlying Part 1 with additional detail and examples. The general applicability of systematic simplicity concepts is further illustrated by Part 3 case studies addressing difficult trade-offs inherent in appropriate discounting of future cash flows, valuing the risk of fatalities and injuries in safety contexts, and scoping the role of requirements for appropriate regulation of commercial organisations.

Modest opportunities involving routine decisions also need a systematic simplicity approach. Ultimately, the goal of any systematic simplicity application is effective and efficient pursuit of all available opportunities to make smarter decisions that can be identified or created by an enhanced understanding and better treatment of uncertainty and risk.

Stephen Ward is Emeritus Professor in Management,
Southampton Business School,
University of Southampton.

Preface and introduction

Most decision makers want to 'keep it simple' in an appropriate way in all decision making contexts. However, even corporate boards and government bodies making extremely important decisions often 'keep it simple' in ways that guarantee serious mistakes, and less important routine decisions frequently waste time and effort in predictable ways. Usually this is at least in part because senior managers and their supporting planners, analysts and other advisors routinely 'keep it simple' in common practice frameworks which deal with both working assumptions and framing assumptions in a defective manner. Helping to replace this defective common practice with much better practice is this book's overall purpose.

Choosing the 'right kind' of simplicity in all decision making contexts is not easy. However, failing to do so can be seriously damaging. The lack of a well-grounded, rigorously tested and generally applicable 'best practice' literature to support practitioners involves a wide range of issues which this book addresses using a 'systematic simplicity' approach. There are no 'silver bullets', but some approaches are much better than others, and we need to seek the best.

A useful starting point for adopting a 'systematic simplicity' approach is making a commitment to avoid all simplistic approaches which mislead and confuse. A central underlying concern is making full use of all the opportunities available to use the 'right' simplifying assumptions, avoiding any significant risks associated with making the 'wrong' simplifying assumptions, as part of seeing the management of all aspects of opportunity as a primary goal, avoiding all relevant risk as a closely-coupled second order goal. A key issue is always asking the 'right' questions and consistently getting 'good' answers, defining 'good' answers to the 'right' questions as 'fit for purpose' in a way which is 'best practice' given the time and other resources available. Being 'fit for purpose' in this sense includes being 'user friendly' for *everyone* involved in an effectively balanced manner, but *always* avoiding inappropriate 'dumbing down' of the approach taken.

The first and overriding goal for this book is persuading you that the systematic simplicity approach explored and promoted by this book can yield *much better* decisions for a *lot less* effort than a lot of common practice in *any context*, including some of your personal and family decisions, although decision making by organisations is the focus.

The closely-coupled second order goal for this book is convincing you that it would be a good idea to help any organisations of interest to you introduce and continue to develop a systematic simplicity approach. These 'organisations of interest' may be commercial organisations (private sector or public sector), or public sector organisations with no commercial goals, or third sector organisations like charitable trusts.

One basic tenet of a systematic simplicity approach is always using words in a plain English sense without resorting to technical terminology unless a technical interpretation is useful. A second basic tenet is all technical terminology *framing* assumptions should generalise as far as possible, *never inappropriately restrict*. A third basic tenet is usefully restrictive closely-coupled *working* assumptions should be clarified and tested appropriately.

For example, the word 'clarity' as used in this book's subtitle can be given a plain English meaning with no restrictions, but when used in the context of the term 'clarity efficiency', 'clarity' means 'relevant insight which can be communicated effectively to everyone who needs to understand'. The term 'clarity efficient' means 'a maximum level of "clarity" (relevant insight which can be communicated effectively to everyone who needs to understand) for any given level of effort and associated cost'. 'Clarity efficiency' is a central systematic simplicity concept, initially explored and illustrated in Chapter 1.

The words 'opportunity', 'risk' and 'uncertainty' as used in this book's subtitle can all be given plain English meanings which are not restrictive, and linked technical concept working assumptions are important. In these three cases it is important to understand from the outset that technical definitions treated as framing assumptions for several common practice approaches are explicitly rejected because they are inappropriately restrictive.

'Framing assumptions' are deeply embedded 'deciding how to decide' assumptions at several interdependent foundation levels which shape the way we see the world. They are inherently difficult to identify, understand, test and revise. 'Working assumptions' are usually much easier to identify, understand, test and revise, but this is not always done effectively or efficiently. The way framing and working assumptions are addressed is a central issue in this book – when not of immediate concern, always an underlying consideration in the background.

A systematic simplicity approach defines the word 'uncertainty' in *framing* assumption terms as 'lack of certainty', a circular but simple plain English definition chosen to avoid any unintended restrictions. As *working* assumptions for analysis purposes, 'uncertainty' is sometimes usefully clarified by association with one or more of five portrayals:

1. variability uncertainty (inherent or the result of composing different sources of uncertainty of any kind);
2. event uncertainty (involving simple events or complex scenarios which may or may not happen, or assumptions which may or may not hold often referred to as 'conditions');
3. ambiguity uncertainty (which may involve underlying complexity not currently understood or a lack of information, both perhaps partially resolvable at a cost, given time and other resources);
4. capability-culture uncertainty (involving systems and people with the potential for surprises ranging from the implications of ill-designed computer systems to badly trained and poorly motivated staff doing wholly unpredictable things as well as reasonably predictable surprises);
5. systemic uncertainty (involving interdependencies between any sources of uncertainty that have been decomposed, which may be unknown and perhaps unknowable – if we take something apart (decompose it), when we put it back together again (recompose it), we have to address systemic uncertainty explicitly).

Sometimes it is useful to associate numeric probabilities with some or all of the uncertainty of interest, but sometimes a purely qualitative understanding is more useful. Drawing a boundary to distinguish between 'risk' and 'uncertainty' based on quantification or non-quantification is an inappropriately restrictive approach adopted by classical decision theory, rejected by modern decision theory 50 years ago, but still common practice. It is explicitly rejected by a systematic simplicity approach, consistent with modern decision theory as advocated by authors like Howard Raiffa (Raiffa, 1968). Some approaches to 'risk' limit their attention to 'event uncertainty', and some go even further and restrict their attention to expected outcomes associated with 'event uncertainty'. Both of these positions are explicitly rejected by a systematic simplicity approach, consistent with a modern portfolio theory approach to 'risk' and all authors following variants of the ideas developed by Markowitz (1959).

Chapter 1 begins to explore and explain the implications of uncertainty, and Chapter 2 begins to explore and explain the implications of 'risk' and 'opportunity', but fully understanding 'uncertainty', 'risk' and 'opportunity' from a systematic simplicity perspective may require abandoning your current understanding of what these words mean in a technical sense, and you may need to read beyond the end of Part 1 before you start to become really comfortable with a new set of framing and working assumptions for uncertainty, risk and opportunity.

Effective communication and collaboration built upon well-founded trust are amongst the central goals of a systematic simplicity approach. When uncertainty is significant and important ethical issues are involved, the need for effective communication and collaboration built upon well-founded trust becomes particularly obvious, but understanding the value of trust and seeking to preserve trust in an effective and efficient manner is always important.

A holistic and pragmatic view of all relevant uncertainty and underlying complexity is central, as is understanding all associated opportunity and risk, viewing them all from the perspective of a *fully generalised* 'risk efficiency' framework. This is a core framing assumption.

The basic approach to 'risk efficiency' developed by Harry Markowitz in the 1950s won him the Nobel Prize for economics in 1990, and risk efficiency is now central to the foundations of portfolio theory in economics. But with effective fully generalised forms as part of a much broader 'opportunity efficiency' concept, risk efficiency should also be seen as central to the foundations of managing all aspects of any organisation's project management, operations management and corporate management. This is not generally the case.

For this book's purposes, 'risk efficiency' means 'a minimum level of risk for any given level of expected reward', understanding that multiple 'reward' attributes may need attention, and some of these reward attributes may not be worth measuring, while measuring other reward attributes in a direct sense may not be feasible. Illustrative reward attribute examples include money (profit, contribution to profit or cost avoided), reputation in positive terms or loss of reputation avoided, fatalities avoided, injuries avoided, and environmental damage avoided.

A central part of the composite 'opportunity efficiency' concept needed to achieve an effective fully generalised risk efficiency concept is a fully embedded 'clarity efficiency' concept, already defined above.

Another central part of achieving 'opportunity efficiency' involves obtaining the most appropriate trade-offs between risk and expected reward for all reward attributes of interest assuming risk efficiency in terms of each attribute, plus the most appropriate trade-offs between attributes, including trade-offs between clarity and the effort/cost involved in a multiple attribute clarity efficient sense.

Achieving opportunity efficiency in this sense is clearly an exceedingly demanding goal. Even understanding what is involved is not straightforward. But doing our best to understand what is involved, and doing our best to achieve 'best practice' defined in terms of *what ought to be done* in these terms, is *the only acceptable option* from a systematic simplicity perspective.

The book *Enlightened Planning – Using Systematic Simplicity to Clarify Opportunity, Risk and Uncertainty for **Much Better** Management Decision Making* (Chapman, 2019) explores a 'systematic simplicity' approach in detail. It argues that all individuals and all organisations ought to seek their version of this kind of simplicity in explicit terms with ambitious goals tailored to their context. It does so in comprehensive 'what needs to be done' terms, with enough discussion of 'tactical clarity' in a range of contexts to provide a foundation for 'strategic clarity' in individual and corporate terms. Endorsements from a range of perspectives for the book *Enlightened Planning* are included in the first backmatter section of this book. You may find it useful to peruse these to help to satisfy yourself that a systematic simplicity approach is worth understanding to the extent that reading this book is an investment of your time that might pay dividends, but starting to read Part 1 first is a reasonable strategy.

In a project management context, further 'how to do it' tactical clarity elaboration of systematic simplicity is provided by *How to Manage Project Opportunity and Risk – Why **Uncertainty** Management Can Be a **Much** Better Approach than **Risk** Management* (Chapman and Ward, 2011). This 2011 book is the re-titled third edition of a 1997 book with Stephen Ward which was widely critically acclaimed, acknowledged worldwide as defining the leading edge of the field, and a modest international bestseller.

Both my 2019 *Enlightened Planning* book and the 2011 book with Stephen Ward are about an approach to decision making in a planning framework driven by a systematic simplicity approach which provides a synthesis of what management decision making and associated planning ought to involve. This synthesis builds on the work of many pioneers of contributing schools of thought drawn from a wide range of disciplines. The foundations of the systematic simplicity concept are well established and widely used.

This book addresses 'introducing' systematic simplicity in a concise but comprehensive sense. It starts in a different place than both the 2019 and the 2011 books, it takes a different route for a much wider target audience, and it is much shorter. All three books have been written in a way which means they can be read in any order, and this is a good book to start with. However, the chapters need to be read in sequence because of the layered development of the material. The early focus of this book is providing an introductory overview of the basic implications for organisations if a systematic simplicity approach is adopted. Part 1 starts by addressing unbiased estimation of parameters like project durations and costs, but a low clarity introductory exploration of the three kinds of efficiency just outlined is the underlying dominant objective of Chapters 1 and 2. The implications of higher clarity analysis is addressed in Chapters 3 to 5, and the implications of a failure to address opportunity efficiency as a whole is addressed in Chapter 6. Part 2 considers the processes underlying Part 1 analysis and key issues involved when introducing these process concepts into an organisation. Part 3 introduces concerns associated with a range of issues needing additional attention in a systematic simplicity framework, which are worth understanding at the level discussed in this book even if they are not about matters of obvious current interest for most readers.

The particular way a Markowitz approach to risk efficiency is generalised creates the clarity efficiency and opportunity efficiency aspects of these three systematic simplicity frameworks as explained in Part 1. It is why, for example, in the 1970s and 80s, BP International adopted an early systematic simplicity approach with my support over an eight year period for planning and costing offshore North Sea projects, with a risk efficient approach to contingency planning that was also clarity efficient and meant that large or sensitive BP projects were delivered on time and within budget on a worldwide basis for a decade. It is also why IBM UK used an early systematic simplicity framework as a central part of a 1990s culture change programme that I contributed to in a significant manner, designed to encourage all staff to take *more* risk at an individual project level, knowing what they were doing, to *reduce* risk at a corporate level, *and* increase expected corporate profitability. Further, it is why the UK Ministry of Defence (MoD) sought advice about a suitable systematic simplicity approach over the period 2010-13 to address how best to plan strategies designed to protect troops from non-conventional weapon attacks which are inherently difficult to anticipate, defend against and mitigate, with a view to being able to justify the high levels of expenditure anticipated.

Senior managers involved in successful past adoption of prototype versions of systematic simplicity approaches by major organisations have attributed an expected payoff of the order of £100 for every £1 invested in the new toolsets, skillsets and mindsets. But sometimes success has been elusive, or achieved and appreciated for a decade or more but then not sustained, for reasons which need to be understood. Sustained investment of effort and energy coordinated by capable reflective practitioners is required. In capable hands this investment pays very handsome dividends, and the prior investment in capability is demonstrably rewarded.

The systematic simplicity approach this book recommends has been developed following a career centred on a practice-research-teaching-practice cycle driven primarily by practice concerns informed by international consultancy assignments involving significant engagements over many decades. Most of the operational and conceptual tools discussed in this book have been directly tested by a range of major and modest organisations.

The practical examples used in this book involve short case-based 'stories'. Some of these stories are drawn from longer case-based 'tales' in the *Enlightened Planning* book, but the ordering, focus and purpose of all of the stories in this book is very different, and this book is a great deal shorter than *Enlightened Planning* for a number of reasons.

This book is focussed on brief and concise but reasonably nuanced answers to three questions:
1. What are the characteristics of the deliverables of a systematic simplicity approach?
2. What is the scope of the resulting benefits?
3. What is the nature of the requisite investment in capability and culture terms?

Question 3 is important because at both an individual and corporate levels there are 'no free lunches' – a systematic simplicity approach can provide deliverables with huge benefits net of the costs of the effort involved, but the required prior and ongoing investments in capability development and perhaps associated culture change need to be understood and addressed effectively and efficiently.

Part 1 of this book gives priority to questions 1 and 2, with attention to question 3 limited to background for later discussion. Parts 2 and 3 address all three questions, with an emphasis tailored to the topic.

This book urges adoption of a systematic simplicity approach to managing decisions explored in introductory but comprehensive terms in this book and elaborated in *Enlightened Planning* (Chapman, 2019). Doing so can lead to an operational basis for *much better* decision making than most current 'good practice', amounting to a significant step change improvement. Even if 'very good practice' is believed to be the current norm in any organisation of interest to you, demonstrating this is the case is an important by-product of adopting a systematic simplicity approach, and one of the many good reasons for organisations formally embracing an appropriate version of the approach advocated in this book. The ongoing organisational vision ought to be seeking to achieve opportunity efficiency with everyone playing appropriate roles in a well-led collaborative effort, whatever the changes in the organisation's opportunities and threats as our economic, political and social landscape evolves.

Part 1
Introducing efficiency and decomposition concepts

Part 1 provides an introductory overview of several basic concepts which underpin the foundations of a systematic simplicity approach.

The focus of the first two chapters is a low clarity level view of the trio of efficiency concepts: clarity efficiency, risk efficiency and opportunity efficiency, beginning with a low clarity exploration of parameter estimation. The next three chapters explore higher clarity levels of the same basic concepts, illustrating how the additional clarity can be provided by effective and efficient decomposition. A sixth chapter concludes Part 1 by exploring a case-based illustration of why organisations that fail to eliminate the common problem of consistently underestimating project costs are demonstrating symptoms of serious underlying problems which need attention from a holistic systematic simplicity perspective.

Everyone interested in understanding why a systematic simplicity approach might be worth adopting needs the level of clarity about the basic concepts provided in the first few chapters, and most need to develop their understanding much further. How much further you will be persuaded to go will depend upon a number of factors you can begin to judge for yourself as your exploration of Part 1 progresses.

Chapter 1
A minimum clarity estimation approach and the clarity efficiency concept

Basic estimation concerns common to all contexts

One important basic concern for all decision making and all of the personal and organisational planning toolsets needed to support decision making *ought* to be clarity of meaning for all parameter estimates of the measurable attributes being addressed. An equally important basic concern *ought* to be a lack of bias (systematic error) in the estimation processes employed.

These concerns affect an organisation's 'operations management' defined in broad terms to include bottom-up change management strategic choice recommendations which may have highly significant corporate strategy implications. They affect 'project management' defined in broad terms to embrace all management of change including programme management and associated portfolio management (of projects and programmes), plus collaboration with all other parties involved in the same changes. They also affect 'corporate management' defined in broad terms to incorporate all decision making not delegated to operations or project management functions, including top-down strategic planning at board level and overall corporate governance. Some of these operations, project and corporate management aspects of an organisation's decision making are not separable, and estimates of parameters used for making decisions are often central to crucial interdependences which may involve complex issues. Important interdependencies may also link relatively simple personal estimates and associated planning decisions, like 'how long will it take to get to an airport to catch a flight?' and 'what is the best time to leave for the airport on a business trip or a family holiday?'.

As a very simple project management example with obvious operations and corporate management implications, if the duration of a project activity is the attribute of interest, a common practice single value (point) estimate approach *should* prompt everyone involved to ask 'is the single number provided by an organisation's estimation process:

1. an optimistic *aspirational target*, often worth using to manage good luck, and also sometimes very useful as a motivational stretch target, but unlikely to be achieved;
2. or is it a pessimistic *commitment target*, with a high probability of being achieved;
3. or is it a *balanced target* somewhere in the middle, perhaps assumed to be the expected outcome, a 'best estimate' of what should happen 'on average';
4. are *all* aspects of uncertainty *fully* addressed in terms of questions 1, 2 and 3;
5. are *all* of the relevant parties clear about the implications of *all* of the answers?'.

Why organisation-wide understanding of the implications of these questions is important is the initial focus of this chapter, with a view to clarifying why mandating an affirmative answer to question 5 is crucial, and *ought* to be seen as a mandatory aspect of best practice.

In practice, often the answer to the question 'which of the three possible target values outlined above is the point estimate provided?' is 'none of them', because the single value provided is based on adding numbers with a variety of different meanings, perhaps including 'most likely' values. 'Most likely' values are not additive in a meaningful sense unless strong assumptions apply, like 'all of the associated probability distributions are symmetric'. This is sometimes a convenient assumption, but it may not be a robust view of the underlying reality.

Even if all three of these target values are provided, and their natures have been effectively clarified for all of the parties involved, there is an important further interdependent question which needs addressing effectively – 'is it reasonable to assume that there is no significant bias associated with any of the values provided?'.

A minimum clarity approach to estimation

This chapter begins to address these issues by considering a minimum clarity approach to estimation that any organisation adopting a systematic simplicity approach ought to mandate as the lowest acceptable level of clarity for the lowest feasible level of effort/cost in most contexts. It uses an illustrative short story based on a tale which is developed more fully in *Enlightened Planning* (the book *Enlightened Planning* (Chapman, 2019), a clarification of a convenient citation simplification emphasised now because it will not be provided again).

In the early 1990s I was providing a report for the UK MoD on how their approach to project risk management could be improved. In part, my report was based on conversations with the Air Vice Marshal responsible for the MoD procurement budget plus several other senior MoD personnel about what they saw as the crucial defects of the prevailing approach. One conversation was with William (not his real name), who was the project manager for a next generation warship. William indicated that he wanted to base our initial discussion on how his team should be expected to address estimating the duration of obtaining permission for a design change with significant expenditure implications that had landed on his desk that morning.

I suggested that his team start with a simple but clearly defined plausible maximum estimate, using a P90 (ninety percentile value) unless there was a good case for some other percentile value. Those involved should believe that there was approximately a 90% chance of achieving the P90 value employed in terms of all relevant uncertainty. For illustrative purposes William suggested that a P90 of 18 weeks seemed reasonable.

They then needed a compatible plausible minimum estimate, using a P10 (ten percentile value) to match a P90. They should believe that there was approximately a 10% chance of achieving the P10 employed in terms of all relevant uncertainty. William suggested 2 weeks was a compatible P10 estimate.

A corresponding minimum clarity expected outcome was $(2 + 18) / 2 = 10$ weeks, a simple arithmetic average.

This minimum clarity approach to estimation was usefully portrayed employing Figure 1.1, showing a uniform probability distribution in density format, followed by a corresponding linear cumulative probability distribution. This is a 'single scenario' approach which will be identified as a special case in the context of a 'multiple scenario' generalisation shortly. It will be further generalised to accommodate multiple sources of uncertainty later.

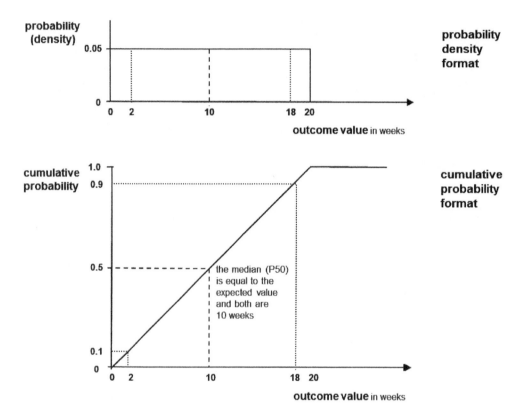

Figure 1.1 A minimum clarity estimation model with the P10 = 2 weeks and the P90 = 18 weeks.

The uniform probability density function model employed by the minimum clarity estimation approach portrayed by Figure 1.1 was usefully associated with an underlying reality which *might* look like the dashed curve in Figure 1.2.

Recognising the uncertainty about the underlying reality is an important characteristic feature of the systematic simplicity approach at all levels of clarity.

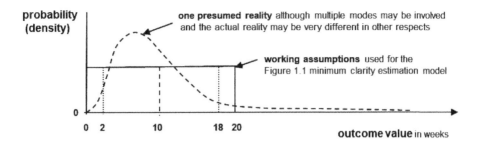

Figure 1.2 One presumed reality underlying the approximation involved in Figure 1.1.

We need to remain aware that what we are assuming to 'keep it simple' involves working assumptions – it does not involve an accurate portrayal of a reality we do not currently know much about and may not be able to fully understand.

This minimum clarity approach was the simplest available, by design. However, its design has been evolved and tested for robustness over many years with widespread use in mind, and:

1. given its simplicity it is surprisingly rich in terms of useful information;
2. its form provides the most flexible available starting point for adding clarity which might be useful if the effort/cost of doing so is worthwhile;
3. it is demonstrably robust.

In terms of information content, the P10 = 2 weeks represented a useful default value for an aspirational target, and the P90 = 18 weeks represented a useful default value for a commitment target. Both of these targets can be given a wide range of interpretations, with no generally imposed restrictions, using different percentile values if this is deemed desirable so long as they are symmetrically spread about a 50 percentile value assumed to define a balanced target equated to the expected outcome. This meant that William's team could use the P10 and P90 values plus the expected value of 10 weeks (assumed to be an appropriate balanced target) in the form of a simple range estimate stated as 10 +/- 8 weeks.

Specification of three separate targets in this simple minimum clarity form was very useful. The ABC of targets (aspirational, balanced and commitment target values) were a starting point for managing uncertainty which *everyone* involved in *creating* or *using* plans at all levels in all areas of an organisation ought to understand *in the same way*. William's team could make base plans using the balanced target (expected value) duration of 10 weeks, contingency plans to exploit good luck if only 2 weeks was required, and further contingency plans to cope with bad luck if 18 weeks was required. Provided everyone involved understood this is what a range (interval) estimate of 10 +/- 8 weeks involved, this was a very rich and useful information set, obtained with very little effort, and expressed concisely for easy communication.

Adding more clarity

If more effort to provide greater clarity looked useful, William's planning team could generalise the minimum clarity model of Figure 1.1 in a number of ways. They could do so within a working assumption that only one source of uncertainty was involved, or they could consider multiple underlying sources of uncertainty, explicitly decomposing different sources of uncertainty for various purposes – effective contingency planning for example.

Preserving the current assumption of 'one source of uncertainty', but relaxing the current 'one scenario' assumption, William's team might use a set of data points from previous experience of design change approvals and basic textbook statistical techniques to construct the five scenario HAT (histogram and probability tree) model of Figure 1.3.

A multiple scenario probability tree portrayal, using five discrete outcomes in this case, underlies the rectangular histogram continuous variable probability density portrayal and the piecewise linear cumulative probability distribution portrayal of Figure 1.3. Using a HAT interpretation of Figure 1.3 initially focussed on the probability tree clearly implies that an expectation of 1 week is associated with the range 0-2 weeks with a probability of 0.1 on the top probability tree branch, an expectation of 3 weeks is associated with the range 2-4 weeks with a probability of 0.4 on a second probability tree branch, and so on. A multiple-

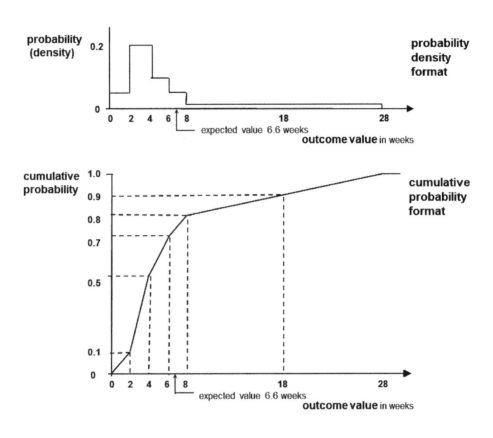

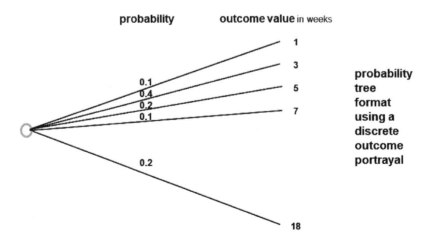

Figure 1.3 A five scenario HAT model with the P10 = 2 weeks and the P90 = 18 weeks.

branch probability tree portrayal like the five-branch portrayal of Figure 1.3 assumed to underlie a continuous variable rectangular histogram portrayal of the same information can be especially valuable as an operational framework for considering both statistical dependence and causal dependence, including addressing different contingency planning responses to particular outcome values. Embedding decision trees whenever contingency planning is relevant is crucial, but so is a flexible approach to associated causal dependence which needs to be decomposed and structured to be managed effectively, and statistical dependence which may not be well behaved but needs a degree of understanding. This *operational* framework also provides an important *conceptual* framework for thinking about uncertainty and its management, even if we sometimes choose not to fully exploit it, comparable to having a general underlying theory to draw on when making simplifying assumptions.

This is an n scenario generalisation of the one scenario Figure 1.1 approach with n = 5, the unrestricted nature of this multiple scenario generalisation of the minimum clarify approach using the HAT framework being another defining characteristic which is a feature of a systematic simplicity approach.

All three of the portrayals used by Figure 1.3 can be useful, but using all three portrayals at the same time will not usually be necessary. Appropriate simplifications can and should be tailored to suit the context.

Planning teams obviously should make the best feasible use of readily available data if they have time to do so. But if William's team were convinced that Figure 1.3 captured the available data and correctly portrayed a 'normal outcome' scenario with an expectation of about 4 weeks in the range 0-8 weeks and a probability of about 0.8, plus a 'high outcome' scenario with an expectation of about 18 weeks in the range 8-28 weeks with a probability of about 0.2, a much simpler two-scenario model might be preferred for contingency planning purposes. This simplified approach might exploit the premise that a 'normal outcome' scenario of 4 weeks with associated modest variability over the range 0-8 weeks was not worth contingency planning effort, but a 'high outcome' scenario of 18 weeks with associated significant variability over the range 8-28 weeks did warrant attention.

Figure 1.4 portrays this two-scenario interpretation, a simpler version of Figure 1.3 in terms of presentation as well as model structure. Figure 1.4 illustrates joint use of continuous variable and probability tree representations in a simple HAT presentation format showing the continuous variable density portrayal plus the discrete variable tree portrayal. It omits the cumulative probability distribution format portrayal to keep the portrayal format simple in a fairly obvious way.

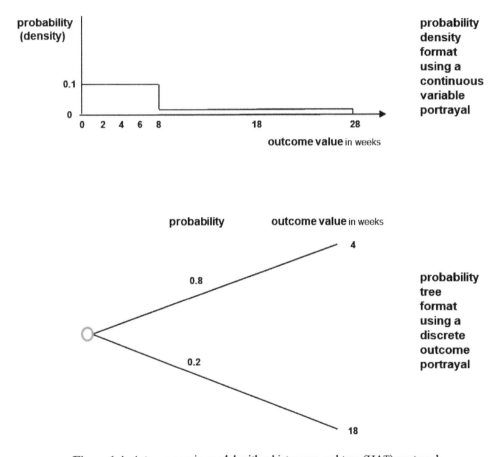

Figure 1.4 A two scenario model with a histogram and tree (HAT) portrayal.

However, had no data been available, requiring a purely subjective estimate by William's team, three scenarios might be the preferred portrayal for both estimation and contingency planning purposes. The grounds might be:

1. most of the people involved thought Figure 1.1 was too simple to be credible for estimation purposes;

2. Figure 1.3 was deemed more complex than necessary;

3. three scenarios seemed to be the most comfortable and useful middle ground.

If William's team wanted to make use of three scenarios, they might choose to employ a format like Figure 1.5. The Figure 1.5 example maintains consistency with the illustrative Figure 1.1 to 1.4 examples, with a P90 estimate of 18 weeks, a P10 of 2 weeks, and a two-week common minimum class width interval. It was defined by also estimating a P80 of 8 weeks and a P20 of 4 weeks.

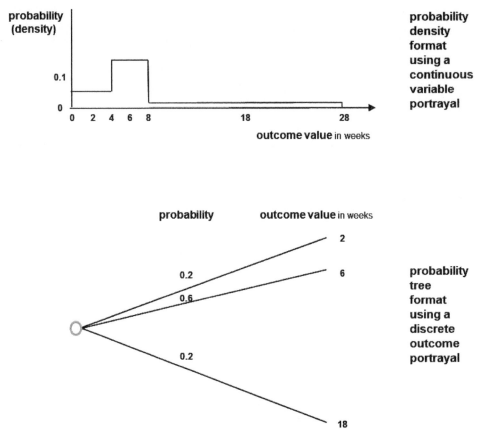

Figure 1.5 A three scenario model with a histogram and tree (HAT) portrayal.

For comparison purposes, compatibility of Figure 1.5 with Figures 1.1 to 1.4 is useful in terms of an illustrative example. But in practice, William's team would not need to worry about this kind of compatibility. Further, they might prefer using a classic three-point Beta distribution specification involving a minimum, maximum and most likely value specification, as discussed by textbooks like Moder and Philips (1970) and used by many project planning teams since the 1960s. Parametric specifications of this kind can be accommodated within a HAT approach, as discussed in *Enlightened Planning*. But using a 'plausible maximum' like a P90 is usually important, and always avoiding direct estimation of an absolute maximum P100 value unless it is clearly defined by the circumstances is a best practice mantra if a systematic simplicity approach is adopted.

Building on this discussion of Figures 1.3 to 1.5, several further points are worth thinking about. First, if they had the data underlying Figures 1.3 and 1.4, this discussion of systematic simplicity approach options *should* get William's team thinking that their data was limited, and their model omits important possibilities beyond the current data set. Second, if they did not have data, when they were thinking about a P90 they might have overlooked the possibility of extremes. For example, in either case, the possibility of a 'very high outcome' scenario with an expected value of 52 weeks (a year) and a probability of about 0.02 (a one in 50 chance) might be important. A 'project cancelled' scenario with a probability of about 0.01 might also be important. If they understood this, and how to address scenarios of this kind, they might begin to see why always starting with a basic minimum clarity estimate as a default position was sound policy. They might also start to see that enhancement of clarity was feasible in a very flexible set of ways. It should then become clear that how *best* to enhance clarity might not involve more refined looking curves and analysis restricted to data, even if reasonable data was available and most of the people involved had a strong current preference for smooth curves based on as much data as possible. They *should* also begin to see why this kind of approach to estimation earlier in a project lifecycle could be extremely valuable. If avoiding the need for expensive design change approvals or a project becoming completely redundant were important potential concerns, these issues might warrant significant early attention in terms of proactive preventative contingency planning, as part of building on a minimum clarity position with a clear agenda for more clarity that was worth the effort and a much better idea about what different kinds of effort might or might not be useful in this context. Precise answers to questions like 'what is the probability of a very long delay?' may not be important, but asking the right questions and then getting unbiased responses in a suitable timeframe for identifying and then making robust choices is always important.

In terms of robustness, if different people believed the presumed reality curve in Figure 1.2 was in different places, these differences of opinion would not actually matter *provided* those involved all believed that the expected outcome and range estimates agreed were reasonably unbiased and the base plan and contingency planning target values being used were appropriate. *However*, a very long right-hand tail associated with the presumed underlying reality would drag to the right *both* the expected value *and* an appropriate commitment target. Experience suggests that this ambiguous long-tailed distribution effect is one extremely good reason why the apparent simplicity of the minimum clarity estimation approach is actually a subtle basis for robustness that is surprisingly sophisticated.

When I used a HAT prototype approach with BP in the 1970s and 80s (as discussed later in this book), BP developed computer software with my support to work with estimate formats comparable to the five-scenario format of Figure 1.3 with the person specifying the estimate choosing to use from 1 to 20 common interval class scenarios as the basic input format. This software could also accommodate Beta distribution specifications using P90 plausible maximums with longer right hand tails than a standard Beta distribution, plus other parametric probability distribution specifications. Monte Carlo simulation approaches embedded in widely available software packages can now perform the same operations with no restrictions on the number of scenarios or the nature of the scenario structure, and HAT approach users can now employ any suitable simulation software. However, you might like to bear in mind that in practice BP planners usually found that from 3 to 10 common interval class scenarios was the most convenient level of precision, sometimes preferring parametrically specified distributions (like a log Normal distribution or a Beta distribution hybrid with Normal distribution tails) converted into a HAT form for computation purposes. Sometimes 10 or more classes associated with scenarios or parametric specifications are useful, but in most client application areas since the 1980s my early preference for the simplicity of a one-scenario approach like Figure 1.1 some of the time, a 2 to 10 scenario approach most of the time, and occasionally more classes or parametric specifications, has steadily moved towards greater systematic simplicity. I now regard the minimum clarity Figure 1.1 approach as a practical first pass approach in many contexts, always assuming that later passes of a multiple pass approach will use more scenarios if the first pass analysis suggests this source of uncertainty needs more attention. An obvious exception is when those involved believe more scenarios are immediately useful and worthwhile. A Figure 1.1 based approach is a systematic simplicity recommended minimum clarity approach in this sense.

Clarity efficiency

A systematic simplicity approach often exploits a deep understanding of underlying complexity to justify the robustness of exceptionally simple tools for routine use. A prior investment in the development of this understanding is required, to ensure that the 'right kind' of simplicity is used and understood, avoiding the 'wrong kind' of simplicity.

Always minimising the overall effort/cost of decision making given the level of clarity required in any given context is the central concern. One useful way to visualise the discussion with William about Figures 1.1 to 1.5 is to consider the concept of 'clarity efficiency', where 'clarity' means relevant insight that can be communicated effectively to everyone who needs to understand. 'Clarity efficiency' is achieved when any given level of clarity is achieved with a minimum level of effort/cost. Clarity efficiency for all levels of clarity which may be feasible can be associated with an 'efficient frontier' as portrayed by Figure 1.6.

Any point on the clarity efficient frontier from point 'a' to point 'd' maximises the level of the clarity provided for any given level of effort/cost associated with acquiring that level of clarity. Point 'c' on Figure 1.6 corresponds to the minimum clarity estimate 10 +/- 8 weeks portrayed by Figure 1.1. The follow-on discussion associated with Figures 1.2 to 1.5 corresponds to an initial exploration of how best to move from point 'c' towards point b_3 on the clarity efficient frontier defined by the boundary from 'c' to 'a'.

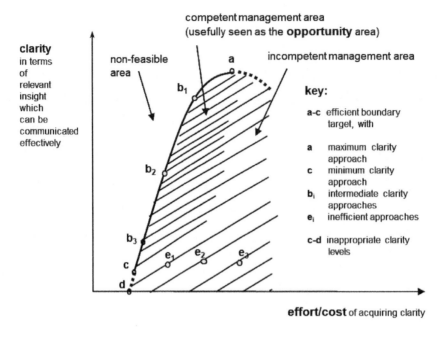

Figure 1.6 Clarity and the effort/cost of acquiring clarity in an 'efficient frontier' portrayal

Any organisation routinely using a probabilistic approach to estimation which does not distinguish low effort first pass approaches from higher effort later pass approaches is arguably failing to manage the opportunity to use less effort to get the clarity needed, potentially operating at points like e_1, e_2 or e_3 instead of a point on the clarity efficient boundary between points 'c' and b_3 on Figure 1.6.

Any organisation using a single value 'point' estimate without clearly indicating its nature is *seriously* clarity inefficient – probably operating at a point *well below* point e_3 on Figure 1.6, using more effort than necessary to get *much* less clarity than needed. A surprising number of organisations habitually persist in working with point estimate approaches that are seriously clarity inefficient. They could simultaneously significantly increase clarity *and* use much less effort if they adopted a systematic simplicity approach involving range estimates like 10 +/- 8 weeks as a starting point in a suitable iterative process, a useful opportunity to use less effort and make better informed decisions.

The region close to the clarity efficient boundary is the competent management area in the sense that best practice *ought* to aim to be on the clarity efficient boundary, and while getting reasonably close to the boundary requires competence, failing to get reasonably close is incompetent. The exact location of the boundary between competence and incompetence is clearly ambiguous and debatable, but the existence of a boundary is not.

A useful way to view the competent management area is as an *opportunity* area in the sense that the approach to opportunity management advocated by this book is about trying to always work in this region, seeking the best point on the clarity efficient boundary. Working in this opportunity area is the clarity efficiency aspect of the overall opportunity efficiency we need to seek, including looking for the optimal trade-off point on the efficient frontier boundary.

Where a planning team should aim to be on the clarity efficient boundary, and how they should proceed to get there, is always highly context dependent, and competence in terms of systematic simplicity approaches is required to make associated judgements. However, if a number of estimates are required as part of any planning analysis, it is generally useful to use an iterative approach to seeking overall clarity efficiency at an appropriate overall level of clarity, starting with clarity efficient estimates at a low level of clarity for all the values of interest. This can include using minimum clarity estimates as a default starting position choice. It should always include adding clarity in an efficient manner to those estimates which seem particularly important.

Starting with a P90 estimate followed by a P10 estimate embracing all relevant uncertainty as the basis of an expected value estimate is a useful first step towards controlling unconscious bias. But much more can and should be done about unconscious bias in a clarity efficient manner if this seems appropriate. Recognising and addressing unconscious bias as approached by authors like Kahneman (2012) can be extremely important.

Conscious bias can also be addressed if relevant, as part of a package of ways of adding clarity and reducing bias. The Air Vice Marshal mentioned earlier in this chapter introduced me to the concept of 'a conspiracy of optimism', a very useful concept embracing conscious and unconscious bias, and a euphemism which I prefer to 'strategic misrepresentation' (Flyvbjerg et al, 2003). 'Strategic misrepresentation' is one version of 'being economical with the truth' which is widely cited in the literature.

All variants of both conscious and unconscious bias need attention in a clarity efficient manner. *Enlightened Planning* provides a starting point for engaging with a very extensive literature.

Expected penalty cost interpretation of balanced target values

Sometimes an 'expected penalty cost' approach to a balanced target using a 'penalty cost function' can be useful for immediate operational reasons, and this option is always useful in the background for conceptual purposes, playing a role comparable to 'useful theory'.

As an illustrative initial example, say we want to move from a personal context estimate like 'it will take me about 90 +/- 30 minutes to travel from my office to the airport check-in desk for a flight that I have to catch to get to a moderately important but routine business meeting' to answering the question 'how long before I need to be there should I leave?'. In this context an expected penalty cost approach lets us weight the 'penalty costs' associated with being early or being late to various degrees using a penalty cost function to weight the amount of time involved. This penalty cost function can reflect the importance of what we think needs doing before we leave, what we can do while waiting at the airport, if we miss our booked flight whether there are further flights later that day that we might get on, the level of importance of the meeting, and so on. At its simplest, being 15 minutes too late has a much higher penalty cost than being 15 minutes early. If B_1 is defined as our basic starting point balanced target time to the airport equal to the expected outcome, it will incorporate a 'provision' for extra time needed on average over and above the aspirational minimum. If B_2 is defined as our balanced target time to the airport incorporating this provision plus an additional 'contingency' of further time not needed on average but useful because being late involves a higher penalty than being early, this higher value incorporating 'provision plus contingency' might be preferred. It could be obtained by weighting possible outcomes by the relevant penalty costs before applying the probability of each outcome to get a weighted expected penalty cost value, with a view to minimising the expected penalty cost value when choosing the time to leave for the airport. This expected penalty cost approach simply involves recognising that all departures from the mean are not equally unwelcome. The weights used will often have to be fairly crude, highly subjective measures of annoyance and anxiety that cannot be assessed with precision. However, imprecise but unbiased weights will do a much better job than no penalty cost weights at all. Equal weights for all outcomes are implicit in using expected outcomes, B_1 instead of B_2. It may be clarity efficient to explicitly use B_2 instead of B_1 with a clear understanding of its meaning and the approximation involved, avoiding bias as far as possible.

One relatively straightforward corporate decision-making example of using a B_2 in this way is setting budgets for projects based on a B_2 estimate. As an illustration, when BP International decided at board level to adopt a prototype systematic simplicity approach to all sensitive or sizable projects on a worldwide basis in the late 1970s, they also mandated using a P80 value to set associated budgets in terms of the measured uncertainty. The BP board appreciated this was not a 'commitment target' in the P90 sense discussed earlier, and not all relevant uncertainty had been measured. They were using a B_2 value balanced target considering the trade-offs between not giving project managers enough contingency (extra money above the expected cost as measured) and giving them too much contingency, addressing *all* the governance cost and incentive implications, bearing in mind not all components of uncertainty had been measured.

In some contexts, the same 'expected penalty cost' approach can help us to understand how to respond to people using and perhaps insisting on single value estimates, plus the implications of insisting on or simply accepting single value estimates ourselves.

For example, a senior colleague you know very well might ask how long it will take you to deliver a project. You might know that he or she wants a single number that they can use with confidence to discuss delivering what others will subsequently expect. In this case you might use a B_2 value balanced target that reflects the pain both of you will feel if you fail to deliver, as well as the rewards of exceeding expectations. You might do so explicitly assuming you have a mutually understood and shared penalty cost function, everyone else involved will understand that you both normally deliver what you say you will deliver in a way which usually exceeds expectations, and you do not need to demonstrate why this is the case on this occasion.

However, if there is a risk of serious problems if everybody involved does not have the same understanding of what a single value means, the results can be painful for everybody. For example, if a senior colleague insists on a lower number for the duration of a project that you have to deliver than you are comfortable with in terms of your own personal B_2 balanced target value, you may be risking your reputation by agreeing, or perhaps even in effect committing yourself to looking for another job just before this project all goes horribly wrong. If those being reported to fail to understand this kind of situation, they may blame you when it goes wrong, your senior colleague, or both of you. Arguably they may also have themselves to blame at least in part for failing to anticipate the muddle which a point estimate approach can create.

What you can infer from these examples is in addition to an expected penalty cost approach to a balanced target using a penalty cost function being operationally useful in a direct way if it is used appropriately, it is also a useful way to view the implications of organisations using single value estimates inappropriately. Sometimes it may be useful to interpret other people's suspected 'strategic misrepresentation' in the Flyvbjerg et al (2003) sense as being driven at least in part by their use of an expected penalty cost approach, implicitly if not explicitly. However, it is important not to confuse the rationale and function of the weights used appropriately in a penalty cost approach with an inappropriate conscious or unconscious bias, with a wide range of possible explanations and associated treatment strategies.

By the end of Part 1 of this book, most readers should be reasonably comfortable with their understanding of uncertainty in terms of B_1 and B_2 balanced targets, how both provide useful information that is quite different to aspirational target values and commitment target values, and why it can be very helpful to understand the roles of all four of these values in some particularly important decision-making contexts.

This expected penalty cost approach provides a useful basis for understanding some aspects of 'risk', but it does not address risk in the risk efficiency sense. By the conclusion of Part 1 all readers should understand why the concept of 'risk' often needs much more sophisticated treatment than a simple penalty cost approach.

Concluding observations

This chapter has briefly explored the use of a very simple minimum clarity approach to estimation, addressing a basic metric for an attribute of interest like the duration of a project activity. It has also used this discussion to provide an initial exploration of the clarity efficiency concept.

The focus of this book is decision making and associated planning by organisations, but most of the systematic simplicity ideas discussed have implications for personal decisions as well. The estimation of parameters is a good illustration of why this is the case.

This chapter's discussion was set within a HAT framework, considering a single source of uncertainty. It explores the generalisation of a basic single scenario portrayal to a multiple scenario portrayal. Later chapters will retain a HAT framework but consider more than one source of uncertainty as the basis of a route to more clarity. This will begin to illustrate the value of developing an understanding of a number of different ways to visualise the decomposition of 'uncertainty'.

One basic form of decomposition involves distinguishing five portrayals of uncertainty as indicated in the 'Preface and introduction' section:

    1. variability uncertainty;

2. event uncertainty;

3. ambiguity uncertainty;

4. capability-culture uncertainty;

5. systemic uncertainty.

The distinction between the first two may involve important inherent differences or just preferred portrayal options. The third involves a lack of knowledge which may be partially resolvable. The fourth involves the capabilities of systems which include computers prone to malfunction plus people prone to human errors, and cultural influences which may be positive or negative. The fifth involves interdependencies which may be simple or very complex.

The complexities associated with systemic uncertainty start to become obvious as soon as we decompose estimates into component sources of uncertainty, the focus of Chapter 3. But they extend beyond the overall estimates used to make decisions. They are also inherent in the processes we use to try to ask the right questions and interpret the answers to act in the right way, and all the associated underlying 'deciding how to decide' choices we make. In this very general sense, they are central to the whole of this book.

Even when employing a minimum clarity estimate using the Figure 1.1 model, it is worth understanding that a very broad view of uncertainty needs to be taken in many contexts. This implies the Figure 1.2 portrayal of underlying uncertainty may not be straightforward to visualise. It is part of the reason that a minimum clarity approach is much more sophisticated than it looks. It is also part of the reason why using a P50 defined by a Figure 1.1 approach as an expected value 'balanced target' is much less pessimistic than it may seem. Many people's first reaction to the suggestion they should use a Figure 1.1 model is 'it is far too pessimistic, and a simple asymmetric model like a Beta distribution is much better'. But the Figure 1.1 model can actually prove far too optimistic. If the reality is a long right-hand tail as Figure 1.2 suggests may be the case, the actual outcome may be a much longer duration than any deemed feasible by a Beta distribution with a P100 plausible maximum as assumed by standard PERT model analysis.

As illustrated with examples later in this book, a systematic simplicity approach generalises key ideas underlying the minimum clarity estimation perspective. It argues that decision making and associated communication is greatly enhanced if *everyone* involved develops a reasonably well-grounded intuitive understanding of the idea that making simplifying assumptions effectively always requires *some* of those involved knowing what very high clarity assumptions to capture requisite complexity can achieve in a reasonably wide variety of example contexts. In some contexts, those providing this expertise may be involved directly. In other contexts, they may be involved indirectly, perhaps by designing processes for others to use as discussed in Part 2. But somebody has to judge which particular aspects of complexity may or may not matter in any given context, even if the contexts currently being addressed are relatively simple.

Those who design the planning and decision-making processes an organisation uses or lead one-off analysis have to understand the implications of alternatives, and everybody else has to trust their judgement if they do not fully understand the rationale. Well-founded trust within an organisation involves everyone trusting their expert advisors in this sense, and experts who cannot be trusted in this sense are a liability needing effective senior management attention, ultimately a board level responsibility. This applies to very simple contexts like estimating parameters, as well as the much more complex contexts we need to move on to now.

Chapter 2
A simple opportunity efficient approach to seeking risk efficiency

The risk efficiency, clarity efficiency and opportunity efficiency trio

A central aspect of effective decision-making is being able to identify and then choose between alternative courses of action to increase expected reward, reduce associated risk, and provide appropriate trade-offs. 'Reward' may need to be addressed in terms of component positive performance attributes like profit, net of component negative performance attributes like cost. Risk-reward trade-offs for any given performance attribute are involved and may need attention, and trade-offs between different performance attributes may also need attention.

One of the core concepts involved is 'risk efficiency'. A 'risk efficient' choice provides a minimum level of risk for any given level of expected outcome in terms of any given attribute of interest. For each attribute of interest, expected outcome and associated risk are two different but interdependent performance criteria which a systematic simplicity approach treats as separate objectives. In the context of a risk efficient choice, 'risk' means the possibility of a 'reward' (positive) objective outcome which is less than that expected, or the possibility of a 'cost' (negative) objective outcome which is greater than that expected, a very general interpretation of 'risk' which is consistent with plain English.

Figure 2.1 portrays expected reward and associated risk in terms of an 'efficient frontier' diagram portrayal, a conceptual tool central to a systematic simplicity perspective.

A diagram comparable to Figure 2.1 was made famous by Harry Markowitz in the 1950s when he developed the foundations of portfolio theory, leading to his 1990 Nobel Prize for Economics, and efficient frontier diagrams for any pair of objectives considered jointly have long been a common practice tool for economics. See *Portfolio Selection: Efficient Diversification of Investments* (Markowitz, 1959) for a classic basic reference.

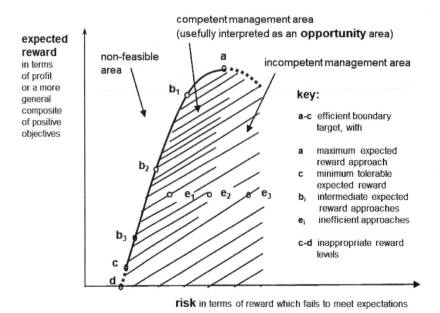

Figure 2.1 Expected reward and associated risk in an 'efficient frontier' portrayal

The clarity efficient frontier diagram of Figure 1.6 employs a similar layout to Figure 2.1 because these two efficiency concepts are comparable and complementary. In both cases we need to seek a point on the efficient frontier boundary with an appropriate trade-off depicted by the slope of the boundary curve at that point. And we should be seeking clarity efficiency and risk efficiency at the same time within a holistic process framework which embraces both, so employing similar layouts to portray both efficient frontier concepts is useful.

The region close to the risk efficient boundary is the competent management region in the sense that best practice ought to aim to be on the risk efficient boundary, and while getting reasonably close to the boundary requires competence, failing to get reasonably close is incompetent. The precise location of the boundary between competence and incompetence is clearly debatable, but the existence of a boundary is not. This is directly comparable to the Figure 1.6 situation.

A useful way to view the competent management region is as an opportunity area in the sense that opportunity management as advocated by this book is about trying to always work in this region, seeking the best point on the risk efficient boundary, again directly comparable to the situation in Figure 1.6. Working in this opportunity area is the risk efficiency aspect of the overall opportunity efficiency we need to seek, including looking for the optimal trade-off point on the risk efficient frontier boundary in a manner that is clarity efficient.

Choosing point 'a' in Figure 2.1 involves ignoring risk and simply maximising expected reward. In many decision-making contexts this may be a preferred and optimal choice, assuming that the risk involved is both bearable and acceptable, because it is clarity efficient. However, in a portfolio of securities context, choosing point 'a' involves 'putting all your eggs in one basket', choosing the one security with the highest expected rate of return. This is not usually considered an optimal portfolio management strategy for a portfolio of securities, the context of direct interest to Markowitz. In a portfolio of securities context, it is usually important to consider taking advantage of the possibility of significantly reducing risk with a minimal loss of expected return by moving towards point b_1. This movement towards point b_1 involves efficient diversification, reducing the level of risk with the minimum loss of expected return to preserve risk efficiency. Points b_2, b_3 and 'c' involve further risk efficient reductions in the level of risk via efficient diversification, with point 'c' associated with the minimum tolerable expected reward.

When Markowitz developed the foundations of portfolio theory using this framework, he assumed that the expected reward on a portfolio of securities could be measured as a linear function of the expected return on individual security rates of return, and a suitable *surrogate* for risk could be measured as a quadratic function of associated variances and covariances. This book and all of my published work since the mid-1970s assumes that this risk efficiency concept needs generalising beyond a mean-variance approach and beyond a portfolio selection context, to provide part of the basic framework for all decision making. This chapter starts to explain the implications. Although most of this book is more directly concerned with choices between two or three discrete alternative options, sometimes it uses this kind of analysis in a pairwise nested manner to address whole portfolios, for corporate strategic planning purposes for example.

Portfolio theory in general terms can address any number of options using any or no subset structures. Part 1 of this book 'keeps it simple' by restricting the focus to choices between two or three options in a project management context.

The focus of a basic Markowitz 'risk efficiency' approach is using quadratic programming to address a single measurable attribute like profit with a view to achieving the highest feasible level of expected reward for any given level of risk measured by variance, understanding the available trade-offs between expected reward and risk, given risk efficiency in this sense, and choosing the maximum level of risk that the decision makers believe is prudent. The focus of the basic systematic simplicity generalisation of risk efficiency is providing a range of low to moderate effort approaches to delivering risk efficiency even if only two discrete option choices are available, and doing so in an effective manner without making any of the restrictive assumptions about the measurement of 'risk' employed by a mean-variance approach, recognising that more than one attribute often needs attention.

Opportunity efficiency builds on underlying risk efficiency and clarity efficiency – it is a higher order composite concept. Opportunity efficiency involves ensuring appropriate trade-offs between expected outcomes and associated risk for all relevant attributes given risk efficiency, plus ensuring appropriate trade-offs between all relevant attributes. This includes the trade-offs between clarity and the effort/cost of acquiring that clarity, bearing in mind the complex multiple attribute nature of 'clarity' and the 'effort/cost' of clarity plus the consequences of insufficient clarity in terms of all relevant attributes.

A simple illustrative example

To initiate discussion of an opportunity efficient approach to risk efficiency, assume that in choosing between alternative decision options only one attribute is of immediate interest, and this attribute is a directly measurable cost. Further, assume that we want to use minimum clarity estimates as discussed in Chapter 1 to choose between the decision options. In this situation a simple low effort decision diagram which uses linear cumulative probability distributions as illustrated by Figure 2.2 can be a valuable tool. Figure 2.2 portrays three decision options with different expected costs and associated cost uncertainty. Consider how such a diagram might be used in a real situation which is very simple for illustrative convenience.

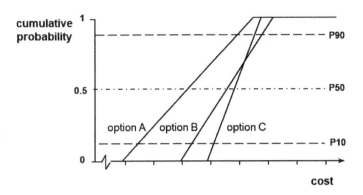

Figure 2.2 Decision diagram: comparison of options A, B and C.

In the mid-1980s, as a newly appointed head of a university academic department, replacing my department's photocopier was one of the first departmental decisions to be made. The need for simple decision diagrams using the format of Figure 2.2 arose at about the same time, and 'the photocopier problem' seemed a useful story to illustrate the low effort and moderate clarity linear decision diagram concept. The intention from the outset was employing this story as a very simple way of communicating an approach that is actually applicable in a very wide variety of much more complex contexts – like the IBM UK illustrations discussed later.

The story begins when my department's only photocopier failed terminally. The service engineer delivering the bad news explained that a new photocopier with appropriate features from his firm would involve a new five-year contract with a rental cost of £x per month plus a servicing charge of £y per copy. The new photocopier could probably be delivered within a few days.

Some idea of the department's likely level of photocopying was clearly needed. The departmental secretary provided records showing copy numbers by months for recent years. This historical record was projected forward for five years, as the basis for an approximate P10 to P90 range estimate for a nominal five-year planning horizon defined by the contract duration. The Figure 2.2 axes were constructed, with the cost scale indicating total cost over the five-year contract period. Contract cost was assumed to be the only attribute of concern as an initial working assumption. The P10 and P90 values were then used along with the service engineer's £x per month and £y per copy contract explanation to obtain the 'option A' linear cumulative probability curve shown in Figure 2.2. Telephoning two alternative photocopier suppliers revealed identical contract structures for photocopiers with comparable features. But the alternative suppliers had higher £x rates and lower £y rates. These rates were used to plot the 'option B' and 'option C' lines in Figure 2.2.

Figure 2.2 suggested option A was the only risk efficient choice, by a significant margin, given the assumptions used to produce it. This was clearly illustrated in terms of what the technical literature calls 'stochastic dominance', because the line portraying option A was well to the left of the lines for options B and C. That is, the expected cost of option A was much lower than the expected cost of options B and C, *and* the probability of options B or C costing more than the expected cost of option A was clearly much greater than the probability of option A costing more than the expected cost of A at all probability levels. Although the cost of option A was more variable than the cost of options B or C, option A was not riskier, because of the significant expected cost advantage of option A. In conventional 'stochastic dominance' terms, option A dominated options B and C. In systematic simplicity terms, option A was the only risk efficient option given these three choices and the other working assumptions.

In terms of Figure 2.1, if option A was associated with the risk efficient point b_2, options B and C might be associated with risk inefficient points in the region of e_1 and e_2.

Continuing to assume that cost as currently measured was the only attribute of interest for the moment, and looking back to the Figure 1.2 *presumed reality* underlying the working assumption for Figure 1.1, the uniform probability density function and associated linear cumulative distribution seemed a reassuringly robust assumption given the size of the gap between the option A line and the lines for the other two options. Formally checking that this was the case was a very basic robustness test, and it was important to be aware of the need to make this kind of robustness test. It involved asking the question 'could plausible assumed alternative realities underlying the measurement of contract cost as portrayed by Figure 2.2 make options B or C preferable?'. The size of the gap between the option A line and the option B and C lines suggested this aspect of the analysis was reasonably robust.

Testing the robustness of the analysis in terms of further attributes which might be relevant was arguably even more important than testing the robustness of the linearity assumptions associated with the measured attribute, and doing so raised very different kinds of issues. Some of these issues were reasonably straightforward to deal with, but others required much more care and attention. In general, a systematic simplicity approach to all comparable decisions requires a 'clarified dominance' generalisation of the conventional 'stochastic dominance' concept which deals with all the further potential attributes that might matter and all related issues that might matter.

The premise that copying speed might matter was tested next. This robustness test began by asking 'was the copying speed of option A faster than that of options B and C?'. Assuming copying speed is measurable simply by consulting supplier specifications, checking the specifications of all three photocopier options confirmed that option A was faster than options B and C – so option A dominated on this criterion too. No further effort was required in terms of the initial working assumption that copying speed did not matter. Had option A been significantly slower than options B or C, the cost of the additional time lost by people waiting for copies might have been estimated in opportunity cost terms. But a simple 'was the contract cost difference worth the speed difference?' question and answer might have sufficed, depending on the figures involved and the perceived importance of copying speed relative to the importance of cost.

The third robustness test began by asking 'was there any evidence that options B or C might be more reliable than option A?'. There was no evidence about B or C, but the departmental secretary assured me that the old photocopier had been very reliable for many years before its terminal failure, so option A seemed to dominate on the reliability attribute in terms of readily available data with no significant incentive to seek more data, and no obvious need to think about reliability-cost trade-offs in opportunity or shadow cost terms.

The fourth robustness test began by asking 'was the departmental secretary happy with the anticipated noise level of the option A photocopier, and any other relevant features or aspects, including its colour and style, given it would be in the departmental office which was her office?'. Enquiring about the noise level, colour, style and any other relevant features of the options and involving the departmental secretary in the choice was an obvious matter of courtesy. It suits the flow of the story to introduce these issues now, but in fact this would have been the best place to start, including asking her at the outset if there were any issues other than those considered above which she thought ought to be explored. She was better placed to see some relevant forthcoming technology and organisational changes than I was. She was also the most directly interested party, and her views were crucial. If colour or style or noise or some combination of these issues mattered, Figure 2.2 was still relevant, but the attributes and associated objectives of interest to the departmental secretary would need very careful, explicit attention, and if they were important enough, they might prove the dominant concerns in shadow cost terms. She liked the option A features on all counts, so it remained the obvious choice, without the need to make extensive comparisons with options B and C.

The fifth robustness test began by asking 'could the supplier of option A actually deliver a new photocopier in a few days?'. If several months might be involved, making the use of option A non-feasible, the choice might move to options B or C.

This raised new issues. Options B and C were *both* risk efficient in terms of the contract cost attribute assuming option A was not available – but option B involved a lower expected outcome cost than C in conjunction with a higher level of risk, indicated by the lines crossing above the expected values. This was associated with option B having a lower £x rate than option C but a higher £y rate, so the expected outcome was lower but the outcome was more variable, and this time the linear cumulative probability distribution curves crossed, implying that option B could cost more than option C.

However, in practice the relatively small additional cost 'risk' associated with option B relative to C was just 'noise' – it was not worth worrying about. It was *bearable* risk and *acceptable* risk, in the sense that my department's financial viability was not threatened by taking this risk and taking it was worthwhile if expected cost could be lowered as a consequence. Because this level of cost risk was just noise which could be ignored, it made sense to go for the lowest expected cost, and choose option B if option A was not available. More generally, it might be *very* important to use Figure 2.2 or a variant directly relevant to a context of interest to explain why 'risk' *should* be ignored, to make decision making both simpler and more effective simultaneously, an improvement in terms of both clarity efficiency and risk efficiency.

Changing photocopier supplier also raised a further new concern. The supplier of option B did not have an established reliability track record with my department, so reliability would now require recognition as a potentially important issue. This in turn clarified the fact that a valuable new option required identification – the option A supplier making an interim machine available until the ordered one could be delivered.

In general, we are always free to think about new options if the current set of options seems unsatisfactory for any reason, an important fall-back contingency planning option to always keep in mind.

It may help you to remember this if you always include a residual 'any other options we have not yet considered' possibility.

Concluding reflections

One key point this story should make clear is that Figure 2.2 is a simple but effective decision diagram portrayal of risk efficiency in terms of one 'primary' attribute, defining the primary attribute in this case as contract cost because that is the attribute that is the initial focus of interest. But the role of this decision diagram is very much richer than the portrayal of risk efficiency in terms of a single attribute. It is a moderate clarity portrayal of option choice implications that also facilitates testing for robustness in terms of *all further attributes which may be relevant,* and trade-offs involving relevant additional attributes can be considered in a manner involving modest effort that is reasonably effective even if some of the relevant attributes are not worth measuring or not amenable to measuring. Figure 2.2 provides all the clarity needed in this relatively simple context, and it demonstrates clarity efficiency at an appropriate clarity versus effort/cost of clarity trade-off position in a way that can be adapted for different contexts which might be much more complex.

A linked point worth noting here is if you are used to using the low effort decision diagram approach of Figure 2.2 and visualising range estimates associated with P50 expected values and a minimum clarity uniform probability density function model, you may not even need to draw Figure 2.2 equivalents to visualise the expected cost and cost risk trade-offs involved, just using spreadsheet equivalents. *Enlightened Planning* chapter 6 explores an illustrative example based on work with IBM UK in detail if you want to pursue this later.

Another related general issue of crucial importance, which this story and Figure 2.2 should clarify directly, is if risk is just noise for some attributes, in the sense that it is both bearable and acceptable when taking risk facilitates improving expected outcomes, then just using expected values is *a very important shortcut* within the risk efficiency framework adopted by a systematic simplicity approach *whatever the approach used to estimate expected values.* A particularly important special case involves ignoring risk, sometimes just using deterministic models based on unbiased expected values for parameters, but always acknowledging the potential importance of uncertainty. Knowing that this is the case *in advance* improves clarity efficiency, because it facilitates a highly valuable opportunity to achieve more insight for less effort/cost. In the right circumstances ignoring risk can be opportunity efficient because it is both risk efficient and clarity efficient.

A further learning point is that variability and risk should *never* be confused – option A involves significantly *greater* contract cost variability than B or C, but much *less* risk. This is clearly demonstrated in Figure 2.2 by the different slopes, but the large gap between the lines for options A and B or C, because the low £x rate for option A which takes the option A line significantly to the left of the B and C lines more than neutralises the cost variability driven by the higher £y rate for option A. This addresses a complication with Markowitz's mean-variance approach to risk efficiency which he clearly understood, but many people using his approach do not. Variance is *never* an appropriate *direct* measure of risk. Variance is only an appropriate *surrogate* measure of risk *given* a particular assumed expected outcome *and given* probability distributions with the same shape can be assumed. Uncertainty addressed using the stochastic dominance approach employed within the decision diagram framework of Figure 2.2 can include *all* relevant uncertainty without restrictive assumptions.

A set of related general points made earlier are worth additional more focussed emphasis here. Potentially important secondary attributes like photocopier speed, which are easily measurable if relevant, may require trade-off consideration. Secondary attributes like reliability, which is more difficult to measure, may not be worth measuring, but consideration of the issues raised may still be needed. Inherently non-measurable issues, like the implications of the photocopier's colour or style, may also prove important. These kinds of secondary attributes may need consideration in relation to a primary attribute like contract cost which can and should be measured, with questions like 'if option B is the preferred choice in terms of a set of non-measurable or simply not measured advantages and disadvantages concisely expressed in verbal terms, is the contract cost difference between options A and B worth it?'. If the choice is a close call, this may suggest further effort and care to consider differences would be worthwhile. *Most* practical decision-making contexts require the consideration of a *primary* attribute (like contract cost in this simple example) *plus* a number of *secondary* attributes. Sometimes the secondary attributes actually prove to be more important than what was initially identified as the primary attribute, and attributes not worth trying to measure or non-measurable may be crucial even if they are not the most important attributes.

Such considerations might reveal preferences not previously articulated. For example, as the decision maker in a variant of this example I might identify a shadow price/cost associated with insisting upon a photocopier with a slightly higher copy speed by constraining the option choice, and use an argument like 'it will cost about £x per month more to have a photocopier which is y% faster, but bearing in mind staff convenience as well as the financial cost of their time, having undertaken consultation I think the extra cost is worthwhile'. If the trade-offs are important for some of the parties involved, and collaboration/trust issues matter, this kind of 'revealed preference' interpretation, yielding an explicit shadow price/ cost explanation of the trade-offs used to make choices, may be useful.

In the 1990s, IBM UK made extensive use of variants of Figure 2.2 in a bidding case study used for a culture change programme and in the subsequent development of bidding processes as discussed briefly in Chapter 5 of this book, extensively in chapters 3 and 6 of *Enlightened Planning*. All of the learning points developed so far in this chapter were central to the IBM UK culture change programme and its *Enlightened Planning* discussion, including the use of a 'traffic light' system of blue to green to red lights to flag concerns that suggest strong positive or strong negative reasons for favouring or avoiding specific options which are not directly measurable, associated with the use of 'smiles' and 'frowns' tests. For example, in the context of bidding for a £20 million contract, option A might involve keeping a significant portion of the contract in-house while option B involved using a subcontractor. The in-house option A might attract a 'frowns test' red light if the in-house staff required are already seriously overstretched on another crucial contract, but a 'smiles test' blue light if they need the work and could provide non-price 'quality' advantages which the subcontractor could not provide and the potential customer would value, a neutral green light if no significant positive or negative issues of this kind were involved. The subcontractor option B might attract a blue light if they are a strategic partner needing explicit encouragement and support at this stage in a developing relationship, a red light if they are not a strategic partner and signs of unreliability are discernible, a neutral green light if no significant positive or negative issues of this kind were involved.

More generally, what is crucial is:

1. starting with a simple low effort approach, which can address more complexity whenever doing so looks worthwhile;
2. comprehensive, effective and efficient assessment of robustness for the simple approach employed initially, testing all relevant simplifying working assumptions to decide whether or not more complexity to achieve further clarity is worthwhile;
3. seeking more clarity of the kind that is needed when and where it is needed;
4. a possible expansion of the option set, with creativity an essential capability;
5. an ability to deal with additional attributes as well as the initially assumed primary attribute, sometimes using formal but simple mechanisms like 'smiles tests' and 'frowns tests', sometimes relying upon informally applied judgements of issues not given any formal analysis treatment.

The starting point for any particular analysis will always be context specific, and the operational toolset employed should be as simple and easy to use as possible, but the conceptual toolset drawn upon should be as general and flexible as possible, to facilitate systematically avoiding simplifying assumptions which are not robust.

Markowitz could use a version of the Figure 2.1 risk efficient frontier diagram as an *operational* tool, because he used variance as a directly measurable surrogate metric for risk. But variance is not a sufficiently general metric for risk for a systematic simplicity approach. The simple linear cumulative probability distribution approach employed by Figure 2.1 might suggest using variance as a metric, but the framing of the Figure 2.1 approach lends itself to asymmetric nonlinear generalisations discussed in Chapters 4 and 5. This means that the risk efficient frontier portrayed by Figure 2.1 is not an operational tool for systematic simplicity purposes. However, the risk efficient frontier concept is still a very useful *conceptual* tool.

Clarity efficiency was usefully portrayed using the efficient frontier diagram of

Figure 1.6, but because 'clarity' and the associated 'cost of clarity' are both multiple attribute concerns that are not measurable in general, the clarity efficient frontier portrayed by Figure 1.6 is a conceptual tool without an operational variant in any framework.

Opportunity efficiency is also a conceptual tool of great importance. But opportunity efficiency cannot even be associated with an illustrative graphical tool like Figures 1.6 or 2.1 in a direct way, because it involves a complex set of trade-offs in more than two dimensions.

An underlying mathematical framework for opportunity efficiency can be exploited as a conceptual tool with operational tool implications in ways touched on later in this book, and some aspects of this underlying opportunity efficiency framework will have been intuitively obvious to some readers from the outset. In brief, for those who are interested now, it is based upon a goal programming approach – see for example a review paper by Tamiz, Jones and Romero (1998). Goal programming generalises the quadratic programming approach used by Markowitz to maximise one 'primary' objective with any number of relevant further objectives labelled 'secondary' objectives and visualised as constraints, initially set at assumed target levels of achievement. An initial optimal solution yields a set of shadow prices or costs defining the trade-offs between the primary objective and all secondary objectives at the optimal solution. An iterative process can then be used to converge to a solution involving an optimal set of trade-offs between all objectives. Expected attribute values and associated risk can be viewed as separate related objectives. The choice of a 'primary' objective is a matter of convenience, and some 'secondary' objectives may in practice be both more important than the 'primary' objective and not measurable. Part 3 of this book will further clarify what is involved, and *Enlightened Planning* will help you to take it further if you wish to.

This chapter used a particularly simple example to illustrate several quite general strategies for seeking clarity efficient approaches to multiple attribute analysis contexts that may be highly complex. For example, one useful strategy involves starting by assuming that an analysis based on the expected outcome and associated risk of the attribute of primary interest may provide a solution which dominates in terms of all secondary attributes. If this is done, then testing the robustness of this assumption for each potentially relevant secondary attribute has to follow, ensuring that no attributes that matter are overlooked, even if they are difficult to measure or completely impossible to measure. More generally, when seeking opportunity efficiency a central concern is testing the robustness of a 'clarified dominance hypothesis' associated with a suitable set of decision diagrams and other supporting tools by repeatedly asking the question 'is it worth trying to measure anything else before we consider making a decision, bearing in mind the costs and benefits of more measurement, and repeatedly asking the question "are there any further concerns which need qualitative attention", whether or not they are measurable?'.

If any potentially important further attribute is not measurable, the only choice may be to look at the difference in cost and ask 'is the difference worth it?' in consultation with all relevant parties, employing a consultation process that all relevant parties will respond to positively and trust. In these circumstances, collaboration/trust may be a crucial concern. If any potentially important further attribute is measurable, it can be important to assess whether or not doing so is worthwhile. We always need to make sensible judgements based on what has been measured and what has not been measured but might be important.

This book is about *systematically simple quantitative* analysis underpinned by appropriate *systematically simple qualitative* analysis, constraining the exploration of complexity to what pays. Most of the time we can keep it reasonably simple. However, there are occasions when considerable complexity must be confronted, including two or more attributes which both really matter. For example, in a safety context one key attribute is lives which might be lost, a second is life-changing injuries which might be sustained, and a third is cost concerns associated with reducing the risk of both lost lives and injuries.

Further, from a systematic simplicity perspective it is very important to appreciate that whatever the level of sophistication of the quantitative and qualitative analysis being used, there are important limitations on both what can be measured in quantitative analysis terms and what can even be considered in purely qualitative terms in a systematic formal manner.

The primary reason for raising these issues now is to explicitly and emphatically avoid the impression that systematic simplicity means quantification is essential or central or even universally feasible. Often quantification is not worthwhile if an effective qualitative analysis is convincing. Frequently further quantification is not worthwhile if effective partial quantification plus appropriate further qualitative analysis is convincing. Crucially, whatever the level of formal quantitative analysis, management decision making almost always also needs further qualitative analysis plus sound well-grounded intuition and informal planning, and it needs to employ creative thinking throughout.

The role of opportunity efficiency is of central importance in terms of any viable definition of what 'best practice' *ought* to be. In addition to the crucial underlying roles of risk efficiency and clarity efficiency, appropriate trade-offs between multiple attributes and between expected values and associated risk for any relevant attributes must be sought in an effective manner for best practice to be achieved.

Chapter 3
High clarity decomposition of sources of uncertainty for contingency planning

Decomposing uncertainty into multiple sources

The single source of uncertainty assumptions associated with the attribute assumed to be the primary or initial concern in Chapters 1 and 2 was a convenient simplification. However, there may be multiple reasons for assuming that decomposing uncertainty into more than one 'source of uncertainty' would provide useful additional clarity in relation to any given attribute of interest. Exploring the clarity efficient boundary of Figure 1.6 in the b_2 to b_1 region needs attention now, decomposing uncertainty into multiple sources to examine the high clarity end of the low to high clarity spectrum.

This chapter explores decomposing sources of uncertainty for contingency planning purposes. The initial concern might be seen as simply increasing clarity to facilitate effective and efficient contingency planning with a view to providing expected outcome and associated variability range estimates which can be trusted. However, further clarity efficiency attribute concerns are involved. They include making effective and efficient use of data, delivering a high level of risk efficiency in a clarity efficient manner, and enhanced overall opportunity efficiency. Yielding a high rate of return on the effort invested in a revised approach to planning is the overall goal – and aiming to achieve risk efficiency in a fully generalised sense is actually at the core of that goal.

A BP offshore projects example

In 1976 I began an eight-year consultancy relationship with BP International in London to advise them on planning and costing approaches for offshore North Sea projects. The primary concern initially motivating the senior BP project managers involved was understanding uncertainty with a view to being able to deliver these £ billion projects on time and within budget. That was achieved to the immediate satisfaction of the senior project managers and the BP board, and later demonstrated more formally to the board by statistical analysis of actual outcomes versus expected outcomes, budgets and associated conditions (assumptions). The focus of this chapter is what was involved when initiating uncertainty decomposition to deliver a clarity efficient approach to completing projects on time and within budget. However, almost immediately effective and efficient contingency planning was seen as the focus, and achieving the risk efficiency concerns addressed in the next chapter soon became the primary goal, closely coupled to a growing *corporate* understanding that *unbiased interval (range based) estimates could be delivered as a by-product of an effective quest for risk efficiency.*

Beginning with a focus on unbiased interval estimates of cost by project planning and costing teams who had to embrace effective contingency planning, we quickly agreed that cost was largely driven by time, so we had to start with an activity duration focus in the E&D (Execution and Delivery) strategy stage of their projects, the first project lifecycle stage which involved them directly. As explained in Part 2 of this book, using the terminology of *Enlightened Planning* as a basis for discussion, the E&D strategy stage can be viewed as the third project lifecycle strategy stage, following a concept strategy stage and a DOT (Design, Operation and Termination) strategy stage, and project management planning and costing staff often have a limited role until the E&D strategy stage is reached. We also quickly agreed that we had to use *much* simpler project planning and costing activity structures than current practice to facilitate capturing the very complex uncertainty relationships involved. Within this simplified activity structure, the uncertainty associated with activity durations and some other cost components needed a flexible approach to decomposition which was designed to be clarity efficient at a fairly high level of clarity. We did not use the terms 'clarity efficient' or 'E&D strategy stage' at that time, but *Enlightened Planning* terminology is used throughout this book as part of simplifying and clarifying the discussion as far as possible, defining this terminology when necessary as this book progresses.

As an example of a simple activity structure component which warranted a complex uncertainty decomposition structure, one activity associated with the first project addressed involved laying a pipeline between an offshore oil production platform and a shore-based terminal. A traditional basic PERT (Program Evaluation and Review Technique) model would associate this activity with a single source of uncertainty defined by a single probability distribution. However, weather defined in terms of wave height for any given working day was a key aspect of the uncertainty involved in this case: summers were generally good, winters were impossible, and shoulder seasons were tricky. Good monthly weather data was available. This meant that a month-by-month analysis (Markovian) framework developed for GERT (Graphical Evaluation and Review Technique) models would be invaluable. We also embedded an understanding of different specific sources of uncertainty for a rich variety of reasons borrowed from the sophisticated fault and event tree analysis approaches to safety analysis used for contexts like assessing the safety of nuclear power station operation. Further, we embedded Generalised PERT (using decision trees to model responses), addressing specific problems as well as delay for combinations of reasons.

The very good data available on wave heights by sea area could be used to estimate the expected number of lay-days (working days) per month that a barge with a given wave height capability could expect to achieve, and associated variability, the first source of uncertainty considered on its own. An anticipated possible start date and an estimated average productivity rate could be used to develop clarity about what weather variability would do to the pipelaying activity duration in a given assumed month given no other sources of uncertainty.

A second source of uncertainty could then be explored within this month-by-month analysis framework, like wet or dry buckles. The pipe is normally laid on the ocean floor using a smooth 'S' shape from the lay-barge, but when a 'wet buckle' occurs the pipe develops a kink which fractures the steel core of the pipe, letting water in. The pipe then rapidly becomes too heavy for the barge to hold. It has to be released very quickly if possible, or it rips itself off the barge. In either case it sinks to the ocean floor, and fills with water and debris. The basic 'repair' response operation has an expected duration of about a month, and is highly weather dependent. The risk of a wet buckle happening in the first place is highly weather dependent, a function of the lay-barge wave height capability specification, and dependent upon other aspects of the capability of the barge and its crew.

A 'dry buckle' was an example of a relatively minor 'productivity variations' source of uncertainty. Productivity variations on their own meant that an expected lay-rate like 3 km per day could be the assumed average rate for laying pipe on days the weather allowed, with variability that could be assumed to cancel out. If a dry buckle occurs, water does not get into the pipe, so the barge can in effect backup, cut off the damaged pipe, and carry on, with a limited loss of time and pipe.

All sources of uncertainty which cancelled out relative to an unbiased expected rate of progress, and would be left to the lay-barge contractor to manage, could be put into this residual 'productivity variations' source of uncertainty. In clarity efficiency terms it was not cost effective to bother decomposing them. But weather variability, wet buckles, plus about a dozen other sources of uncertainty needed separate treatment and careful BP contingency planning attention to enhance risk efficiency as well as increasing clarity to avoid biased estimates.

The assumed response to any source of uncertainty can give rise to 'secondary sources of uncertainty', part of the complexity which may need to be understood. For example, 'repairing' a wet buckle involves sending down divers to cut off the damaged pipe and fit a 'cap' with valves to release the water in the pipeline when a 'pig' (a torpedo shaped object) is sent through the pipeline under air pressure from the shore end to 'dewater' the pipeline. The pig may get stuck on rocks or other debris in the pipeline during this dewatering activity, and a 'stuck pig' was a secondary source of uncertainty of potential importance. It needed effective prior contingency planning.

In many cases it may be important to understand a number of these secondary sources, and in some cases further higher order uncertainty may prove crucial. For example, a stuck pig might be overcome by sending down divers to cut off the pipeline behind the pig, fitting another cap, and trying again. But this may involve the loss of a lot of coated pipe which will be difficult to replace without delaying the whole project significantly. Another stuck pig response is turning up the air pressure to pop the pig through. But this could damage the pipeline and lead to even more lost pipe.

Knock-on dependency issues may be very important, like the need for more coated pipe which may not be available without significant delays. In this case, ordering extra pipe in advance is one possible approach. This raised questions like 'should BP use a common pipe specification for successive projects, so pipe ordered for one project which does not get used for that project can be used for the next?' It also raised questions about how far dependencies and immediate knock-on effects plus wider implications were worth exploring in detail to achieve clarity efficiency at an appropriate level.

A total project activity set in the range 20 to 50 activities was the target for BP offshore projects. Not all of these activities benefited in clarity efficiency terms from the use of the month-by-month analysis framework, but almost all benefited from about 5 to 15 separate 'primary' sources of uncertainty associated with each activity, with 'secondary' sources of uncertainty associated with some after-the-fact 'reactive' responses and 'preventative' responses. Systematic identification of both 'specific' responses which dealt with specific sources of uncertainty and 'general' responses which dealt with sets of sources, including unidentified sources, was widely seen as crucial to clarity efficiency and risk efficiency, at board level as well as within the project planning and costing teams.

The PERT, Generalised PERT and GERT ideas were discussed in a book I was familiar with (Moder and Philips, 1970), and I had used these approaches a year earlier as a consultant on a very large Arctic pipeline project in Canada, working for Acres Consulting Services. The separate specific sources of uncertainty and follow-on specific response structure ideas were the result of a new synthesis of this experience plus nuclear power station seismic (earthquake) risk consulting experience with Acres, which BP were persuaded to try out, and quickly accepted as a crucial step forward in terms of effective contingency planning.

The multiple key roles of high clarity sensitivity diagrams

To facilitate understanding the multiple roles of uncertainty decomposition, and to link this chapter's discussion of BP high clarity decomposition of uncertainty approach to the discussion of earlier and later chapters, consider BP use of a high clarity 'sensitivity diagram' for a 'jacket fabrication' activity. The 'jacket' is the steel structure pinned to the ocean floor which supports the facilities used to produce the oil by the 'platform'. Fabrication of the jacket took place in a 'yard' (dry dock). Figure 3.1 is the variant of the BP sensitivity diagram used to plan its fabrication at the time.

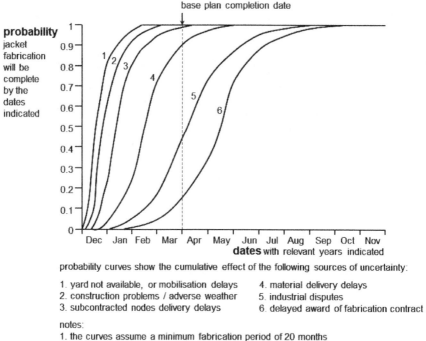

probability curves show the cumulative effect of the following sources of uncertainty:

1. yard not available, or mobilisation delays   4. material delivery delays
2. construction problems / adverse weather   5. industrial disputes
3. subcontracted nodes delivery delays   6. delayed award of fabrication contract

notes:
1. the curves assume a minimum fabrication period of 20 months
2. no work is transferred offsite to improve progress
3. no major fire, explosion or other damage

Figure 3.1 Sensitivity diagram: North Sea oil project platform 'jacket fabrication' example.

Figure 3.1 curve 6 portrays the joint effect of six 'sources of uncertainty' which had been quantified (using a prototype HAT approach) and combined making appropriate statistical and causal dependence assumptions. Some of these 'sources' involved further decomposition not portrayed by this diagram (source 1, for example – with two components explored shortly). Curve 1 portrays the effect of source 1, curve 2 portrays the effect of sources 1 + 2, curve 3 portrays 1 + 2 + 3, and so on. The gap between the curves portrays the potential impact of each successive source. For example, Figure 3.1 indicates that source 1 might have zero impact or lead to an assumed maximum delay of about two months, and source 2 adds about a week to the minimum, a couple of weeks to the maximum.

The 'base plan completion date' at the end of March was an estimate initially inherited by the project manager from earlier feasibility studies, to be adjusted if necessary. Curve 6 suggests a chance of achieving this date in terms of the assumptions used of about 15%.

Sources 2 and 3 were clearly relatively unimportant, source 4 slightly more important than 2 or 3, but less important than sources 5 or 6. Figure 3.1 and variants of this kind of sensitivity diagram could be used by all the people involved in undertaking and interpreting the analysis, in different ways at different times, to communicate effectively, and to drive the way the analysis was pursued effectively. Everyone needed to be aware of the relative size and importance of the complete set of sources as currently assessed in quantitative terms. They also needed to understand the role of the conditions (associated assumptions) flagged by the notes, an important form of qualitative analysis of uncertainty that required understanding for unbiased interpretation of the quantitative analysis.

There was no role for a variant of Figure 3.1 underlying the line A portrayal of option A in the Figure 2.2 decision diagram discussed in Chapter 2, because the Figure 2.2 approach used only one source of uncertainty. However, in the BP context Figure 3.1 proved itself very helpful at several levels for a number of purposes, and the way it was used provides an initial illustration of both the value of decomposing uncertainty and the value of an iterative approach to using the results.

The ordering of the sources in a sensitivity diagram like Figure 3.1 has three kinds of rationale which need understanding.

One is the value of ordering sources of uncertainty in a way that reflects time sequence and causality directions for storytelling purposes. For example, source 1 in in Figure 3.1 is the first source of uncertainty encountered, and source 2 cannot be encountered until source 1 has been overcome.

A second rationale is the importance of ordering to reflect dependence relationships which may need formal causal modelling or formal conditional dependence specification structures. If the nature or characteristics of source n depends upon source n-1 outcomes, that is the ordering needed. Sometimes source n may have a very complex relationship with source n-1, n-2 and so on, what is often referred to as a 'cascade effect'. Facilitating a sophisticated understanding of relevant aspects of dependence can be a very important aspect of the ordering of uncertainty sources.

A third rationale is the value of ordering sources to facilitate delivering specific messages. For example, the ordering of the sources in the Figure 3.1 format, with the potential impact of source 6 added last, provided a very useful basis for encouraging those responsible for letting the contract to avoid delays if possible. The project manager who selected the Figure 3.1 format initially had a message he wanted to communicate effectively to the managers responsible for possible delays to the award of the contract: 'if the chance of delayed award of the fabrication contract can be eliminated, then the 0.15 probability of achieving the base plan completion date at the end of March (as indicated by curve 6) is increased to 0.45 (as indicated by curve 5)'. That is, curve 6 portrays the effect of all six sources, and removing source 6 means curve 5 becomes the new overall total.

Other people subsequently made effective use of Figure 3.1 in other ways. For example, the planner who initially estimated the source 5 contribution based it on extensive industry knowledge but no direct analysis of data. He was motivated by the relative size and importance of this source to systematically search for data and analyse it carefully. Analysis of available data confirmed he had sized the uncertainty correctly, but indicated he had misunderstood the underlying causes and how they might be dealt with. The industrial disputes in his data set had all occurred towards the end of contracts when no more work was coming into the yard – the workforce was facing layoffs. This was one of the consequences of a 'feast or famine' unstable market for this kind of dry dock facility, and unstable prices and market inefficiencies were probably further consequences. If energy majors could collaborate on the timing of their demand for these facilities, they could probably get better prices for jacket fabrication contracts in addition to reducing industrial dispute problems, a recommendation which the project manager later took to the board.

Key roles for underlying source-response diagrams

The planner who sized the two components of source 1 needed to separate them initially to think about two mutually exclusive issues which might delay getting started at the contracted date: unfinished work in the yard might require completion, causing delay to BP's project, or if the yard had not been used for some time, acquiring a fully trained workforce might lead to significant delays. Combining them as source 1 was subsequently convenient for most purposes, but they needed initial consideration separately.

Everyone concerned with formulating and interpreting Figure 3.1 needed to be aware that a carefully composed qualitative analysis framework underlay the Figure 3.1 portrayal of the quantitative analysis results. Figure 3.2 illustrates the portion of it associated with source 1.

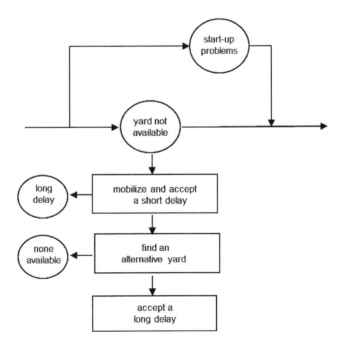

Figure 3.2 Source-response diagram: source 1 in Figure 3.1.

The qualitative analysis portrayed by Figure 3.2 clarified assumptions which the planner who produced curve 1 on Figure 3.1 had to understand before he addressed quantitative analysis, and his colleagues might need to understand to interpret curve 1. BP would not respond to 'start-up problems', leaving the yard to deal with them. A short delay due to 'yard not available' would be accepted, with 'mobilise' involving perhaps the delivery of steel to an adjacent site. If a long delay was involved, BP would try to find an alternative yard. But if an alternative yard was not available, BP would have to accept a long delay.

Further specific decomposed sources of uncertainty which could all happen followed on to the right, for as many pages as necessary. 'General responses', dealing with an uncertainty residual of all specific responses to identified specific sources, were shown on the far right-hand side. Preventative responses which could be specific or general were discussed in notes above. All relevant dependencies were highlighted in appropriate ways. The systematic generation, discussion and documentation control associated with the use of Figure 3.2 variants addressing all sources of uncertainty and all proactive and reactive responses for all project activities plus all the identified interdependencies was central to the process developed for BP and the understanding of uncertainty which that process delivered.

Everyone involved agreed that the quality of the qualitative thinking and associated formal analysis underlying the quantitative analysis was greatly improved by this flexible approach to the portrayal of the qualitative analysis, and effective communication of the rationale for all recommended decisions was greatly enhanced as well. Further, the way Figure 3.1 and 3.2 variants for all project activities contributed to a systematic documentation of the basis of decisions was soon seen as invaluable for a wide range of reasons, including 'capturing corporate knowledge' for reuse on later projects as well as later on in the current project.

Concluding reflections

In terms of the Figure 1.6 discussion of clarity efficiency in Chapter 1, the discussion of this chapter is about points in the region from b_2 to b_1 on the clarity efficiency boundary. The pipelaying discussion might be associated with point b_1, and the jacket fabrication discussion might be associated with point b_2, because the fabrication activity did not require a month-by-month analysis approach or the same level of sophistication in terms of primary or secondary sources of uncertainty. The discussions in Chapters 1 and 2 were about point 'c' and the region between point 'c' and point b_3. Most organisations in most contexts need enough operational knowledge about the region between point 'c' and point b_2 to understand in broad terms the implications of the simplifications they are using on a routine basis when working in the region between points 'c' and b_2. But they also need some conceptual understanding of the region between points b_2 and b_1 to enrich their operational skills and provide the insight necessary to seek help when levels of clarity beyond their current skillset seem to require attention.

What this implies will become clearer in following chapters. In some respects, seeking clarity efficiency is a very simple idea, but in other respects seeking clarity efficiency is a very subtle proposition which requires an evolving understanding.

A key aspect explored in this chapter is the clarity enhancement provided by decomposing uncertainty about how long a project activity might take. Using the pipelaying examples, some source of uncertainty components might involve variability uncertainty (weather in terms of wave heights, for example). Other components might involve event uncertainty (wet buckles, for example). Ambiguity uncertainty was often involved (detailed plans deemed not worth addressing until later in the lifecycle, like the use of a simple productivity variations provision per month, with considerable concern for lack of bias for the expected value, but little concern for variability which would cancel out over the activity duration). Systemic uncertainty was generally crucial. The HAT approach facilitated a sophisticated approach to general and specific contingency planning responses to deal with causal dependency structures as well as sophisticated approaches to statistical dependence. Capability-culture uncertainty sources were not addressed in these studies, and were not a problem at that time.

To some extent the additional effort associated with this detailed decomposition of uncertainty sources was offset by using a much simpler activity decomposition structure for the strategic planning being addressed than had been the practice earlier – a target of 20 activities with an upper limit of about 50 for £ billion projects, instead of the hundreds of activities used before a prototype systematic simplicity approach was adopted.

To help to clarify the relationship between the Figures 3.1 and 3.2 treatment of jacket fabrication duration and the Chapter 1 single source of uncertainty treatment of William's design change activity, first observe that the Figure 3.1 note 1 assumption 'the curves assume a minimum fabrication period of 20 months' was a starting position minimum feasible duration assumption comparable to a P0 for William. It was used to define the x-axis dates scale origin point as the beginning of December. Source 1 on its own could account for a delay of more than two months in terms of the P100 for the curve 1 estimate. A possible delay of more than 10 months was implied by the P100 value of curve 6. The P0 value of curve 6 was late January, but an arguably much more useful curve 6 plausible minimum was defined by the P10 in March, close to the end of March 'base plan completion date'. A diplomatic way to refer to the 'base plan completion date' might have been a 'plausible stretch target', but a need for diplomacy about this issue did not arise. A comparably robust plausible maximum associated with curve 6 was a P90 in mid-July, implying an eight-month P10 to P90 range. Note 3 indicates the kinds of adverse extreme events which curve 6 does not attempt to measure, and note 2 indicates the nature of further contingency planning which might marginally improve the outlook – a possible opportunity not yet explored.

Everybody using Figures 3.1 and 3.2 who understood the overall approach appreciated what had been measured, what had not been measured, and the implications for the base plan completion date which the project had inherited from a much earlier concept strategy stage estimate that the current project manager and his team had not been involved in. They also understood that the additional clarity relative to the approaches used earlier was very worthwhile, and it had been acquired using a very effective and efficient process for clarifying preventative and reactive contingency planning that all well-founded plans facing complex uncertainty needed to address.

This chapter has outlined the nature of the planning process BP developed based on a gradually evolving perspective that was ultimately driven by a clarity efficient quest for risk efficiency in an opportunity efficiency framework. But this chapter has not discussed the central role of the decision diagrams used to achieve risk efficiency. By the time prototype systematic simplicity analysis of the first BP offshore North Sea project was complete, the quest for risk efficiency was seen as the central issue by everyone involved.

The next two chapters focus on some key features of risk efficiency which you need to understand in a high clarity framework in order to understand why seeking risk efficiency is important, and why from a systematic simplicity perspective any approach to management practice that does not explicitly address risk efficiency needs to be replaced by one that does.

Chapter 4
A high clarity demonstration of risk efficiency and enlightened caution

A high clarity demonstration of risk efficiency

As explained in Chapter 2, a 'risk efficient' choice provides a minimum level of risk for any given level of expected outcome in terms of any given attribute of interest. For each attribute of interest, expected outcome and associated risk are two different but interdependent performance criteria treated as separate objectives. In the context of risk efficiency, 'risk' means the possibility of a 'reward' (positive) objective outcome which is less than that expected, or the possibility of a 'cost' (negative) objective outcome which is greater than that expected. Figure 2.1 portrays the risk efficient boundary we want to be on, and Figure 2.2 provides a simple linear decision diagram tool for achieving this in many circumstances. However, a higher clarity portrayal of risk may be important, especially if the probability distribution associated with any of the possible option choices involves significant asymmetry.

Figure 4.1 is a useful illustration of a high clarity decision diagram portrayal of risk efficiency illustrating an enlightened caution choice. It was used initially during the assessment of the first BP project using the prototype systematic simplicity approach.

Figure 4.1 was employed by a BP project manager to compare the use of a 3.0 m (metre) wave height capability barge and a 1.6 m barge to complete a 'hook-up' activity. This hook-up activity involved using a 'hook-up barge' to connect an installed platform to the pipeline laid by a lay-barge. The initial base plan assumed this hook-up activity would take place in August using a 1.6 m barge. However, the analysis of all relevant sources of uncertainty prior to completion of both pipelaying and platform installation, in addition to sources of uncertainty during the hook-up activity, suggested hook-up being completed in August was unlikely; October or November were more plausible targets, and there was about

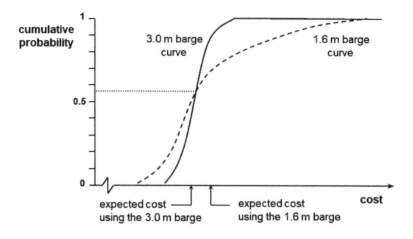

Figure 4.1 Decision diagram: one risk efficient choice example.

a 10% chance that a spring completion would be needed if the 1.6 m barge option was selected. The knock-on costs of 'going into a second season' were of the order of £100 million. It was the 10% chance of an extra £100 million that initially triggered considering a 3.0 m barge, which would cost more than twice as much per working day, but cope with much worse weather. There was a better than 50% chance that the 1.6 m barge would prove cheaper than the 3.0 m barge, as shown by the point on Figure 4.1 where the two curves cross; but the expected cost of using the 3.0 m barge was less, by about £5 million; and the risk associated with the 3.0 m barge was also less.

What the project manager understood clearly from this decision diagram was in terms of cost as measured he only had one risk efficient choice – the 3.0 m barge. Its expected cost was about £5 million less, *and* it was much less risky, because its cumulative probability curve rose relatively vertically. The exact shape of the 1.6 m curve did not matter, but the long right-hand tail driven by a possible delay until the following spring had two implications which both mattered. The asymmetric uncertainty associated with the long tail of the 1.6 m curve dragged the expected cost value to a level well above the 3.0 m barge option, *in addition* to exposing BP to the risk of a cost outcome well above the expected value.

What later users of this high clarity approach to achieving risk efficiency understood was this was a good example of using what became known as 'enlightened caution'. Using enlightened caution involves understanding how to look for and choose options that will be more expensive most of the time, but risk efficient (less expensive on average and less risky), because the alternatives which are less expensive most of the time have a highly asymmetric probability distribution involving very high possible values. Another way to look at this is avoiding 'unenlightened gambles', defined as gambles which are not risk efficient – on average it does not pay to take them.

Using this example to illustrate clearly why risk efficiency matters

When the project manager eventually completed the analysis of his whole project for the E&D strategy stage and used it to seek approval for his strategic plans by the board, with a budget and a mandate to start detailed planning, he took Figure 4.1 to the board with the 3.0 m barge for hook-up associated with a revised base plan. He used Figure 4.1 to help explain the concept of risk efficiency now being sought as a central driving concern for the new planning process which this project had been pioneering. He explained that this one decision to switch from a 1.6 m hook-up barge to a 3.0 m hook-up barge increased the expected return (reduced the expected cost) by about £5 million, *and* simultaneously reduced the risk of cost overruns.

He emphasised that this particular decision was a close call – what later became known as an example of 'enlightened caution' – because it needed a high clarity decision diagram supported by a high clarity decomposition of uncertainty to identify and communicate what was involved. He did not use the term 'enlightened caution' at the time, but he clearly understood the usefulness of this particular example, and he explained that his project planning team had often uncovered massive increases in risk efficiency which were more obvious, comparable to the 3.0 m barge curve being even farther to the left. He emphasised Figure 4.1 played an important role in his planning team's understanding because it made them all clearly aware of the need to search for opportunities to employ specific and general responses which were both proactive and reactive to reduce expected cost and risk simultaneously.

He also believed it was an especially useful example for demonstrating clearly to the board why planning based on the use of high clarity decision diagrams like Figure 4.1 to ensure all important choices were risk efficient was an investment in much better decision-making which provided a high expected rate of return at a lower level of risk. This new planning process was not just about giving them comfort that duration and cost estimates were unbiased. It was about *reducing expected cost in order to increase expected reward in conjunction with less risk.*

He did not cite the £100 return for every £1 invested in this kind of analysis later used regularly by a very senior MoD colleague, who implemented the MoD study discussed in Chapter 1 and many others. Nor did he spend a lot of time explaining that the proactive response to hook-up activity delay, which a change to the 3.0 m barge involved, could be seen as both a *specific* response to dealing with bad weather during the hook-up activity and a *general* response to delays to the preceding pipelaying activity and all of its preceding activities plus delays in the preceding jacket installation activity and all of its preceding activities. However, he did make it clear that in terms of the project as a whole, the new planning approach delivered a massive expected return on investment in terms of reducing expected overall project cost, *and* associated overall project cost risk was reduced, *and* he believed unbiased estimates providing well-founded confidence in project duration and cost estimates should now be the norm.

Budgets based on enlightened provisions and contingencies

The board approved his plans plus a budget set in a new manner based on clearly defined contingencies as well as provisions, and the project came in on-time and within budget, despite some surprises. Provisions were expected expenditures based on all quantified sources of uncertainty reflecting statistically and causally modelled dependencies using the HAT framework. Contingencies involved a further uplift, which should not be needed on average as assessed using quantitative analysis, to provide an 80% chance of staying within budget in terms of the quantified uncertainty. In the board's judgement this was deemed to be an appropriate level of confidence for a budget figure. It was comparable to a commitment target in some respects, but it was explicitly based on the B_2

penalty cost approach to a balanced target addressing too much versus too little contingency. It did not embrace the full set of more general 'commitment target' properties which could be associated with a P90 mentioned in Chapter 1. But it did address some governance and other cost trade-offs. And from the outset it formally recognised that some of the identified conditions might not hold (not all identified sources of uncertainty had been quantified, as illustrated by the 'notes' on Figure 3.1). Later it also acknowledged that some previously unidentified surprises should be expected.

It is important that some 'unknown unknowns' – as 'surprises' were referred to later – should be anticipated, even if their nature was inherently unpredictable. Indeed, a very important part of the role of 'general responses' in terms of achieving risk efficiency was coping with what was inherently unpredictable *plus* what was not worth predicting given the robustness of a rich general response set.

Further, in terms of setting budgets and controlling expenditure, dealing with unknown unknowns effectively and efficiently is important. The term 'enlightened provisions and contingencies' was not used at the time, but it might be a useful term to apply now, *if* the complete set of provision and contingency sums *explicitly* covered both the known and unknown unknowns *and* the uplift associated with the 80% confidence level for the quantified uncertainty in a way which reflected an appropriate corporate penalty cost function associated with being under or over budget.

Concluding reflections

In addition to approving this particular project, the board also endorsed the new project planning process it had pioneered and decided to mandate it on a worldwide basis for all future large or sensitive BP projects. After about five years the unbiased nature of the new approach to estimates was verified by statistical analysis of estimates and outcomes. The eight years that I worked with BP was one of my career's most successful partnerships, and I remain deeply impressed by all the BP people that I worked with. Robin Charlwood, an Acres Consulting Services colleague I am still in touch with, introduced me to the BP project managers to trigger the initial contract, and BP software as well as BP prototype systematic simplicity approaches were subsequently used for a series of Acres' clients in Canada and the USA.

After about a decade the mandated BP systematic simplicity prototype approach to project planning was changed again, as part of a significant portfolio of other changes in approach. The driver of these changes was BP moving away from direct management of project risks towards letting their contractors manage risk. The overall consequences of the board changing approaches again after a decade were complex, relevant to the next chapter, and touched on again later in this book.

Chapter 5
Enlightened gambles and enlightened prudence

Sometimes taking more risk as a culture change proposition

In the 1990s I accepted an invitation to play a role in the IBM UK Forum 2 programme which had a significant impact on my understanding of a systematic simplicity perspective. The Forum 2 programme was designed by IBM senior executives and training staff with my support to change IBM corporate culture. The change involved a new focus on *most* IBM decision makers taking *more* risk as well as systematically seeking risk efficiency, understanding that both achieving risk efficiency and taking more bearable and acceptable risk were essential to avoid important corporate level risks associated with changes in the marketplace and the nature of their competitors. The idea that it might be desirable, even essential, for *any* decision makers to deliberately take *more* risk was initially counterintuitive for many of those involved. But the necessary culture change required everyone becoming convinced that *in most contexts* they needed to take more risk *knowing what they were doing*, always embracing a risk efficiency driven approach to all management decision making, sometimes exercising prudence. Clarity about the role of enlightened caution coupled to a distinction between enlightened and unenlightened gambles and the role of enlightened prudence was enthusiastically welcomed by everyone involved, and seen as central to both knowing what they were doing using a new decision-making approach and the behavioural changes needed. Taking more of the right kind of risk as well as less of the wrong kind of risk was the explicit IBM goal, within a process based on achieving risk efficiency. This is a crucial aspect of understanding opportunity efficiency, which needs to be fully understood to achieve 'best practice' in any meaningful sense. But it is not a recognisable aspect of most common practice. That is part of the reason why organisations need to introduce *and sustain* the ongoing development of a systematic simplicity approach with a reasonably nuanced understanding of what is involved.

Building on an elaboration of the Figure 4.1 story

All senior and middle level IBM UK managers attended one of about 40 two-day sessions, with about 30 people at each session. The IBM UK Chief Executive Officer (CEO) spent about half an hour opening the first day of each session, introducing the agenda and explaining the objectives. I then spent the rest of the first morning on presentations. In the afternoon I used a carefully designed case study to link the morning's messages to outlining what IBM staff had to do to implement the ideas. The second day was spent discussing implementation by the IBM staff in terms of their particular concerns, building on day 1.

My morning presentations on the first day started with the use of Figure 2.1 to provide an overview explanation of risk efficiency in terms of an efficient frontier perspective. Figure 4.1 was then used to explain how employing decision diagrams in a high clarity form by BP demonstrated to everyone involved that higher expected reward as well as less risk could be achieved even in very complex circumstances.

The 'enlightened caution' aspect of the 3.0 m barge choice decision made using Figure 4.1 was then explained, contrasting it to the 'unenlightened gamble' of the 1.6 m barge choice. The explanation outlined in the last chapter was then elaborated, starting by pointing out that the hook-up activity actually took place in October, in good weather. Given this outcome it was very important for the project manager's reputation and future career prospects that the analysis provided after-the-fact evidence that the project manager had made the right choice, *and* managed the project very effectively to get to the hook-up by October, *and* BP had been lucky with the weather. The message being emphasised by this elaboration was that using a prototype systematic simplicity approach had been crucial to BP making the best available choice in the first place, *and* it was also crucial to recognising that the best choice had been made *after* the activity had been completed *when they might have got away with an 'unenlightened gamble'*. IBM needed comparable capability, based on in depth understanding of what always seeking risk efficiency involved, although in practice they might use much simpler tools than BP required, and formal analysis would not always be needed once the culture change took place.

A hypothetical 'enlightened gamble' decision was then considered using Figure 5.1. Creating Figure 5.1 for the Forum 2 programme involved simply moving the 3.0 m barge curve on Figure 4.1 to the right, so that the £5 million expected cost advantage for the 3.0 m barge on Figure 4.1 was transformed into a £5 million expected cost disadvantage for the 3.0 m barge on Figure 5.1. If the probability estimates involved in the actual case portrayed by Figure 4.1 had been different, Figure 5.1 might have been the result obtained by the BP planners.

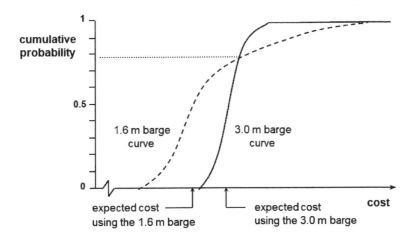

Figure 5.1 Decision diagram: two risk efficient choices example.

Two questions for IBM staff to address using Figure 5.1 were:
1. 'if this was the case, what would BP project planners probably do?';
2. 'what messages should IBM staff take from this in terms of the need to sometimes take more risk, knowing what they were doing, as emphasised by their CEO?'.

To address the first question, I suggested that the 10% chance of an extra £100 million associated with the long right-hand tail for the 1.6 m barge choice clearly needed to be understood by the project manager and communicated effectively to his board. Assuming that this was done, it was reasonable to assume the risk would be accepted to take advantage of the expected cost advantage of £5 million. The rationale was that this kind of project had an expected cost of about

£1 billion in late 1970s £s, with possible 'very bad luck' scenarios doubling or trebling this amount. To cope with this level of risk, BP often collaborated with other oil majors, sharing risks and rewards, a form of insurance/diversification. Having put these arrangements in place to cope with this high level of risk, at the £100 million level of risk involved here they could afford to accept the risk and maximise expected reward by minimising expected cost, and it was actually very important to see doing so as an opportunity.

In this case the 1.6 m barge choice would be an 'enlightened gamble', worth taking. And in this case, if the enlightened gamble did not pay off because they were unlucky, the risk involved was big enough to be worth using Figure 5.1 *in advance* to explain the nature of the gamble and the rationale for taking it to the board, so that if the extra £100 million 'bad luck' scenario arose, this outcome would not be inappropriately associated with 'bad management'.

If, over all of their projects, BP made 20 comparable decisions per annum, on average they would save about 20 x £5 million = £100 million, an important further boost to the expected profit increase driven by getting on the risk efficient frontier portrayed by Figure 2.1. In terms of the Figure 2.1 portrayal, in addition to moving from points like e_1 to points like b_2 for less risk and higher expected reward, they would be moving from points like b_2 towards points like b_1 for higher expected reward involving a bearable and acceptable increase in risk.

All IBM staff needed to appreciate that risk at a corporate level needed effective management, and at a corporate level a very complex portfolio of corporate strategic management issues was involved, some of which required enlightened prudence. However, most IBM staff were focussed on operations and project management concerns at a level where taking enlightened gambles as well as achieving risk efficiency should be the focus most of the time. They needed to be aware of the need for 'enlightened prudence' in some circumstances, and when appropriate they might need to test for a possible reduction in risk in a risk efficient manner to avoid taking an imprudent level of risk. They also needed to be aware that the boundary between enlightened gambles and enlightened prudence was sometimes not a simple or straightforward matter. But they needed to be clear that avoiding risk because of prudence concerns was not the central issue most of the time *at their level of decision making.*

In a context like Figure 4.1, the 1.6 m hook-up barge choice was an 'unenlightened gamble' in the sense that it was risk inefficient – it involved less expected reward and more risk. The 'enlightened caution' 3.0 m hook-up barge choice was the only risk efficient option in the context of Figure 4.1. Most of the time a single risk efficient choice would be much more obvious, with any risk inefficient choice curves further to the right. Crucially, once people understand what they are looking for, and how the relevant supporting tools for making decisions within a systematic simplicity approach work, they might not even need to use the tools in an operational form much of the time. The tools would become part of a conceptual toolset and mindset which would help to transform the culture.

In a context like Figure 5.1, the 1.6 m hook-up barge choice was an 'enlightened gamble' in the sense that a risk efficient choice involving less risk was available, but the risk involved was well within the organisation's risk-taking capabilities, and the risk involved was worth accepting to achieve the additional expected reward. The organisation should have a 'risk appetite' concept defined in a risk efficiency framework which facilitated taking this level of risk and recognised that some enlightened gambles would involve unfavourable outcomes.

If the 'bad luck' scenario associated with Figures 4.1 or 5.1 was not a 10% chance of an additional cost of £100 million, but a plausible chance of an additional cost of £100 billion, arguably the gamble would clearly be imprudent and inappropriate whether or not a higher expected reward was involved.

Selective use of decision diagrams like Figures 4.1 and 5.1 can be the key to corporate clarification of the difference between bad luck and bad management, or between good luck and good management. This can help to drive a very fundamental and important culture change, based on all relevant decision makers taking the right kind and level of risk based on the right kind of analysis. Very clear corporate understanding of why inappropriate risk avoidance and associated counterproductive 'risk appetite' concepts unrelated to risk efficiency need to be eliminated has to be part of this movement to a new kind of 'managing opportunity culture'. Taking appropriate gambles with a 'no *inappropriate* blame' culture should be a clear goal that everybody understands, with everyone accountable for the quality of their decision making. Avoiding confusing good or bad luck with the quality of the decision making can be a fundamental and transformative aspect of a required culture change.

All of these culture change ideas need to be understood by all relevant parties to effectively implement a systematic simplicity approach. Further, organisations need to invest in a comprehensive understanding of the underlying conceptual tools, like the clarity efficient frontier portrayal of an opportunity region provided by Figure 1.6, and the risk efficient frontier portrayal of an opportunity region provided by Figure 2.1. Operational tools matter too, like decision diagrams and sensitivity diagrams. Relevant staff need an appropriate conceptual level of understanding of high clarity decision diagrams like Figures 4.1 and 5.1, plus high clarity sensitivity diagrams like Figure 3.1 and underlying source-response diagrams like Figure 3.2. They also need to be comfortable with operational use of lower clarity variants of decision diagrams like Figure 2.2. If this can be achieved, *much* better decision making using a *lot* less effort should become the norm, a step change in terms of a whole new vision of what 'best practice' *ought* to mean, and why introducing systematic simplicity to manage decisions in terms of seeking opportunity efficiency is essential.

Developing an effective understanding of how to use Figure 2.2 format simple linear decision diagrams was central to the IBM Forum 2 case study exercise, building on the understanding of Figures 4.1 and 5.1 developed during earlier presentation discussions. The IBM case study exercise began to explore the multiple attribute concerns associated with opportunity efficiency as discussed in Chapter 2 of this book, using a bidding context which all IBM staff could associate with, even if they were not directly involved in sales. The context was suggested by a senior IBM executive who helped to guide my design of the overall approach. It drew on my understanding of the kinds of issues discussed in Chapter 2, but it soon took me well beyond my prior expectations of what was feasible, and it proved to be a significant learning experience for me as well as for the IBM staff. For example, I built into the case study an option to use a subcontractor which involved a lower expected cost but the risk of a hostile takeover with possible adverse effects that could be significant. My purpose was to see if they would take account of the 'red light' test aspects of this risk. One IBM bidding team came up with a 'friendly takeover' strategy which generated a 'blue light' linked to the longer term corporate advantages of keeping this subcontractor available to IBM, unanticipated creative thinking built into the *Enlightened Planning* chapter 6 discussion. In my view, just over the first day of their Forum 2 programme many of the IBM staff developed a much more sophisticated and nuanced understanding of opportunity efficiency in terms of multiple attributes and the importance of attributes that were not easily measured than some of the BP project planners I worked with for several years, although the IBM staff clearly did not acquire the depth of understanding of BP project planners in some other areas.

Concluding reflections

One general lesson which I drew from the Forum 2 programme was the importance of all the IBM staff involved understanding how the high clarity tools operate in conceptual terms, *plus* how simpler low clarity variants can often meet the required decision-making needs with less effort if the higher clarity option is used as an effective alternative to 'useful theory'. This was clearly illustrated by the conceptual importance of Figures 4.1 and 5.1 coupled to the practical application of Figure 2.2 variants.

A second general lesson was how important creativity is, illustrated by the friendly takeover counter to the hostile takeover threat identified by IBM staff during their case study exercise.

A third general lesson was how different people working in different areas can take advantage of the same basic systematic simplicity frameworks and concepts to achieve significant management decision-making improvements involving creative adaptation to the context. This was illustrated by IBM safety management staff developing a very sophisticated understanding of how to justify a much simpler and significantly less expensive approach to meeting UK building regulations on fire safety *as well as* IBM international corporate rules using my consultancy support on a separate contract triggered by Forum 2.

For any organisation, a carefully designed in-house programme comparable to the Forum 2 programme should be able to equip people engaged in a wide range of roles with sufficient understanding of what is involved to get them started in their areas of particular focus. But the design of a Forum 2 programme equivalent which is best suited to all the context features of any given organisation is not a simple matter, and there are many other alternative routes to organisations adopting and developing a systematic simplicity approach. Some recommended options are briefly explored in the final chapter of Part 2.

Chapter 6
Bias as a symptom of multiple sources of opportunity inefficiency that matter

Basic uncertainty decomposition concerns

Using systematic decomposition of uncertainty as part of achieving opportunity efficiency involves a complex set of interdependent issues that are highly controversial. This chapter addresses some of these issues and their implications. Later chapters address some more.

Very basic and obvious concerns most management decision-making processes *ought* to address are how to decompose uncertainty into multiple sources of uncertainty in a clarity efficient manner, and what level of clarity ought to be sought in terms of this decomposition. When addressing these concerns, less obvious underlying issues include what exactly is the set of purposes and associated priorities of the decomposition process, and does everybody involved have the same well-founded understanding of the rationale for uncertainty decomposition at an appropriate level of clarity in any particular context.

The rationale for all decomposition of uncertainty in a systematic simplicity framework is 'the additional clarity provided is worthwhile because the right kind of decomposition has been chosen and the level of effort expended pays dividends'. People who do not understand opportunity efficiency and the component risk efficiency and clarity efficiency concepts invariably see the nature of decomposition choices very differently, and sometimes the implications are seriously inept decision making for complex sets of reasons which are not easily explained but need broad understanding. This chapter provides an overview of some the common misconceptions which are usefully addressed before finishing Part 1 of this book.

A UK Highways Agency example

Prior to 2007, the UK's Highways Agency (now Highways England within

England) adopted a very widespread common practice approach to these issues when estimating the cost of the UK roads they were responsible for. When a House of Lords enquiry severely criticised the Highways Agency because of routine serious cost overruns, the Secretary of State for Transport responded by commissioning a report from Mike Nichols (Nichols, 2006). I worked with Mike and a small team to help write his report, and when this report was accepted by the Highways Agency, I worked with a Nichols Associates consulting team to initiate the implementation of suggested changes. This assignment began by re-estimating the cost of about £20 billion worth of highway projects in various stages of development.

Nichols consultants and Highways Agency staff used a variant of Figure 6.1 to re-estimate the costs of a sample of proposed new motorway projects in the first stage of their lifecycles, the 'concept strategy stage'. 'Concept strategy stage' is *Enlightened Planning* terminology, and Figure 6.1 is an averaged and normalised version of the individual diagrams actually used for each of the sampled Highways Agency (HA) projects. Figure 6.1 uses a base estimate value of 100% as employed by Hopkinson, Close, Hillson and Ward (2008), also used by *Enlightened Planning*, to preserve confidentially and summarise the sample involved.

Figure 6.1 is a linear sensitivity diagram using three sources of uncertainty to provide a simple but carefully designed moderate clarity portrayal of uncertainty sources. It is a variant of the Figure 3.1 high clarity sensitivity diagram portrayal of six sources of uncertainty used in Chapter 3 to discuss uncertainty associated with a BP offshore oil project's 'jacket' fabrication activity duration.

The original HA estimation approach involved starting with the 'base estimate value' associated with Figure 6.1, a traditional single value point estimate of this project's cost as estimated in the concept strategy stage. This was followed by the HA using a traditional project risk management estimate of the 'risk adjustment' needed to eliminate what was referred to as 'optimism bias', as required by HM Treasury guidelines at the time (HM Treasury, 2003a and 2003b).

After the HA estimator who provided each base value estimate was given an

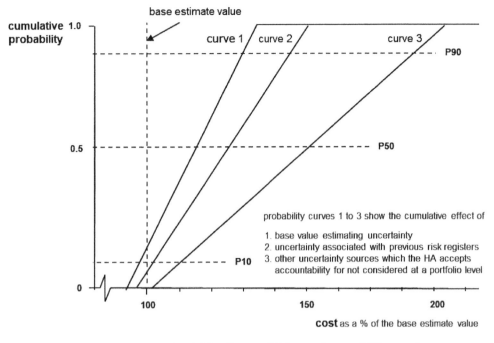

Figure 6.1 Sensitivity diagram: Highways Agency (HA) example.

introductory overview of the whole re-estimation process, so they understood each step of what was coming, they were asked to begin the re-estimation process.

Curve 1 was addressed first. The estimator was asked to review their understanding of all the uncertainty that they had considered when assessing the original 'base estimate value', using any notes or other records available, with a view to defining curve 1.

The estimator was then asked to estimate the P90 value followed by the P10 value defining curve 1, a minimum clarity estimate portrayed in cumulative probability distribution form. Estimators were initially surprised and concerned that the P50 interpreted as an expected value was about 15% larger than their base value. However, after unconscious bias associated with effects like 'anchoring' when initially focussing on most likely outcomes given reasonably optimistic working assumptions was explained, and the way this bias can be reduced by an initial focus on a plausible pessimistic outcome like a P90, plus the way a very long tail on the right-hand side of the presumed underlying reality Figure 1.2 curve as discussed in Chapter 1 can pull the expected value to the right, they became comfortable with curve 1 and its implications.

Curve 2 was then addressed, first assessing its P90, then its P10. Curve 2 involved adding the additional uncertainty associated with the original 'risk adjustment' so the sum of source 1 plus source 2 was portrayed by curve 2. The simplest available interpretation of the process required to produce curve 2 was used – a separate minimum clarity estimate of the 'risk adjustment' cost probability distribution provided by the traditional project risk management approach was assessed in terms of its P90 and its P10. This source 2 probability distribution was then added to source 1 to define curve 2 assuming 100% positive dependence between these two sources.

The 100% positive dependence assumption, implying all percentile values coincide as a simple but flexible and general interpretation of perfect positive correlation, can seem excessively pessimistic to people who are not familiar with its use. Statistical independence (0% dependence) is a common default assumption which many people initially prefer to 100% positive dependence. But 100% positive dependence is usually much closer to the underlying reality than 0%, it is easier to use, it usually (not always) errs on the pessimistic side to a modest degree which helps to offset other residual optimism bias, and if its use suggests an intermediate percentage dependence or a more sophisticated dependence framework would be worthwhile, there are a rich range of options available for seeking more clarity in an effective and efficient manner.

Two sources of uncertainty which needed consideration at portfolio level by the HA were then explored to clarify their exclusion from the current assessment, referred to as source 4 and source 5. Source 4 was inflation, which clearly applied to all projects and needed consistent treatment for all projects. It was best addressed separately at a much later stage in the project lifecycle. Using money of the day estimates and avoiding accepting accountability for this source of uncertainty until a contract was signed had now become recommended HA policy. Source 5 was all other portfolio level sources of uncertainty which the HA could reasonably be deemed accountable for, best addressed later at a portfolio level, like changes in the 'quality' of motorways due to changes in EU regulations or comparable HA policy changes – stronger crash barriers between separated lanes for travel in opposite directions, for example.

Curve 3 was then addressed, first assessing its P90, then its P10, as a separate probability distribution for source 3. Source 3 involved all sources of uncertainty which the estimator could now see were:

    1. specific to this project (not part of sources 4 or 5), and

    2. the HA could reasonably be held accountable for them, but

    3. they were not covered by sources 1 or 2.

Examples included a wide range of working assumptions which were unlikely to hold exactly, addressing issues like the type, nature and effectiveness of contracts with the main contractors and all their subcontractors, the capability of the main contractors and all the subcontractors, the actual length of the route between the outcome versions of the assumed route points, the availability of the assumed materials of preferred types and qualities, and market pressures affecting a wide range of prices and other supply concerns with implications not covered by general inflation. The competence of all relevant HA employees was also part of this residual source 3 uncertainty, plus the timeliness of required government decisions which might be influenced by the project team with consequences attributable to the HA.

In effect, source 3 has to be seen as an explicit 'closure with completeness' concept, a category or component of uncertainty *explicitly* addressing all sources of uncertainty not included in sources 1, 2, 4 or 5.

Source 3 was added to sources 1 + 2 to define curve 3 assuming 100% positive dependence.

Estimators were not surprised that sources 1 + 2 + 3 provided an expected 50% uplift to their base value estimate starting point, because this was the level of bias typically involved in their original estimation process in terms of these three sources. And they were very comfortable with the approximately 15% + 10% + 25% contributions associated with sources 1, 2 and 3.

Estimators were surprised, and very pleased, that simply asking them a new set of simple but very different questions produced an answer that seemed approximately correct. So were *most* of the other HA staff involved.

However, a few of the HA staff who were responsible for the extensive decomposition of source 2 using 'traditional project risk management' methodology were concerned that this result was directly critical of their approach.

To clarify the term 'traditional project risk management' methodology in terms of key defining features for present purposes, it used:

1. a 'risks' concept limited to sources of event uncertainty associated with events or conditions which do or do not happen/hold, portrayed using probability-impact grid representations, often involving long lists (significant decomposition detail);
2. no direct consideration of sources of variability uncertainty;
3. no direct consideration of sources of ambiguity uncertainty;
4. limited attention to interdependencies between risks and systemic uncertainty more generally;
5. no recognition of the important difference between specific and general responses;
6. a focus on reducing the impact of 'risks' without any direct explicit attention to risk efficiency and the associated issues addressed earlier in this book, including clarity efficiency and opportunity efficiency.

Those who were concerned about Figure 6.1 did not say so directly, but they seemed to believe that the traditional approach they had advocated was 'good' practice even if it was not 'best' practice because it was common practice that they and their colleagues had used for some time. They interpreted what Figure 6.1 demonstrated as a direct criticism of their professional judgement. In a sense it was. However, I am inclined to blame the profession collectively rather than the individuals. That is, any individuals who begin by following conventional common practice, and at some stage appreciate why changing to much better practice would be a good idea, have nothing to be embarrassed about as I see it. But professional bodies that continue to defend inappropriate approaches in project risk management guides and standards, despite widespread knowledge of the problems this causes, should not be allowed to keep getting away with it without increasing levels of public criticism. In this context you might like to know that HM Treasury (2014) acknowledged and supported the Nichols (2006) report, and *Enlightened Planning* provides evidence of significant further support for the need to revise project risk management guides and standards so they reflect a more enlightened perspective.

Just in terms of eliminating bias, Figure 6.1 clearly suggested that the focus on source 2 of the traditional methodology involved wasting time and effort, some of which could and should have been used much more effectively addressing the more significant overlooked concerns associated with sources 1 and 3 plus portfolio level uncertainty sources 4 and 5.

The very simple decomposition structure for sources of uncertainty used for Figure 6.1 was clarity efficient for its intended re-estimation task. As part of this task, it clarified the need to recognise explicitly the very wide uncertainty range associated with the expected construction cost of a new motorway in the concept strategy stage of its development, and it started to clarify the need to distinguish this initial uncertainty from the uncertainty underlying risk when construction contract commitments were made, as discussed in the 2006 Nichols report using a variant of Figure 6.2.

The terminology employed by Figure 6.2 has been taken from the Nichols (2006) report discussion used in chapter 7 of *Enlightened Planning*, which explains the rationale of the underlying project lifecycle structure. In brief, the concept strategy gateway stage is the board level approval process which completes the concept strategy stage, following the concept strategy process aspect. This gateway stage sanctions spending more time and money on developing design, operation and termination strategic plans (the DOT strategy stage). The DOT

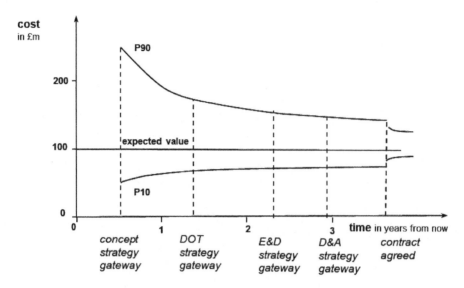

Figure 6.2 Cost uncertainty-time profile graph for the construction cost of a new motorway assuming
four strategic planning gateways followed by a contract agreement with no big surprises
and no inherent bias in the estimation processes.

strategy gateway stage is the board level approval process which completes the
DOT strategy stage. It sanctions spending further time and money on execution
and delivery strategic plans (the E&D strategy stage). In addition to these first
three strategy stages in their basic progress and gateway stage forms, it can be
very useful to employ separate devils and angels in the details (D&A) planning at
a strategic level with an associated D&A strategy gateway stage prior to contract
agreement, assuming that detailed planning for implementation purposes will
follow contract agreement.

Figure 6.2 assumes no big surprises as well as no bias causing the expected value
to change over time. In practice there may be big surprises. For big surprises
to be forgivable, the accountable parties should be able to provide reasonable
explanations, and a systematic simplicity approach can help with these issues in
ways discussed briefly in this book, more extensively in *Enlightened Planning*.
For example, documentation can be crucial to help to demonstrate the difference
between good luck and good management, bad luck and bad management,
related to enlightened caution and enlightened gambles. Also, general responses
can be designed to accommodate some (not all) 'unknown unknowns', to avoid

them becoming 'big surprises' if at all possible. Some big surprises are invariably beyond effective anticipation.

Routine persistent bias involves a failure to use systematic simplicity in very basic ways. An illustrative example of how this can happen is provided by the significant detailed attention given to source 2 on Figure 6.1 while ignoring sources 1 and 3. For any organisation using traditional project risk management 'risk adjustments' linked to initial point estimates, the resulting serious understatement of the uncertainty considered at the concept strategy gateway means that the range of possible outcomes is severely understated. As illustrated by the discussion associated with Figure 6.1, the result will be an expected outcome which is seriously optimistically biased.

The wide P10 to P90 range associated with the expected cost estimate at the concept strategy gateway in Figure 6.2 is not all uncertainty relevant to 'risk' associated with the expected outcome *when a contract is signed and commitment is made*. It is largely uncertainty because of ambiguity which *should* be partly resolved prior to a contract being agreed. But the asymmetry of the associated probability distribution contributes to the expected value, and ignoring it contributes to biased expected value estimates. A key 'risk' which needs particular attention at the concept strategy gateway stage in a project's development is a failure to achieve unbiased estimates of expected outcomes and associated ranges, leading to inappropriate decisions and failures of trust with knock-on implications that can be very serious – *including projects done in the wrong way by the wrong contractors as well as doing the wrong projects*.

The decomposition structure of the three sources of uncertainty used for Figure 6.1 was designed to capture what was *currently* being assessed (source 2) plus what *could* be captured immediately (sources 1 and 3) and should be captured later (sources 4 and 5) to get a complete picture of a variability uncertainty portrayal of all relevant uncertainty specific to this particular project to avoid biased estimation. Designing the decomposition structure to emphasise the need to deal effectively with two portfolio level concerns separately at a later point in time goes beyond immediate bias implications, but it was done to clarify the partial treatment of bias associated with sources 1 to 3 as well as the need to deal with sources 4 and 5 later.

A revised HA approach to estimation for ongoing use in all project lifecycle stages had to build on the insight provided by Figure 6.1 plus Figure 6.2. To do this it had to use a significantly modified decomposition of uncertainty structure, tailored to achieving clarity efficiency, risk efficiency and overall opportunity efficiency in the concept strategy lifecycle stage, with planned further tailoring adapting the process used as the project lifecycle evolved.

Any other organisation considering moving from a traditional project risk management approach to a systematic simplicity approach to all aspects of project management needs to consider the same issues, adapting their approach to the context. Earlier chapters in this book provide clear indications about some key aspects of what this involves, Part 2 of this book elaborates briefly, and chapter 7 of *Enlightened Planning* elaborates further.

People who are skilled at designing and developing clarity efficient approaches suitable for a range of different contexts need a familiar toolset to draw upon. One useful toolset component is an understanding of the range of levels of clarity that can be provided by different aspects or features of alternative approaches to uncertainty decomposition.

To begin to understand these issues and the nature of associated controversy is difficult because of the complexity, but they matter a great deal, so a broad understanding of the role of *all* relevant kinds of uncertainty which *all* approaches to decomposing uncertainty *ought* to facilitate thinking about is very worthwhile. As noted earlier, one way to visualise the decomposition of uncertainty involves five portrayals of uncertainty: variability uncertainty, event uncertainty, ambiguity uncertainty, capability-culture uncertainty and systemic uncertainty.

Variability uncertainty plus event uncertainty are clearly central concerns, and the discussion earlier in this book should have made it reasonably clear how these two aspects can be captured using a systematic simplicity approach to decomposing sources of uncertainty.

Especially very early in a project lifecycle, ambiguity uncertainty (what we do not know or understand) is clearly a somewhat different source of uncertainty. Ambiguity uncertainty will in part resolve itself as time passes, but we have to identify it, and we can also choose to proactively resolve some aspects.

Systemic uncertainty in causal dependency terms becomes directly relevant as soon as explicit contingency planning is introduced. Systemic uncertainty in statistical dependence terms is always relevant when decomposition is involved, because statistical independence is rarely a realistic or robust assumption. It needs a systematically designed framework, like the HAT approach, used effectively and efficiently.

How people behave in terms of capability and culture uncertainty includes, but is much broader than, 'human error' concerns. An example is the 'wrong kind of contract', perhaps with 'the wrong kind of contractor', motivating the 'wrong kind of behaviour', perhaps driven by pressures from a board who do not fully understand the issues, leading to a breakdown in trust. How people behave in terms of these kinds of capability and culture issues is an issue that is always important, and can be crucial. Managing decisions in these terms matters.

Underlying market behaviour, social and economic issues can also play a role in terms of this set of five portrayals of uncertainty. More than one perspective, further kinds of uncertainty and a variety of structures can be used to ensure everyone is comfortable with addressing *all* relevant sources of uncertainty in a simple, effective and efficient manner.

A summary to conclude Part 1

A common practice 'traditional' event uncertainty focus for 'project risk management' almost invariably means that cost estimates will be consistently optimistically biased, often to a significant extent, an obvious indication of underlying problems. But this commonly observed bias is just one particularly obvious *symptom* of a very complex set of interdependent underlying problems. The really big issue is not the bias caused by these problems. It is the lost opportunity to be risk efficient and clarity efficient in a way which is opportunity efficient – to deliver better projects at lower cost with less risk and less effort in a way that all parties can trust by making much better management decisions using systematic simplicity to manage decisions in a holistic manner.

The focus of Part 1 is why systematic simplicity is worth seeking in terms of the role of a trio of efficiency concepts: clarity efficiency, risk efficiency and opportunity efficiency.

Starting to elaborate this brief summary of Part 1, one symptom of a failure to understand all relevant management of decisions concepts is bias, in terms of both expected outcomes and the potential range and nature of departures from expectations. Biased expected outcomes is an obvious bias issue in the sense that it really cannot be overlooked – outcome costs consistently above expectations by non-trivial amounts, outcome delivery dates consistently late, and achieved rewards consistently disappointing. A more subtle bias issue *which should be obvious* involves the expected scope and character of possible departures from expectations – the anticipated range of outcomes from the concept strategy stage onwards. Those who consistently have biased views about expected outcomes also invariably have consistently biased views about associated uncertainty. A closely-coupled issue *which should be obvious* is the need to appreciate the ABCs of target values and the need to avoid point estimates, always working with interval estimates with clarity about aspirational targets, commitment targets, and balanced targets which may be expected outcomes but might be weighted expectations using a penalty cost approach to reflect asymmetry.

Chapter 1 deals with the basics you need to understand about bias and clarity efficiency to understand why a systematic simplicity approach to avoiding bias when a minimum clarity approach may be appropriate is a well-grounded starting point. Chapter 2 deals with the basics of risk efficiency and opportunity efficiency. Chapters 3 to 5 then elaborate on what is involved in Chapters 1 and 2. Chapter

6 addresses bias, directly linked to the Chapter 1 discussion, but also linked to the concerns of Chapters 2 to 5 plus the side effects of a failure to achieve opportunity efficiency.

A basic tenet of this book is everybody needs a well-grounded shared understanding of why 'risk efficiency' in the flexible and nuanced sense associated with a systematic simplicity approach is central to both clarity and opportunity efficiency, with this trio of efficiency concepts playing a framing assumption role relevant to all best practice planning and associated decision making.

Part 2
Making systematic simplicity operational on a corporate basis

The first four chapters of Part 2 provide an introductory overview of the basic process concepts which underpin making a systematic simplicity approach operational for all aspects of management – in operations management and further corporate management contexts as well as project management. A fifth chapter then provides a broad understanding of what is involved in evolving an organisation's commitment to systematic simplicity.

If you are interested in a playing a role in an organisation introducing a systematic simplicity approach, you need the overview introductory level of clarity about the basic process concepts provided in all five Part 2 chapters, and you may need to develop your understanding further in the areas covered by some of them. How much further, and in which areas, will depend on a number of factors you can judge for yourself.

Chapter 7
A universal process (UP) concept

Meeting a basic planning framework, process and model concern

In any organisation decision making and all of the associated planning can be viewed in terms of a nested *framework-process-model* hierarchy of assumptions.

Framework assumptions may apply to broadly defined contexts in generic forms, sometimes given specific forms for specific applications. As a useful simple example, in a broadly defined project management context there is a commonly acknowledged need for a project lifecycle framework, usually explicitly associated with the asset produced by the project, which in a basic generic form is often defined in terms of four steps referred to as 'stages':

1. a concept stage;
2. a planning stage;
3. an execution & delivery stage;
4. a utilisation stage.

An example *process* within the planning stage (stage 2) of this example framework is the Critical Path Method (CPM), which involves a process defined by a sequence of steps referred to as 'phases':

1. identify the set of required activities;
2. diagram the activities to portray precedence relationships (what has to take place in an ordered sequence and what can proceed in parallel);
3. estimate expected durations for the activities;
4. use the expected activity durations to compute an expected project duration;
5. test the results for consistency with all relevant underlying assumptions and expectations, iterating back to earlier phases if any problems are identified, like a project expected duration which is unacceptably long.

An example *model* within the diagram phase (phase 2) of this example process is the widely used activity-on-arrow model for portraying activity precedence relationships graphically and providing a mathematical basis for computing project duration.

Many other lifecycle stage structure *frameworks* could be used, as well as different embedded *processes* for each stage, and alternative *models* within the processes.

A fundamental basic concern in this and all other contexts is answering the question 'is our organisation using the best available *framework-process-model* combination?' All organisations need a means of making this judgement in a way that can be relied upon for all situations. Some situations may involve a unique one-off decision-making context and a choice that is of very great importance; other situations may involve routinely addressed roughly comparable contexts with sets of choices that are individually of modest importance but collectively matter a great deal; and there is a very wide variety of intermediate situations.

An essential basic tool for approaching all of these issues in all contexts from a systematic simplicity perspective is a '*universal* planning and complexity management *process*' concept, contracted to 'universal process' or 'UP'.

A 'universal process' or 'UP' is as general as possible, by definition and design. The full name implies that the role of a universal process is managing all of the uncertainty of interest and its underlying complexity in any planning context, viewing all decision making within a planning process that spans all the relevant interconnected components. The uncertainty addressed underlies the opportunity and risk which may sometimes be viewed as the immediate or dominant concerns – but dealing effectively and efficiently with the interdependence of opportunity, risk, uncertainty and complexity is crucial. Uncertainty management is the interfacing central concern, and both uncertainty and underlying complexity are always directly relevant.

This universal process concept is general (unrestricted) in more than one sense:
    1. it provides maximum flexibility by beginning with minimal limiting assumptions but facilitating quickly adopting robust limiting assumptions which exploit context characteristics to enhance process

effectiveness and efficiency;

2. it can be used on its own;

3. it can be inserted in other processes;

4. it can draw on other processes which might provide useful components;

5. it can be used as the basis for designing specific processes; and

6. it can be used to test specific processes developed by other routes.

This UP concept is a synthesis of Operational/Operations Research (OR) traditional 'hard' and more recent 'soft' approaches, other Management Science (MS) approaches in a broadly defined and integrated MS/OR approach, other cognate discipline approaches, plus any other approaches that its users deem relevant. *Enlightened Planning* chapter 2 assumes that readers may not be familiar with any of these underlying disciplines, and outlines their contributions after exploring the nature of the UP in considerable detail. This book also assumes that readers may have no relevant background knowledge, but limits itself to just exploring the key features of the UP relatively briefly in the next section with a view to providing the basic understanding needed by all readers to see the point of organisations having an agreed UP concept available as needed without elaborating the background history or implications.

The simplest situation in which to envisage the effective use of this universal process involves a one-off decision-making context needing urgent attention when there is no immediately obvious off-the-shelf framework-process-model combination readily available, and you should assume this is the context when reading the next section. If we believe we have a best practice UP to use in this situation, the same universal process can be adapted to develop a 'specific process' (SP) for a set of all comparable specific contexts. Further, the way this UP tests the opportunity efficiency of the evolving and final SP choices can be applied to the assessment of any SP equivalents developed in any other way. There are additional layers of complexity associated with designing an SP instead of just making one set of decisions. There are further layers of complexity associated with testing an approach that has been designed in some other way. However, these additional complexities need separate focussed attention and suitable illustrative examples in any case, and they can all be addressed in an effective and efficient manner by an organisation which has the capability to use one universal process (UP) to deal with one-off situations plus requisite specific processes (SPs), as illustrated in *Enlightened Planning*.

A basic tenet of the systematic simplicity approach is every organisation would find it clarity efficient to subscribe to the need for an explicit UP concept, and seek corporate clarity about the nature and planned use of the UP concept that it subscribes to. It follows that clarity about basic features of a UP relevant for all organisational contexts should be of interest on an organisation-wide basis.

An overview of the universal process (UP) structure

The universal process (UP) structure is portrayed in flowchart form by Figure 7.1.

The UP portrayed by Figure 7.1 involves seven sequential phases in an iterative structure plus a capability-culture concept composed of assets and liabilities.

An example of a broadly defined capability aspect of the asset set is 'immediately available knowledge and skills required for immediate use'. People available who have clarity about appropriate framing assumptions plus nested working assumptions and how to use them to create appropriate approaches to address planning practice is a more specific illustration within this broad example.

An example of a broadly defined culture aspect of the asset set is 'fully developed teamwork and cooperation at all levels within the team structure involved'.

Examples in the middle ground of the capability-culture asset set are 'corporate mechanisms which encourage positive behaviours for all relevant parties and discourage negative behaviours', applying the mantra 'promote and protect the good, contest and constrain the bad'.

Corresponding capability-culture liabilities are a lack of any of these capability and culture aspects of the capability-culture asset set.

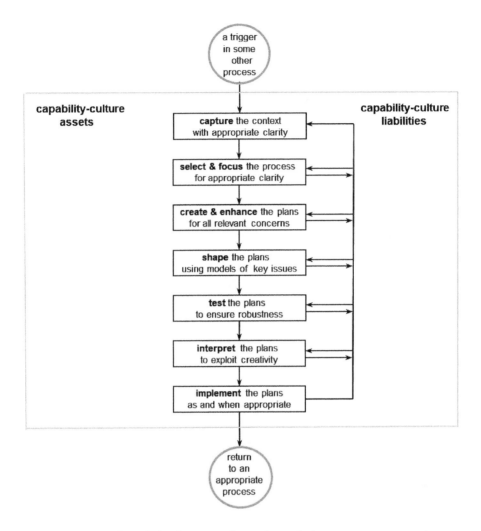

Figure 7.1 A 'universal planning uncertainty and complexity management process',
contracted to 'universal process' or 'UP'.

Organisations need to ensure that they make full use of all available capability-culture assets, and resolve or work around any capability-culture liabilities in an effective manner.

The first phase, 'capture the context with appropriate clarity', addresses the basic idea that everyone directly involved in shaping the process to be applied needs to begin by agreeing to an initial set of simplifying working assumptions about all relevant aspects of the context within the framing assumption set provided by the capability-culture assets, perhaps initially testing some key assumptions with key players later. This provides a basis for initial testing that all relevant assumptions about the context are understood and appropriate. It also provides a basis for later process selection and focussing assumptions, plus still later ongoing assumption testing and revision.

The second phase, 'select and focus the process for appropriate clarity', can then use the current context assumptions to choose and focus a suitable process. This facilitates gaining process effectiveness and efficiency by making use of the first phase plus knowledge about appropriate process selection and focussing (shaping or tailoring) choices. For example, if the first phase context assumptions suggested a relatively simple project planning context was involved, the second phase assumptions might suggest that a basic project planning technique involving a simple method and embedded model like Critical Path Method (CPM) would be appropriate for what looks like a straightforward project planning 'problem'. However, a very different set of initial context assumptions in the first phase might suggest a relatively sophisticated Soft Systems approach is needed, to untangle a very complex 'mess' of interdependent 'problems' and 'issues'. A wide range of other possibilities may involve different forms of complexity needing different kinds of simplification, preserving and exploiting different aspects of the complexity deemed relevant to the context. At least one member of the planning team involved in this UP phase needs the requisite capability to make appropriate choices. This obviously requires a full understanding of the options. It also requires a full understanding of the associated framing and working assumptions. Continuity may suggest the ongoing involvement of this person in the first two and all of the later phases, but each phase could be led by different people with different experience and skills who work collaboratively as an effective team, or one person whose team leadership skills are the basis of his or her role.

All seven phases of the overall process are separable in the sense that it makes sense to think of each phase as different components of the overall process addressed in the sequence indicated, but a nested pairwise separability structure perspective means that the first two phases are actually fully interdependent, and the third phase can build on the composite nature of what the first two phases achieve. In practice this means early trial assumptions about a suitable 'soft' (mess oriented qualitative) or 'hard' (problem oriented quantitative) approach, which may or may not have MS/OR roots, using the frameworks this provides to describe the context, with early tests that this approach to the first two phases seems to be working, frequently iterating between the first two phases in an approximation to doing both in parallel.

The third phase, 'create and enhance the plans for all relevant concerns', can then use the current context assumptions plus the current process choice assumptions to provide an initial plan, making use of the first and second phases addressed in an integrated manner to initiate planning. Most members of planning teams involved in this phase need to acquire the capability to contribute to this third phase aspect of planning in their areas of responsibility, if they have not already got the requisite capability, including understanding the implied working assumptions as plans emerge.

The fourth phase, 'shape the plans using models of key issues', can then use the outcome of the first three phases to employ models which further simplify and clarify aspects of the plans in ways that are useful. Again, most of the planning team members involved need to contribute, acquiring requisite capability first if necessary, and they need to be clear about the implications of the fourth set of working assumptions involved.

The fifth phase, 'test the plans to ensure robustness', can then systematically test all sets of working assumptions from the first four phases. At this point the earlier decomposition of the identification of working assumptions in the first four phases can prove extremely helpful, as can the separation of a clearly defined and communicated 'capability-culture asset' concept plus a 'capability-culture liability' concept. In all phases it is important to be aware of and fully exploit all available capability-culture assets, and to accommodate all capability-culture liabilities. In this fifth phase it may also be very important to test the assumptions made about capability-culture assets and liabilities – a fifth set of working assumptions. This fifth phase must ensure that *all* working assumptions will withstand scrutiny, including assumptions which may be implicit at this stage about the capability and culture of all the people who will be involved later in interpreting and implementing plans.

The sixth phase, 'interpret the plans to exploit creativity', may involve parties who did not contribute earlier, like board level senior managers, or contractors who may implement aspects of the plans.

The seventh and final phase, 'implement the plans as and when appropriate', may involve ongoing iteration, to update plans as expectations change and exploit new reactive contingency plans as well as prior contingency planning.

Separating the 'capability-culture assets' and 'capability-culture liabilities' from the seven UP phases serves several different purposes which are worth understanding. Two basic ones were outlined discussing the fifth phase above. Another purpose worth noting is an ongoing reminder for *everyone*, including senior managers who are not involved in the details of planning processes, that both base plan and contingency plan performance is conditional on the validity of all capability-culture assumptions.

The initial inspiration for separate treatment of capability and culture concerns in this way was Gawande (2011), a book by an American medical practitioner based on planning techniques and associated teamwork integrated in a way inspired by a surgery career. Atul Gawande borrows planning techniques and other concepts that have MS/OR origins, but his contribution to the UP concept is usefully viewed as a contribution from his medical practice perspective, as an illustration of the diversity of relevant contribution sources.

Concluding reflections

Looking back at the evolution of my current universal process concept to the Figure 7.1 portrayal, it began when I was initially introduced to a simple interpretation of the OR process as described in my undergraduate textbooks of the 1950s and 60s, in retrospect a useful place to start. Its five phases were:

    1. describe the problem;

2. formulate a model of the problem;

3. solve the model;

4. test the solution for robustness; and

5. implement the solution.

What this process instilled was a lifelong concern for testing the robustness of solutions in terms of the working assumptions being used to simplify the uncertain complexities of the reality being addressed using 'models'. Initially 'models' were interpreted as the graphical and mathematical abstractions of a more complex underlying reality discussed in basic textbooks. However, I soon realised that 'methods' in the relatively simple process sense could be usefully seen as qualitative models as well as the embedded graphical and quantitative models. For example, the simple phase structure of the Critical Path Method is a process level model with an embedded graphical model which has a mathematical basis defining project duration and activity criticality. CPM was initially developed in the USA by consultants for a specific organisation (Westinghouse), but then widely adopted. By the time I developed the SCERT process for BP, I saw my role as a practising consultant as providing clients with a specific process (SP) using my prototype UP (without calling it a universal process prototype) based on my ongoing generalisation of the OR process. When I became President of the OR Society, my inaugural address urged the OR profession to develop this line of thinking as one important line of development of OR conceptualisation of its professional role (Chapman, 1992a). In a sense what the universal process of Figure 7.1 does is just take this generalisation to its logical conclusion, making what is involved explicit with a view to making it easier to use for the members of all professions, in teams which integrate all the requisite knowledge and skills. In my view corporate effectiveness and efficiency requires all relevant professions work in a collaborative team within a hierarchy of shared assumptions. 'Deciding how to decide' framing assumptions are at the top of this hierarchy of assumptions, framework assumptions which we recognise are context dependent working assumptions next, then 'planning the planning' process and model assumptions.

What the process of formalising the UP of Figure 7.1 made very clear to me is a formalised systematic approach to this hierarchy is useful in terms of simplifying the way we avoid making inappropriate simplifying assumptions too soon in the process, and later systematically test for robustness in a comprehensive manner. For you to become convinced about this you may have to see it in action, but reading chapter 5 of *Enlightened Planning* might do the job – that is the intention.

It is clear that what is involved is not new. It is just 'applied science' in the 'creative synthesis of ends and means' sense which engineers subscribe to. It is also clear that no profession has a monopoly on what this involves in terms of capabilities and cultural contributions.

The origins of the UP concept lie in MS/OR for me, set in a broad applied social and physical sciences context. However, you and your colleagues need to use this particular vision of the UP concept as a starting point to consolidate and then evolve your own joint understanding of the best practice basis of all specific best practice approaches relevant to your organisation.

If you would like to understand what needs to be done to make use of this universal process in a one-off context, and how this approach might differ from a textbook OR process application, chapter 5 of *Enlightened Planning* provides a detailed example which is a good place to start. This book concentrates on why we need an UP, given a broad overview understanding of what an UP is, not the details of its use.

An exploration of the role of the UP in all project management contexts in the background to a set of frameworks and specific processes for project management is the most effective next step for this book's attention now – the topic of the next chapter. We can then widen our exploration to direct and background use of the UP concept in other management areas.

Chapter 8
Project management: frameworks, processes and models

Meeting basic systematic simplicity concerns

The conceptual and operational tools provided by a systematic simplicity approach are most effectively applied as mindset plus linked conceptual and operational toolset components used by processes for planning and associated decision making which have been designed for repeated use in specific contexts. This facilitates exploiting the features of that context, including the capability and experience of *all* of the people working in that context. Tailoring a systematic simplicity process to a specific context involves a cost, but that cost is an investment which will provide a high rate of return if the process is used effectively and efficiently on many occasions. Tailoring a systematic simplicity process for multiple use in a specific context also involves a loss of generality, but for a single use occasion, or to explore a new context, or to explore a context which has just changed significantly, we can start with the universal process (UP) discussed in the last chapter.

All organisations should employ systematic simplicity processes which are both effective and efficient for all contexts, using a systematic approach which moves from the most general approach available to those designed for multiple use in very specific contexts when a high degree of specialisation is clarity efficient.

To keep it simple systematically it is useful to distinguish just two basic process types. A *universal* process is as general as possible, by definition and design. A *specific* process is tailored to a specific context, by definition and design. However, relevant specific processes and associated frameworks cover a very wide range of kinds and degrees of specialisation.

Making prior assumptions to create specific processes can be a matter of degree, and sometimes we can take a nested approach to developing approaches tailored to specific contexts. For example, in a project management context we can use a 'generic' approach to all projects in all organisations defined in very broad 'management of change' terms. In addition to single use application of this kind of very flexible generic process, we can use the generic process as the starting point for tailoring a less flexible but more efficient multiple use variant for 'project planning in organisation A'. If significant multiple use makes it worthwhile, we can then work towards even more tailored variants, like 'project planning in organisation A for projects of type A_1, type A_2 and so on'.

The interdependence between the roles of universal and specific processes in a systematic simplicity approach is central and crucial. It is explored in some detail in five extensive tales in the part 2 chapters of *Enlightened Planning*, including a tale addressing project management in a private sector UK water and sewage utility in chapter 7. In this book this chapter outlines the broad understanding needed by everyone involved to maximise overall success if a systematic simplicity approach is adopted for an organisation's project management.

In any context, decision making and associated planning in organisations can be associated with a nested framework-process-model hierarchy, as explained at the outset of the last chapter. In a project management context, we can use the 'four Fs' (four interdependent frameworks) to make high level assumptions which structure the advocated approach to planning and associated decision making in all project contexts. The design of the four Fs was evolved and tested using the universal process in the background.

The four Fs (four interdependent frameworks) for project planning

The four interdependent frameworks (four Fs) for project planning are:
1. a project lifecycle framework;
2. a seven Ws (who, what, why and so on, plus associated plans) framework;
3. a goals-plans relationships framework;
4. a project planning process framework referred to as the 'basic specific

process for **p**rojects' (basic SPP) plus the rest of the SPP pack.

A systematic simplicity perspective on project management is built upon *explicit* use of the four Fs, arguing that the four Fs are implicit in any good practice approach to project management, and systematic explicit use is essential for a best practice approach.

A project lifecycle framework provides context foundation assumptions for the other three Fs. The basic idea of a project lifecycle concept for all project planning has been used by project managers for centuries in many long-established common forms. One mentioned earlier involves four stages: a concept stage, a planning stage, an execution & delivery stage, and a utilisation stage. A systematic simplicity approach decomposes these four stages (and all other portrayals) in two different ways in two separate steps, sometimes overlooking the second step divisions if they are not immediately relevant.

One way, applied first, involves decomposing the lifecycle into nine 'nominal' stages:
1. a concept strategy stage;
2. a design, operation and termination strategy (DOT strategy) stage;
3. an execution & delivery strategy (E&D strategy) stage;
4. a devils & angels in the details strategy (D&A strategy) stage to try to ensure that tactical plans are tested for the traditional 'devils in the details' plus any comparable 'angels in the details' (opportunities not seen at an earlier strategic planning level) prior to finalising the strategy;
5. an implementation tactics stage (finishing tactical planning for implementation purposes);
6. an execution stage;
7. a delivery stage;
8. an operation stage (using, maintaining and updating the asset created by the project);
9. a termination stage (selling an asset no longer required, like an office building, or removing an asset which is a liability at the end of its lifecycle, like a nuclear power station or an offshore oil platform).

Some organisations may need more than nine nominal lifecycle stages, and some may be able to combine some of the nine nominal progress stages, but for present purposes these nine nominal progress stages are the 'nominal' concern. The first three of them are the current focus, anticipating the other six to follow.

The second way of decomposing lifecycle stages involves recognising that each of the nominal stages defined by the first decomposition step is usefully interpreted primarily in terms of its *progress* stage component, associated with getting the planning and other relevant activity done, to make *progress*, and this needs to be followed by a separate *gateway* stage component, associated with approving what was done during the *progress* stage component. That is, we need to make it clear when we are talking about separate gateway stages, without necessarily repeatedly using the 'progress' label when doing so is not necessary.

For example: the first progress stage can be referred to as the 'concept strategy stage', followed by the 'concept strategy gateway stage'; the second progress stage can be referred to as the 'DOT strategy stage', followed by the 'DOT strategy gateway stage'; and so on.

These gateways stages must address approving what has just been done prior to moving on to the next stage. They should also address documenting important lessons learned with wider implications than this particular project. Effectively capturing corporate learning as an asset which needs ongoing attention can be important, not just maintaining a 'lessons learned' log.

The rationale for this overall separability structure is it makes it *much* easier to recognise:
1. changes in who is usually responsible for what is the focus of attention;
2. the nature of what is being done;
3. the nature of the collaboration and communication which is essential to avoid inappropriate independence assumptions.

For example, as more extensively discussed in chapter 7 of *Enlightened Planning*, the concept strategy stage for a new sewage works for a water and sewage utility might be initiated by the utility's operations director because of anticipated operations' needs, and in any organisation the people initiating a potential project will usually want a significant degree of 'ownership' of what is a corporate strategy option or 'proposition' in the concept strategy stage. However, corporate planners who may be part of the finance director's domain may feel that they are responsible for business case plans, especially for issues like what discount rate ought to be used. Project planners who will ultimately have to plan and cost the delivery of the new sewage works are often given a negligible role at the concept strategy stage, but a projects director who understands a systematic simplicity approach can and should make an invaluable contribution by initiating an outline version of the work that their staff will later have to do in the execution & delivery (E&D) strategy stage. Further, if this projects director was able to persuade the operations director to ensure their operations management planning staff contribute a compatible outline design, operation and termination (DOT) strategy stage analysis to the business case assessment even if the business case plans are initiated and managed by the finance director's staff, working collaboratively with all corporate planning and project planning staff, the progress components of the first three strategy stages could build a holistic view of the required strategy in a much more effective and efficient manner than more siloed common practices. Further still, if gateway stages after each of these first three progress stages allow the utility's board of directors to monitor progress and test key working assumptions from a board perspective, then progress/gateway stage separability assumptions serve a different but complementary purpose in all six of the first progress-gateway-progress ... gateway stages.

The 'basic specific process for projects', the 'basic SPP', is the systematic simplicity process designed for the first three strategy progress stages, all three addressing project strategy development in a highly interdependent manner using a common structure applied with context differences in interpretation. The 'specific process for projects pack', the 'SPP pack', is the complete set of SPs used for project management. The focus of this chapter is the basic SPP and why its use to develop project strategy matters. Applying the rest of the SPP pack is just outlined very briefly, but those who are interested are provided with references at 'what needs to be done' and 'how to do it' levels of detail.

Two further frameworks lie between the project lifecycle framework and the process framework, building on the project lifecycle framework to provide clarity efficient and user-friendly foundations for the process framework.

The 'seven Ws' framework builds on the lifecycle stage framework in terms of very basic questions like 'who are the parties involved in each lifecycle stage?', 'why? (their motives and objectives, bearing in mind different parties may have different motives and conflicting interests may be important)', 'what will be the project deliverables? (as seen from the perspective of all parties)', 'when will the key milestones be achieved? (bearing in mind different parties may have different priorities)', and so on.

Figure 8.1 is a useful summary portrayal of the seven Ws concept.

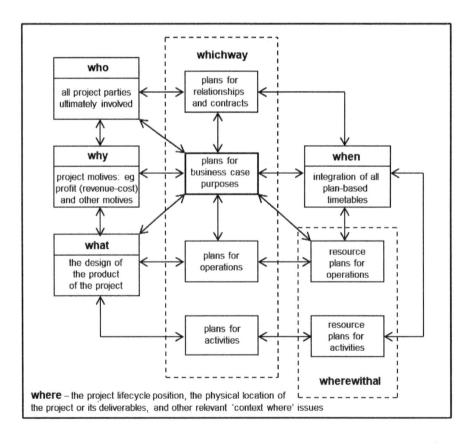

Figure 8.1 The basic project definition process – the clarified seven Ws structure.

Figure 8.1 elaborates long understood planning notions about the 'who', 'what' and 'why', and it complements standard project lifecycle concepts in a crucial manner which is now widely employed. It was initially developed by Stephen Ward in the 1990s using a basic soft OR 'influence diagram' approach, explicitly drawing upon a poem by Rudyard Kipling as a cited source of inspiration, implicitly using Stephen's 1990s prototype UP to draw on both soft OR tools and the much earlier project management wisdom described by Kipling.

A goals-plans framework has to clarify the linkages between all the important motives of all the key players in terms of all the plans identified in Figure 8.1 to the treatment provided by the basic SPP and the rest of the SPP pack, addressing concerns like preferred trade-offs between duration, cost and quality, acknowledging the importance of non-quantifiable aspects of 'quality'. That is, this third member of the four Fs has to build on the first two, to complete a basis for the fourth framework, provided by the basic SPP and the rest of the SPP pack.

The basic SPP is portrayed in a flowchart form by Figure 8.2.

An outline of the basic SPP as a tailored version of the UP

The basic SPP of Figure 8.2 involves nine phases, and there are other differences relative to the seven-phase portrayal of the universal process or UP in Figure 7.1. However, there are also clear similarities. This is because the basic SPP is a version of the universal process that has been tailored to a specific context (project management in the first three strategic planning progress stages of the project lifecycle) in very general (unrestrictive) terms.

Beginning with the first stage of the project life cycle and the first phase of Figure 8.2, 'capture the context with appropriate clarity', the phase label and stated purpose is *exactly the same* as the first phase of the UP portrayal of Figure 7.1. But there is an important interpretation difference because we can make the prior assumption that the context is 'project planning', we are addressing the concept strategy stage within the project lifecycle using the four Fs to structure the planning involved, and it is clarity efficient to start using the basic SPP in

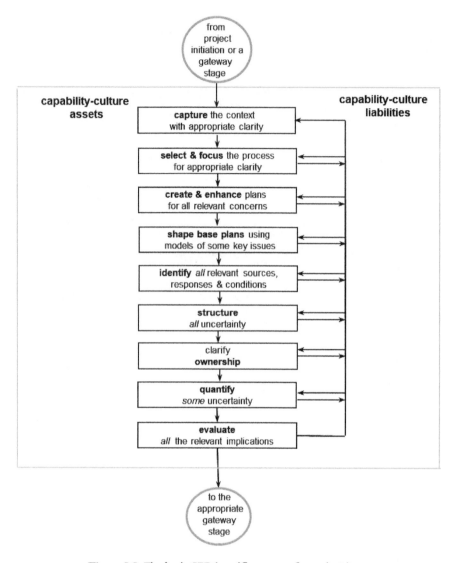

Figure 8.2 The basic SPP (specific process for projects) .

the concept strategy stage anticipating using the same basic process for the two following strategy progress stages as our development of the four Fs evolves. This implies that even if corporate strategic planners thinking in a top-down mode initiated this project, and their priority is the business case plans, they will recognise the need to involve operations management planners who can work towards an outline strategic planning model for the DOT (design, operation and termination) progress strategy stage from the outset. Further, they will recognise they need to also involve project management planners who can work towards outline strategic planning models for the E&D (execution and delivery) strategy progress stage from the outset. In terms of Figure 8.1, the initial focus in the concept strategy stage may be the business case plans, but these business case plans rest on all the other plans, and it makes sense to use the four Fs in a closely-coupled interdependent manner, drawing upon all relevant capabilities and a culture which facilitates the kind of effective teamwork projects need from the outset.

The BP examples discussed earlier in this book involved a SCERT (Synergistic Contingency Evaluation and Review Technique) planning process (Chapman, 1979) developed for the E&D strategy stage because that was the first stage involving the project managers I was working for. When Stephen Ward and I wrote the first edition of *Project Risk Management* (Chapman and Ward, 1997), we argued that project *risk* management needed full integration with all planning aspects of project management, and the approach we were advocating needed to be employed from the outset of the concept strategy stage, but we explained how the approach worked from an E&D strategy progress stage perspective to cater for the expectations of most people we were writing for as a starting point and initial focus. Even the retitled third edition (Chapman and Ward, 2011) adopts this approach.

However, this book explicitly confronts the need to change project management cultures and capabilities in an integrated manner at an organisation-wide level, arguing for a rebooted approach to projects from the outset, as does *Enlightened Planning*. The rationale is those currently involved in project *risk* management are not the primary target audience, and *everybody* needs to understand the need to start managing project opportunity, risk, uncertainty and underlying complexity in the very first stage, the concept strategy stage, with a fully integrated holistic approach. Using this approach to the first phase of the basic SPP immediately increases the effectiveness and efficiency of the overall project management approach relative to using a universal process in what I believe is an optimal manner, basing that belief on the gradual evolution of all the ideas underlying Chapman and Ward (2011), building directly from Chapman (1979) and the BP SCERT approach. *Enlightened Planning* chapter 7 explains the nature and importance of the relationship between the first phase of the basic SPP and the UP concept in detail, as well as the role of each of the four Fs.

Moving on to the Figure 8.2 second phase, 'select and focus the process for appropriate clarity', again the phase label and purpose is exactly the same as the Figure 7.1 second phase, but because we know we are working with the basic SPP within the four Fs, initially in the concept strategy stage, with a view to using the basic SPP over all of the project strategy lifecycle stages to develop strategic plans treating concept business case, DOT and E&D concerns holistically, the effectiveness and efficiency of the approach is immediately enhanced.

The third phase, 'create and enhance plans for all relevant concerns', embraces a holistic perspective on *all* aspects of project planning, in both formal and informal terms, explicitly fostering a creative 'big team' approach using all relevant aspects of best practice.

The fourth phase, 'shape *base* plans using models of some key issues', implies all traditional project planning models which do not usually explicitly address uncertainty concerns can be considered and selected for initial use *before* the planning team move on to address uncertainty explicitly in the following phases, as a basis for fully integrating 'project uncertainty management' with all other aspects of project management. There is a place here for a simple minimum clarity approach to estimating expected parameter values for the business case models central to the concept strategy stage.

These first four basic SPP phases all correspond to UP phases in a way developed for the first time in *Enlightened Planning*, as part of the joint evolution of the SPP pack and the UP, as elaborated in chapter 7 of that book. The key new features for the SPP pack are addressing *all* aspects of project planning, not just project uncertainty management, starting with *base* plans in the concept strategy progress stage when the project is first conceived, drawing on widespread general understanding of project management knowledge in this area.

The fifth phase, 'identify all relevant sources, responses and conditions', then moves on to begin a sequence of five phases which serve the same role as the last four UP phases but use a different structure. This different structure is based on an extensively tested project uncertainty management process previously published in Chapman and Ward (2011), as elaborated in *Enlightened Planning*. The examples used in the *Enlightened Planning* chapter 7 discussion for all phases involve a water and sewage utility creating and delivering new water mains and sewage treatment plants. The examples used in the Chapman and Ward (2011) discussion also include a more detailed treatment of the BP examples used earlier in this book.

The sixth, seventh, eighth and ninth phases complete this five-phase basic SPP variant of the final four UP phases which have evolved via previously published prototypes of the basic SPP.

The basic SPP is a nine-phase variant of the seven-phase universal process, adapted to gain effectiveness and efficiency by exploiting what we know about clarity efficiency in a project planning context. It is a 'generic' process in the sense that it has a 'select and focus the process' (for appropriate clarity) phase to exploit the characteristics of any particular project context and deal effectively and efficiently with what really matters in this particular context in terms of achieving clarity efficiency.

A key feature of all *generic* specific processes *ought* to be this explicit built-in flexibility of focus to exploit the characteristics of any particular context within the scope of the generic process. This requires a team who know how to use this flexibility effectively and efficiently. They have to share the requisite mindset and collectively have the requisite capability-culture skillsets and craft skills to choose appropriate variations.

An outline of the rest of the SPP pack as further tailored variants

Once a project strategy has been developed through the progress portion of each of the project strategy formation stages, it clearly needs gateway testing by a board or other senior managers who do not have a personal vested interest in the plans, to avoid the obvious bias concerns as far as possible. This requires a related but different process, executed by different people for different purposes, in a coordinated manner.

Especially if a contractor is going to do the detailed planning for a large project on behalf of a client project owner, a final strategy testing stage concerned with the well-known notion of 'devils in the detail' plus potential 'angles in the detail' can be useful, in 'progress' and 'gateway' forms.

At this point, given a final approval, contracts may be let, and a commitment to the escalating investment of tactical planning can begin. We are now on to more conventional project management territory, making effective and efficient use of all earlier plans, with further process and model variants adapted to the evolving situation, as discussed in 'how to do it' terms in Chapman and Ward (2011) and the many sources it builds on.

Some readers may want to look at *Enlightened Planning* and then take this further. Others may have a limited interest in project planning, but still find it useful to briefly reflect on the relationship between the UP and the role of the basic SPP plus its variants in the four Fs for project management as part of the process of understanding the overall role of UP and SP relationships underlying a systematic simplicity approach.

Concluding reflections

Using the UP concept and perspective to clarify the nested four Fs structure for a generic approach to all project management is one way to begin to understand the range of relationships between the universal nature of the UP and the specific nature of SPs, and it is a useful one for this book's purposes.

What you may have found initially perplexing is the large number of nominal 'progress' lifecycle stages (nine) relative to the common practice four lifecycle stages for an approach explicitly focussed on keeping it simple, plus a separate set of associated 'gateway' stages. The rationale is the focus of the planning effort in all of these different stages tends to be led by different people on behalf of different parts of the organisation pursuing a different balance of linked objectives with different trade-off preferences using different tools to do different things. Separability is essential to recognise and respond to this, to keep it simple within each stage. But separability does not imply independence, and dealing effectively with interdependence is an extremely important focus of concern. That is why the concept strategy stage which initiates the project lifecycle may be led by a corporate planner with a business case plan focus, but this chapter has emphasised the need to involve an operations management planner who can visualise his or her input as a preliminary outline analysis for the DOT strategy stage to follow, plus a project management planner visualising their input as a preliminary outline E&D strategy stage analysis to complete the first three strategy progress stages. We need to keep it simple *systematically* to achieve clarity efficiency at a corporate level, recognising the importance of differences in perspective of people who need to work together, to some extent in an ordered sequence, but to some extent in parallel.

Another aspect of this chapter's approach you may have found perplexing is the large number of phases in the basic SPP and the complex relationship between this basic SPP and the UP relative to many common practice portrayals of project planning processes. Again, the rationale is keeping it simple *systematically*. We need to accommodate *all* aspects of *all* best practice approaches in a framework which allows us to test which aspects are appropriate for any particular context of current interest. There is no one best specific way to approach all projects. The current project of interest may be viewed as a one-off, but once we acquire some understanding of and skill with a generic process for all project planning, we can start to increase clarity efficiency by developing a more specific version for a specific organisation, and then still more specific versions for specific project types within that organisation. As we do so, some aspects of common practice, which may look attractive because they may be familiar and they seem usefully simpler, can be tested. They may prove robust and effective, but they should be rejected if more clarity efficiency can be achieved via alternative approaches.

What is involved is a systematic learning process, building on being aware of the assumptions being made because of awareness of less restrictive approaches, and testing the reliability and robustness of those assumptions, using a creative synthesis of ends and means.

Chapter 9
Corporate strategy formation frameworks

A basic framework using a specific example context

The universal process concept discussed in Chapter 7 plus all of the systematic simplicity conceptual and operational tools discussed in Chapters 1 to 6 can be adapted to operations management and corporate management contexts as well as the project management contexts discussed in Chapter 8. When this adaptation has been completed, many operations management, corporate management and project management frameworks can be viewed as remarkably similar once the terminology differences are clarified. Although some differences are important, and central to a good deal of discussion in *Enlightened Planning*, giving most of them direct attention in this book would not be helpful.

The corporate strategy formation aspect of corporate management does raise significant differences which need some focussed attention now. This chapter also needs to clarify the recommended framework for holistic integration of corporate management, operations management and project management which a systematic simplicity approach to strategy formation provides.

A central issue in a number of earlier chapters was the need to decompose uncertainty into five portrayals (variability, event, ambiguity, capability-culture and systemic) to ensure that all relevant uncertainty is perceived and addressed in all management contexts in a manner appropriate to each kind of uncertainty within an integrated and holistic approach to all kinds of uncertainty. For example, as discussed in Chapter 6, a common practice approach to project risk management which is appropriate for dealing with uncertainty perceived and portrayed as an event which may or may not happen during the construction of a motorway is clearly not appropriate for dealing with uncertainty perceived and portrayed as ambiguity which should resolve itself over time as the project lifecycle evolves prior to the contract for construction being let. However, both need coordinated treatment when the initial estimate of a motorway's cost is prepared and explained, and persistent optimistic bias associated with estimated costs is a symptom that important relevant concerns are being overlooked.

A related central issue addressed in this chapter is the need to decompose corporate strategy formation *and implementation* into five component areas of corporate planning (short-term, medium-term, long-term, futures and goals) to ensure that each is approached efficiently and effectively *and all relevant sources of uncertainty plus interdependencies* are managed efficiently and effectively. Managing uncertainty in all five of these corporate planning areas in different ways appropriate to each area is certainly not a new idea. However, ensuring that all five get portrayed and addressed in a holistic uncertainty management manner in all corporate management contexts in all organisations is not common practice. It needs to be, and an overview of how to approach this concern is provided by this chapter.

Figure 9.1 portrays a formal corporate strategy formation and implementation framework which is useful for exploring the basic issues. In any corporate strategy formation context, it plays the same foundation framework role as the project lifecycle framework does in a project management context.

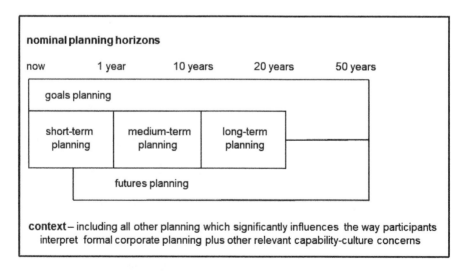

Figure 9.1 Formal corporate planning portrayed in terms of five different planning categories using four nominal planning horizons plus a comprehensive view of all the relevant context issues.

Figure 9.1 was used in chapter 8 of *Enlightened Planning* as the basic framework for the Canpower tale of corporate strategy formation and implementation central to that chapter. This Canpower tale was based on the published report (Chapman, 1992b) of a review of Ontario Hydro's strategic planning which began in 1990, significantly broadened and updated to reflect a 2020s' perspective. The 1992 report was prepared for an Ontario Government review of Ontario Hydro's strategic planning when Ontario Hydro were seeking permission to add ten more nuclear power stations to their already significant portfolio of nuclear power three decades ago. I was hired to prepare this report by the Independent Power Producers Society of Ontario (IPPSO), using funding IPPSO obtained from Ontario Hydro as an official 'intervenor'.

My report was highly critical of Ontario Hydro's approach to their variant of Figure 9.1. It explained in some detail what should have been done as a starting point for explaining why what had been done was seriously flawed. Empirical evidence that the basis of my critique was sound emerged and received significant press attention a few weeks before I was due to give oral evidence. Ontario Hydro then withdrew their plan.

One central feature of the Figure 9.1 portrayal which is relevant to strategy formulation for all organisations is a set of separate component frameworks for short-term, medium-term and long-term planning, using three different planning horizons, and assuming the use of three different kinds of models and processes to address three different kinds of uncertainty management issues. This component separation is crucial, but so is recognising formally and explicitly the need to address important interdependencies.

A key feature of all three of these short-term, medium-term and long-term component frameworks is they should address *base* plans for all potentially desirable choices involving options that are known to be feasible in technical terms, explicitly excluding all options that are not *known to be feasible in technical terms*. However, the overall planning framework also needs to consider *contingency* plans for all possible relevant opportunities as well as risks, including currently non-feasible options becoming feasible because of new technological developments, and options currently deemed non-feasible for inappropriate corporate culture or capability reasons becoming recognised as potentially desirable, an important ambiguity uncertainty management feature of the advocated systematic simplicity approach.

A key related feature is a separate fourth framework for futures planning that addresses a range of planning approaches for options that are not feasible currently, for technical, economic or capability-culture reasons. They require separate consideration because some of them *might* become both feasible and demonstrably desirable. This might be as a result of the efforts of others, simply requiring patience. But helping to make some of them feasible might be an attractive option, requiring the planned allocation of effort and financial resources for this purpose in a way which proved successful. Addressing this kind of uncertainty separately using appropriate tools is important. It is an important kind of ambiguity uncertainty.

Interdependencies between futures planning and long-term, medium-term and short-term planning that operate in both directions need attention. For example, any options reasonably likely to become feasible should be addressed via contingency planning to take advantage of possible new opportunities in the medium-term or short-term frameworks if that is feasible. And short-term, medium-term and long-term planning might assess economic feasibility gaps in opportunity cost (shadow price/cost) terms to inform futures planning if that was useful.

Another key related feature is a separate fifth framework which addresses corporate goals planning. Effectively clarifying corporate goals on a top-down basis, and then integrating this with all futures, long-term, medium-term and short-term planning, is left until the end of the current discussion and the *Enlightened Planning* discussion for expository reasons. However, in practice goals planning *ought* to be the starting point when implementing a Figure 9.1 approach.

This book will focus on a Canpower interpretation of Figure 9.1 initially, because context considerations have to be part of its interpretation, but any organisation of interest to you will need some variant of Figure 9.1 which reflects the kinds of key differences in organisational context concerns illustrated towards the end of this chapter.

Most organisations are reasonably effective and efficient at short-term planning, using a planning horizon of about a year. For most organisations it is the medium-term planning or the long-term planning, or both, which is the usual *obvious* problem. This was the basis of my 1992 Ontario Hydro report.

In any electricity utility context, long-term planning involves a planning horizon of about 20 years, and the basic central issue is what *portfolio* of sources of baseload electric power by type (nuclear, hydro, gas, oil, coal, wind, solar and all other sources) should be the current target given current knowledge and uncertainty. Peak and shoulder period electric power provision may require different types of sources than baseload for reasons usefully addressed separately at a later point in the planning process, and later decomposition of baseload types into different nuclear technology options, various kinds of large and small hydro options, and so on, will also need attention. The directly relevant uncertainty is about prices, demand levels, regulations and geopolitics at a planning horizon about 20 years into the future. It is extremely risky to assume that any one source of electric power type will be best in all foreseeable futures, which means that *efficient diversification* should address the trade-offs between expected cost and associated risk as overall portfolio level risk is reduced to an appropriate level. What is an 'appropriate' level of risk *ought* to be judged in a manner which considers the preferences of *all* parties with a legitimate interest in the choice. Even if all baseload electric power produced by units of one type is the eventual decision, it may be very important to achieve approval via a process which is judged appropriate by an effectively informed public concerned about domestic, industrial, commercial and public services electricity supply with due consideration of all relevant geopolitical concerns.

The details of what needs to be done and how to do this using a pairwise separability structure so that all the risk efficiency, clarity efficiency and opportunity efficiency concepts and tools discussed in Part 1 can be exploited in this particular portfolio management context are outlined in *Enlightened*

Planning, further developed in terms of any portfolio management context in references provided. For present purposes you may find a brief explanation of a pairwise separability approach useful.

As an example, oil and gas fired power stations might be considered first, as an initial component portfolio, asking the question 'what ratio of oil to gas power station output GW (gigawatt) capability is the preferred risk efficient choice at the planning horizon given any relevant assumed oil plus gas capacity?' If either oil or gas has an expected cost per GW which is significantly lower and the risk reduction associated with diversification is negligible, 100% use of a single risk efficient choice can be appropriate. But if the expected costs are similar, and the correlation between oil and gas prices is not perfect, diversification may be appropriate, and making the ratio a function of the oil plus gas capacity may also be appropriate. High clarity sensitivity diagrams can be used to clarify underlying sources of uncertainty, and high clarity decision diagrams can be used to assess the preferred ratio.

The resulting oil plus gas composite might then be considered in conjunction with coal power station output, asking the question 'what ratio of coal to oil plus gas power station output GW capability is the preferred risk efficient choice at the planning horizon given any relevant assumed total fossil fuel (coal plus oil plus gas) capacity?' As for the first level pair, if either coal or the conditionally optimised composite of oil plus gas has an expected cost per GW which is significantly lower and the risk reduction associated with diversification is negligible, 100% use of the risk efficient choice can be appropriate. But if the expected costs are similar, and the correlation between coal and oil plus gas prices is not perfect, diversification may be appropriate, and making the ratio a function of the fossil fuel capacity may be appropriate. High clarity sensitivity diagrams can be used to clarify underlying sources of uncertainty, and high clarity decision diagrams can be used to assess the preferred ratio.

The resulting conditionally optimised portfolio of fossil fuel power stations could then be considered in relation to nuclear power. A portfolio of hydro, wind, solar, tidal and any other renewable sources might then be addressed, later combining this with the fossil plus nuclear portfolio. Understanding the pattern of correlations in the uncertainty associated with expected prices at the long-term planning horizon is a central concern, to understand risk efficiency and an opportunity efficient approach to risk-return trade-offs plus clarity efficient achievement as part of a holistic approach to managing opportunity. Unbiased expected outcome estimates are clearly crucial, but direct measurement of covariances making specific probability distribution assumptions may not be helpful. The central concern is understanding the nature of the *portfolio* management decision making required, in terms of opportunity efficiency plus component risk efficiency and clarity efficiency.

Assuming this is done, and given a resulting current target portfolio at the long-term planning horizon, which we know is going to be revised as time progresses, the basic medium-term decision making concern is planning how to get there with a focus on the medium-term horizon. A key consideration is as far as possible avoiding *committing* to any medium-term plans which will be difficult or expensive to revise when long-term plans require adjusting. The relevant uncertainty this time is very different. It involves making timing decisions, understanding the costs of getting them wrong when commitments are or are not made. Examples of some of the key issues are when to plan to commit to contracts to design a new unit, when to plan to commit to begin its construction, and when to commit to producing power from it. The medium-term planning horizon of 10 years assumed for Figure 9.1 relates to nuclear power stations, which have a lead time of about 10 years between committing to construction and first power. Some medium-term planning not addressing nuclear power will involve a variety of shorter planning horizons. Medium-term planning can be seen as the domain of project planning using the specific project planning (SPP) pack discussed earlier in Chapter 8, with corporate, operations and project management staff involved jointly as appropriate in all strategy 'progress' stages, and different corporate management staff including the corporate board involved in the associated 'gateway' stages.

Medium-term planning in these terms has to address clarity efficient controls as well as clarity efficient estimation, planning and corporate board approved decision making within an overall planning horizon structure which is clarity efficient in holistic terms.

Short-term planning has to work within the available portfolio of operational power stations to meet demand and deal with other short-term planning concerns. Most of this may involve routine operations and corporate management concerns. But some issues may give rise to key interdependencies with important strategic implications needing careful board level attention.

For example, all types of power stations are prone to failures, and a planned overall system GW capacity 'provision' (needed on average) for the expected average level of outages plus a further 'contingency' (not needed on average) for outage levels above expectations is standard practice. However, three concerns which are important in the context of the Canpower tale need a mention here.

One is that a strong corporate culture-based preference for large nuclear power stations plus large power station units of other kinds means a need for much more 'contingency' spare capacity than a willingness to develop significant portfolios of relatively small units. If this is not fully reflected in the cost estimates for long-term planning purposes, an inappropriate expected cost bias in favour of large unit and against small units will seriously distort corporate strategy.

Secondly, nuclear power stations are prone to design failure problems which do not surface until many years of operation, and extensive use of a single design type can lead to late realisation that a large proportion of a system's power stations must all be shut down permanently at once. This is a low probability catastrophic event in economic terms for everyone affected, and its possible occurrence needs addressing as part of long-term planning, decomposing the portfolio of nuclear power stations and diversifying appropriately. If it happens at a serious level it is a board level failure, as well as a failure for all the managers at all levels who should have advised the board. It is also a failure for all the relevant regulators and their controlling governments who failed to see the problem coming.

Thirdly, nuclear power stations are prone to accidents, some possibly catastrophic.

The risk involved is not just a matter of expectations, and the implications of the scope for departures from expectations arguably need careful treatment beyond current common practice.

Clarity to deal efficiently with the different kinds of uncertainty associated with different kinds of decisions in the long-term, medium-term and short-term, plus all the interdependencies between them, is the early focus of the *Enlightened Planning* Canpower tale for several good reasons. The issues are complex, frequently addressed inappropriately, and of great importance. They obviously need competent treatment.

Separate but interdependent treatment of futures planning involves separating the initial analysis of further different kinds of uncertainty associated with different kinds of decisions, to deal with this different kind of uncertainty in a clarity efficient manner. Once the approach to long-term, medium-term and short-term planning for feasible options is clear, it is relatively obvious that a comparable approach to futures planning for all relevant non-feasible options is clarity efficient. 'Horizon scanning' approaches to a distant futures horizon like 50 years can become more focussed technical feasibility studies at a nearer long-term futures planning horizon. In the still nearer term, research and development expenditure may become relevant, then pure short-term development. More than three 'short', 'medium' and 'long' term equivalents may be needed, to capture what can be viewed as a continuous spectrum approximated by discrete stages.

Separate but interdependent treatment of goals planning involves yet another separation of the initial analysis of further different kinds of uncertainty associated with different kinds of decisions, to deal with the implications in a clarity efficient manner. In the Canpower context the key uncertainty identified is 'what are the consequences of the fact that Canpower is a public sector organisation owned by the people of the province it operates in, but the current board's decisions and some of their current directors' approaches to their domains do not reflect this fact, with an implied 'privatisation risk' which is not being recognised or managed effectively?' *Enlightened Planning* chapter 8 concludes with an exploration of these issues linked to Ontario Hydro's recent history and likely future, relating it to the UK's privatisation of the Central Electricity Generating Board (CEGB). The overall position on private and public sector ownership which I favour is politically neutral, with the case for either highly dependent upon the context in ways which can require very careful analysis to capture what really matters, explored briefly in chapters 7, 8, 9 and 10 of *Enlightened Planning*.

All of the organisations investing in prototype variants of the enlightened planning perspective on systematic simplicity described in earlier chapters of this book have been convinced that the corporate return on the investment made would be significant before they started, none were disappointed, and some were delighted. The Canpower framework of Figure 9.1 has not been used directly apart from its IPPSO role, but it builds on the successful use of its basis for IPPSO to provide an updated framework which has features clearly needed by most organisations, and all of these component features have been successfully used by other organisations.

Adapting the approach just outlined to other contexts

Organisations that are very different to Ontario Hydro may require variants of Figure 9.1 which involve some very different features. For example, a pharmaceutical company might want to focus its initial attention on the futures planning aspects of finding new products and bringing them to market with levels of complexity involving both portfolio and timing issues which are interdependent in ways that need much greater attention than electricity utilities, carefully focussed on what matters most. Most pharmaceutical companies have considerable expertise in the futures planning area. A commercial or military aircraft company might have futures planning concerns that are different in very important ways, but managing the gap between what is definitely technically feasible and what might become feasible within a portfolio of other uncertainties will involve some common concerns. A small family-owned organisation which markets lawn mowers and other garden machinery currently mainly manufactured in-house may have very limited need for futures planning in the pharmaceuticals or aircraft industry sense, but significant need for clarity about goals and product portfolio issues involving both the markets for its manufactured products and the markets for outsourced products plus all input markets. An insurance company or a hedge fund organisation will be very different again. There is no simple 'one size and shape fits all', but common features treated via portable conceptual and operational tools is feasible, and recognising the value of decomposing corporate strategy formation into component areas as illustrated by Figure 9.1 is an important aspect.

In some organisations most of the 'propositions' addressed by the corporate strategy formation processes may be initiated by operations management functions engaged in bottom-up strategic planning, supported by a project management function. Corporate strategic planning has to integrate all bottom-up strategic planning with top-down strategic planning goals clarified at board level. Corporate management more generally has to integrate and coordinate all separate operations management and project management activities, in addition to managing all activities not allocated to operations management or project management functions. *Enlightened Planning* explores several examples in terms of how they might fit into an overall framework like Figure 9.1, to illustrate what is involved in adapting the approach. In practice most organisations will have important individual characteristics which need attention.

Understanding how to adapt a framework like that of Figure 9.1 to a new and very different context is not necessarily a straightforward matter. It involves crucial capability-culture attributes that an organisation may have to develop, perhaps with support from new members of staff or external consultants. However, once they have been acquired, most systematic simplicity mindsets, toolsets and skillsets are portable and universally relevant.

Concluding reflections

A central goal for a systematic simplicity approach is achieving 'strategic clarity' in the general sense this term is used in *Enlightened Planning*. The approach taken in the last chapter and this chapter are very different in most respects, but they share a concern for strategic clarity.

The focus of Chapter 8 was initiating planning for a project at the outset of a 'context strategy progress stage' with a clear vision of the need to proactively 'plan the planning' as well as 'planning the project', a higher order form of planning that is to some extent instinctive and intuitive for experienced planners, but needs explicit acknowledgement and support for all planners. This involves systematic simplicity which is not remotely simplistic. Chapter 8 did not explore 'planning the planning', but Chapman and Ward (2011) does, explaining in 'how to do it' detail the 'what needs to be done' outline provided by *Enlightened Planning*.

The focus of this chapter's treatment of formulating corporate strategy was understanding the need for a framework structure which will facilitate an organisation starting to think about 'planning the planning' at a corporate strategy formation level. This framework has to facilitate clarity efficient integration of all relevant components. This too involves systematic simplicity which is not remotely simplistic. It involves organisational strategic clarity of a different kind at a different level than that involved in Chapter 8, but they are not independent or unrelated.

The approach to separability used to structure a portfolio analysis treatment of long-term planning in this chapter based on pairwise separability was illustrated in very simple terms, but the underlying interdependence captured is clearly not simplistic. The nature and role of the pairwise separability structure approach used to address important correlation patterns central to risk efficiency in a portfolio context like long-term planning in this chapter is directly comparable to the nature and role of the same pairwise separability structure approach to the way successive phases of the basic SPP build on previous completed phases and full iterations discussed in the last chapter, but there are clearly very important differences too. Perhaps the most important associated general message is the need to always see separating components of whatever is being analysed as a basis for systematic treatment of what kinds of interdependencies need attention as well as what kinds of different aspects need different treatment within the component structure. Independence between components is always a very strong assumption special case, and developing a feel for a variety of different kinds of interdependence as well as different ways to structure decomposition is an important part of acquiring strategic clarity.

These comments may not strike you as immediately useful, but because Chapters 8 and 9 take such different approaches to very different aspects of systematic simplicity, linking them to the common strategic clarity goal may serve as a useful strategic clarity starting point for the next two chapters.

Chapter 10
Operations management and further corporate management concerns

A bidding process example of the specific process (SP) concept

Most specific processes are much more extensively tailored to a particular context than the generic SP example illustrated by the basic SPP (specific process for projects) in Chapter 8. This means they sacrifice much more generality, but they do so to gain much greater efficiency and ease of use. It also means they provide strategic clarity in a relatively focussed manner. This makes them a relatively straightforward and 'user-friendly' way for all the members of an organisation employing them to contribute to an organisation's best practice in a direct manner as part of their basic organisational role.

As an illustrative example, chapter 6 of *Enlightened Planning* discusses the development of a moderately sophisticated specific process which still provides a great deal of built-in flexibility. The context is the regional branch of an international computer systems company called Astro developing a 'SP for bidding' specific to their needs while bidding for a particular systems integration project contract worth about £20 million. The Astro tale builds directly on the IBM UK Forum 2 programme case study example discussed earlier in this book, plus later consultancy work for IBM UK on much more complex bidding processes for contracts worth £100 million plus. For simplicity the IBM Forum 2 case study used a single stage bidding process, but the Astro tale bidding process uses three stages for significantly enhanced clarity efficiency even when relatively small contracts may be the concern. The way a multiple stage process delivers more clarity efficiency is a useful feature of this example.

Figure 10.1 portrays what is involved in this Astro SP for bidding at an overview level.

Stage 1 involves an effective and efficient *simple early qualitative* process, asking

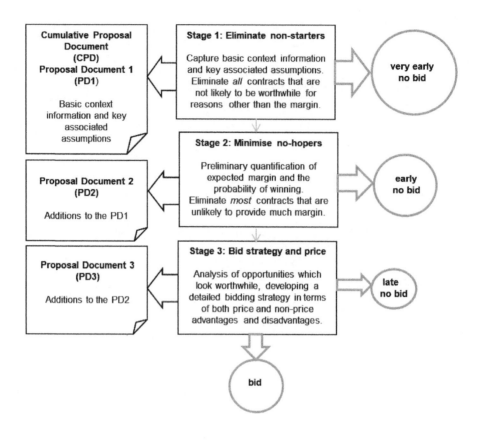

Figure 10.1 The overview plan of Astro's SP for bidding portrayed as a flow chart.

questions like 'is the prospective client a reputable organisation which pays its bills without difficulty, and is the nature of the work aligned with currently underemployed corporate resources and our corporate goals?' For each question a green light can indicate a neutral 'yes', a blue light can indicate a very enthusiastic positive 'YES', a red light can indicate a negative emphatic 'NO'. Yellow and orange intermediates can be used between. Multiple red and orange lights may signal the possible value of a very early 'no bid' decision, to save wasted effort. However, if the bid progresses to stages 2 and 3, then ongoing clarity about all blue and yellow lights as well as any red and orange lights remains important, to ensure ongoing consideration of all qualitative assessments of issues that may matter is both effective and efficient. This is a useful, relatively simple example of the general systematic simplicity concern for consideration of the right questions at the right time in an operations management context which is going to be used extensively by a number of people who do not need to design the process – they just need to understand its rationale and use it in a capable manner.

Stage 2 is focussed on an effective and efficient *simple early quantitative analysis* of potential profitability, to finish an early filtering of projects not worth the effort involved in a much more sophisticated stage 3 assessment which explores issues like what package of features to offer the potential customer as well as what price to bid. Stage 2 is a simple non-iterative (one-pass) five phase process portrayed by Figure 10.2.

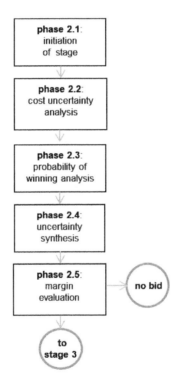

Figure 10.2 The stage 2 plan of Astro's SP for bidding.

The first phase in stage 2, phase 2.1, addresses planning the following four phases, combining the functions of the first two phases of the UP (and basic SPP) in terms of 'capture the context' and 'select and focus the process' roles given that we know the results of stage 1.

The second phase, phase 2.2, involves a very simple cost uncertainty analysis using the minimum clarity estimation approach and the closely related simple variants discussed in Chapter 1 to assess the total expected cost and associated range. This phase and the remaining three phases in this stage are all grounded on the basic bidding process developed for case study use for the IBM Forum 2 programme. However, phase 2.2 is simpler, to reduce the level of effort put into 'costing' in phase 2 given a significant chance that an early 'no bid' decision will be made in stage 2.

The third phase, phase 2.3, addresses assessment of the probability of winning the bid if any bid over a plausible range is used. It first assesses the probability of winning if a plausible maximum bid is made. It then assesses the probability of winning the bid if a plausible minimum bid is made. A very simple graphical model can then assume a linear relationship between these points to define the probability of winning over the plausible range of bids.

The fourth phase, phase 2.4, uses a simple table to synthesise phase 2.2 and 2.3 results, plus a summary of any key issues from the stage 1 analysis.

The fifth and final phase, phase 2.5, involves using the table provided by phase 2.4 to evaluate the margin which the stage 2 analysis suggests could be achieved with a plausible range of bids and associated probabilities of winning. In stage 2 there is no need to select a bid, but the bidding team does have to assess whether an early 'no bid' decision looks sensible, or bidding looks promising enough to invest the effort and cost involved in proceeding to stage 3.

Stage 3 involves a much more sophisticated version of the stage 2 process which builds on stage 1 and 2 in both qualitative and quantitative analysis terms. As part of its increased sophistication, the stage 3 process employs an iterative approach to enhanced variants of the same five phases as stage 2, as portrayed by Figure 10.3.

The first phase in stage 3, phase 3.1, addresses 'planning the planning' in terms of planning the current pass through the following four phases. This combines the functions of the first two phases of the UP (and basic SPP) in terms of 'capture the

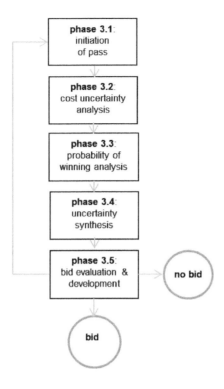

Figure 10.3 The stage 3 plan of Astro's SP for bidding.

context' and 'select and focus the process' roles given that we now know stage 3 of a three-stage bidding process is the concern *plus* the details of the stages 1 and 2 results. The iterative nature of the stage 3 process means that for experienced users anticipating future stage 3 passes will be part of planning the current pass as well as reflecting the results of past stage 3 passes.

The second phase, phase 3.2, addresses cost uncertainty analysis using a more sophisticated cost component breakdown than phase 2.2. For some bid components, when more than one approach to meeting the requirements has been identified, in-house or subcontractor options for example, the minimum clarity estimation models discussed in Chapter 1 of this book can be used to assess expected costs and associated ranges for all available options, followed by the use of the simple linear decision diagrams discussed in Chapter 2 to make choices. These approaches to making decisions are reasonably straightforward to use, and were employed directly to discuss the IBM culture change case study during the Forum 2 programme.

The third phase, phase 3.3, addresses assessment of the probability of winning the bid over the plausible range of bids like phase 2.3. It takes a much more sophisticated approach than any demonstrated during the Forum 2 programme, although some of the underlying ideas were discussed. Its basic premise is if it is worth breaking down the cost estimate into five or six different components and assessing alternative approaches to some components when options are available, as undertaken in phase 3.2, then it is also worthwhile decomposing Astro understanding of 'the competition' on this occasion. It is worth thinking about the market leader who is the 'key competitor' on their own, then separately addressing the 'other competitors'. In addition, it is worth thinking about probability of winning a bid curves estimated in a way which is conditional on what bid the 'key competitor' makes. The rationale is based on dealing directly in an effective and efficient manner with relative non-price advantages and disadvantages, inferring how much effort a key competitor has *probably* put into this from a possible level of their bid, without trying to predict what they will bid. The additional sophistication of this approach actually makes it easier to use, for reasons developed and explained in *Enlightened Planning* chapter 6. This is sometimes a feature of successful additional 'constructive complexity' in a systematic simplicity framework which is particularly rewarding, a 'pleasant surprise' increase in opportunity efficiency, a useful explicit complement to the 'constructive simplicity' concept (Ward, 1989). As discussed in *Enlightened Planning*, it may be worth thinking about further decomposition of 'other competitors', but if this form of additional complexity does not pay it can be ignored.

The fourth phase, phase 3.4, uses a more sophisticated variant of the simple table developed for stage 2 to synthesise phase 3.2 and 3.3 results, plus a summary of any key issues from the stage 1 analysis.

The fifth and final phase on this pass through the process, phase 3.5, involves using the results provided by earlier phases to evaluate the margin which the stage 3 analysis suggests could be achieved with a plausible range of bids and associated probabilities of winning. In phase 3.5, a crucial option in early passes is a systematic search for non-price advantages which will increase the probability of winning at the level of margin being sought, or increase the level of margin at the probability of winning being sought. If this search proves positive, a loop back to phase 3.1 for another pass can revise the earlier analysis. This searching for non-price advantages and looping back should continue until a satisfactory bid is identified or a late 'no bid' decision seems appropriate.

The move from a single stage process to a three-stage process is a useful example of how to acquire strategic clarity in a bidding process context. It illustrates the strategic value of 'planning the planning', initially in the sense that the first stage operates as a very useful filter to save effort if an early stage 1 'no bid' decision is made, plus a valuable source of highly relevant qualitative information often overlooked if proceeding to further stages is the result, in effect 'strategic clarity' at the level of deciding whether a single stage bidding process is good enough or a multiple stage process needs consideration for multiple reasons. But these benefits of a separate stage 1 are just the 'tip of the iceberg', with a number of further strategic clarity spinoffs to follow.

Enlightened Planning chapter 6 discusses this Astro process and its relationship with initial and later bidding processes developed for IBM and other organisations, suggesting that the new features of phase 3.3 and their implications for the rest of the stage 3 process could *on their own* provide a basis for a significant improvement in bidding effectiveness and efficiency for a wide range of organisations in many different contexts.

Further specific process applications

This SP for bidding is just one example of a specific process to support operations management decision making developed in a particular way for a particular purpose. In this case the concern was bidding as a particular approach to marketing on the demand side of the organisation's operations, and the approach started by examining a simple bidding process developed for a culture change process case study and asking the question 'how could it be made more effective and efficient for actual bidding purposes – increasing strategic clarity in a directly comparable actual bidding context'.

A wide range of other operations management contexts plus an equally wide range of other corporate management contexts could be provided with clarity efficient specific processes for repeated use using similar development approaches for similar strategic clarity enhancement reasons. However, there are also a wide variety of very different routes into the development of specific processes to enhance strategic clarity across any organisation, helping to build on the corporate strategy formulation framework outlined in Chapter 9 as well as addressing other operations management concerns.

As an example of one very different sort of approach, the universal process variant adopted by an organisation can also be applied directly whenever this looks useful for one-off analysis, and specific processes might be developed by building on the results. *Enlightened Planning* chapter 5 discusses another operations management decision making context, this time using the UP explicitly in the foreground in a default mode, initially focussed on using it like a traditional basic OR process. This *Enlightened Planning* chapter 5 analysis initially works with a set of traditional inventory models (as discussed in OR textbooks) to address supply side operations management, starting with very basic simple models, gradually adding more complexity which successive robustness tests suggest is necessary. But the testing of working assumptions eventually results in a significant departure from even the most complex of the standard inventory models, leading to more sophisticated supply chain management strategies, and introducing a range of 'propositions' on the supply, production and demand side which all need top-down corporate planning in formal and informal terms. All of this planning might then benefit from a wide range of specific processes, developed using a fully evolved UP. Indeed, most organisations need a wide range of SP variants which require development by fully evolved UP variants, sometimes setting out to provide an SP like the SP for bidding discussed in this chapter, sometimes setting out to address what initially looks like a simple one-off issue that soon reveals a complex set of interconnected ongoing concerns.

This *Enlightened Planning* chapter 5 demonstration of the operation of the UP might be interpreted as testing the use of simple inventory models as applied in very basic OR textbooks using a simple classic hard OR process, and finding this particular specific process and model set approach unsatisfactory. A more useful interpretation is that chapter 5 of *Enlightened Planning* is a simple demonstration that *any* model used within *any* specific or general process which may be too simple in an inappropriate way can be tested by embedding that model and process combination within a UP, and the results can be built on in a variety of ways.

Concluding reflections

To conclude this sequence of four Part 2 chapters on universal and specific processes, it is worth emphasising several points which draw together some implications of using a systematic simplicity approach.

One is that many people in organisations adopting a systematic simplicity approach may want to use some of the basic concepts and operational toolsets, but not get directly involved in using a universal process (UP) or developing a sophisticated specific process (SP). For example, they might find the minimum clarity estimation approach discussed in Chapter 1 and the linear decision diagram approach discussed in Chapter 2 directly relevant and useful, but struggle to see the relevance to their responsibilities of becoming directly engaged in the development of sophisticated models or processes comparable to some of those discussed in this chapter. However, almost everyone makes some use of both models and processes, and these models and processes can all be assessed for possible improvements using a UP, by appropriately skilled colleagues if not by those using the models and processes. A freely available corporate source of advice of this kind can be a very useful corporate capability.

A second point is that any organisation which does not have an explicit corporate UP concept can be assumed to have some individuals and groups of people who are each using different relatively restrictive (narrowly framed) UP variants. It follows that an agreed corporate version of the UP concept, which is fully evolved to a form that is as general as possible, should improve the quality of all corporate decision-making processes, provided it is employed effectively and efficiently by competent people whenever doing so looks worthwhile.

A third point is the systematic simplicity mantra 'promote and protect the good and contest and constrain the bad' has a very general role in the UP concept which can sometimes be usefully embedded and given more focus in an SP developed using the UP. The general nature and value of this mantra is explored and developed in *Enlightened Planning*, but it is particularly clear when relationship management is directly involved, including relationships which may cross organisational boundaries. For example, the 'clarify ownership' phase of the basic SPP portrayed by Figure 8.2 evolved to provide a suitable focus on the need to plan forms of contract which were designed and interpreted in a way that encourages all those involved to work in a collaborative 'win-win' manner, fostering mutual trust and give and take. All contracts and associated relationship features should include incentives to promote and protect appropriate capabilities and motivation as well as more directly observed 'good' behaviours, and penalties to contest and constrain all unhelpful 'bad' behaviours. In a project management context, a crucial direct concern is the ownership of managerial and financial responsibility for risk and opportunity with a view to making the contractual relationships work in the best interests of the project owner. In operations management and corporate management contexts, adopting the mantra 'promote and protect the good and contest and constrain the bad' generalises this idea. Viewing it as an explicit part of all systematic simplicity processes by building it into the UP can be a useful way to remember to make use of it in a wide range of circumstances, as illustrated in all *Enlightened Planning* part 2 chapters.

A fourth and final point is the three points above imply that one central source of corporate expertise on UP usage should be helpful, but there are many very different ways this might be approached.

For example, a significant central group providing both strategic leadership and a direct source of support for all parts of the organisation is one route, perhaps supported by additional distributed expertise with knowledge and skillsets reflecting particular application areas, including special areas of focus within broad operations, project, and corporate management areas. Within this approach particular strengths might be associated with small teams which focus on subsets of these sources of expertise, related to testing and adjusting any existing processes to better suit changing circumstances, or building new SPs, or solving one-off messes (interdependent problem sets), for example.

As a quite different example, a significant central group providing strategic leadership plus wide range of support in general terms might be explicitly rejected at the outset, starting with an existing portfolio of groups with area-specific expertise and loyalties which are deemed too valuable to lose. A relatively modest central group might be envisaged, set up to coordinate and market the expertise of all the existing groups. Strategic clarity about where on a spectrum between these kinds of extremes an organisation should be might be obvious in some cases, worth careful thought in other cases.

Those involved in providing this corporate expertise might collectively play an internal consulting and corporate education role, perhaps operating as part of a wider set of related corporate services. They clearly need team or group or departmental labels reflecting their collective roles and their corporate context. Further, there needs to be a flexible approach in place for developing their short-term, medium-term, long-term and futures planning, driven by goals which are fully understood and appropriately shared by all relevant senior managers.

Chapter 11
Evolving a corporate commitment to systematic simplicity

A 'smiles test' starting point

This chapter addresses two related but separate questions:

First, 'what are the implications of using the processes for approaching planning and associated decision making outlined in Chapters 7 to 10 plus the conceptual and operational toolsets outlined in Chapters 1 to 6 in terms of an organisation of interest to you evolving a corporate commitment to systematic simplicity?'. 'Evolving' in this context implies adopting and then developing in a sustained manner.

Second, 'what does this imply in terms of you evolving your personal commitment to systematic simplicity?'.

Figure 11.1 is a useful way to portray some key interdependences associated with addressing these questions about a systematic simplicity approach.

Figure 11.1 is almost identical to a comparable figure in the last chapter of *Enlightened Planning*. You can interpret Figure 11.1 in terms of the corporate benefits of your organisation adopting any systematic simplicity approach which has been initially based on the approach advocated in this book, assuming adaptation during implementation and subsequent use to best suit the needs of your organisation with effective and robust testing of the variations adopted.

The prototype of Figure 11.1 was initially created by Stephen Ward more than 20 years ago, long before the development of the *Enlightened Planning* 'frowns' test and associated traffic light test concepts. In its initial form it was based on a 'smiles test' story which I used to tell people attending 1980s public courses on prototype systematic simplicity approaches. I began my story by explaining that I had been aware that a prior expectation of many people was any formally

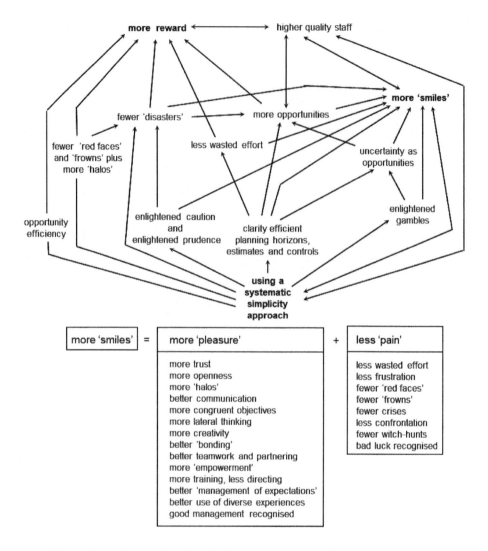

Figure 11.1 Corporate benefits of using a systematic simplicity approach with a focus on 'smiles' and associated capability-culture concerns, including the way these concerns drive 'reward' (profit and other positive objectives).

structured processes would be boring and restrictive, and they might have this prior belief too. But I had observed that when the kind of process I was advocating was adopted, the reverse was in fact the case. Systematic simplicity approaches were creative and liberating, and those using them were excited by the immediate implications of the changes and the follow-on implications. I had literally observed 'more smiles' when client organisations successfully adopted these approaches, some client staff members I worked with actually commented that they were both excited and pleased by the changes with a sincere big smile on their faces, and I had subsequently started suggesting the use of a 'smiles test' as a way of observing whether or not effective and efficient use was being made of all the relevant tools. Promoting the management of change as a quest for more smiles seemed a good way to improve morale.

Achieving 'smiles' in this sense can be associated with staff who tend to smile in the plain English sense because of good morale. From this starting point, the way a corporate focus on achieving 'smiles' in all senses can influence a corporate culture is portrayed by Figure 11.1.

To read what the influence diagram structure of Figure 11.1 is saying, opportunity efficiency achieved in any way will result in more reward, as indicated by the first arrow on the left-hand side in Figure 11.1. All forms of analysis concerned with opportunity efficiency will contribute directly in this way. The arrows to the right pick up additional positive effects with associated knock-on and feedback loops.

For example, fewer red faces and frowns plus more halos will also result in more reward, as indicated by the second arrow moving towards the right. 'Red faces' are frowns with an important ethical dimension, like the potential subcontractor that one option would use may be cheap, but they do not have acceptable ethical standards, a particular kind of red light that matters a great deal and is worth distinguishing from red light frowns with no ethical implications. There are several reasons people may see these distinctions as important. One is some managers want to make very sure that on important ethical issues their positions and the corporate stance is unambiguous, to protect the organisation's reputation and their reputation. Another is some managers may not want to burden staff with trying to make ethical choices on the organisation's behalf because they care about the implications of pressure this puts on staff.

'Smiles' are important positive reasons which do not lend themselves to quantitative treatment for considering making particular choices, like the staff one option would require are currently underutilized and developing this kind of work is a corporate priority, one trigger for the 'blue lights' discussed earlier.

'Halos' are special cases of blue light smiles, when positive ethical implications are involved, the opposite of a red-light-red-face situation. However, the rationale for explicitly signalling a halo is not necessarily a simple reversal of the red face concerns. For example, the corporate position may require financial measurement of the extra cost involved in 'doing a favour' for a charity before deciding whether or not to proceed, to explicitly consider the trade-off between the cost to the organisation and the benefit to the charity, but never contemplate putting a price on ignoring unethical actions, and formally mandate rejection of all red face test failures as a matter of principle.

This second arrow also generates more smiles via fewer disasters and more opportunities, which in turn generate more reward via higher quality staff.

Further arrows moving right keep amplifying this effect, the final right-hand arrow portraying the two-way relationship between adopting a systematic simplicity approach in terms of an enlightened planning perspective and higher quality staff feeding back up through all the arrows to more reward.

An initiating catalyst and one possible evolutionary path

For an organisation to begin the process of evolving a commitment to systematic simplicity, someone in the organisation needs to act as an initiating catalyst. Ideally, they need to begin by forming a team with agreed goals involving at least one demonstration application area where a need for change is clear to some of the key players. Consider one example that is reasonably typical of many of the contexts where I have some direct relevant experience.

In 1989 I led a two-day seminar in London on the prototype systematic simplicity approaches outlined earlier in this book. After attending this seminar, the Engineering Director of National Power (NP) approached me. He wanted a simplified form of the variants developed for BP and some of my other early clients which the seminar had used as examples. He wanted this simplified form adapted for use on the planning for all new NP electric power station projects. NP was a significant proportion of the UK's recently privatised Central

Electricity Generating Board (CEGB), and he wanted to improve on the current NP approaches to project management inherited from the CEGB.

We quickly agreed that the most effective way forward was probably an in-house NP seminar for all of the staff involved, followed by choosing a suitable demonstration project and NP selection of what this book will refer to as an in-house 'project processes team' leader who would take responsibility for ongoing adaptation of *project* uncertainty management *processes* plus adaptation of embedded operational frameworks and other tools for all NP projects under the Engineering Director's control using current prototype systematic simplicity approaches as the starting point. This project processes team leader would have consultancy support provided by me on an 'as required' basis. Initially this support would be quite intensive, but it would taper off over time. Initially I would be the only member of his team, but he would gradually add in-house staff to his team and train them with my support as his role developed.

Each project manager who reported to the Engineering Director would be responsible for using their whole project team to undertake the overall project planning and management their projects required. The project processes team and its leader would act as members of the teams reporting to project managers. The project processes team and its leader would help project teams with all of their uncertainty management, seeking opportunity efficiency in the systematic simplicity sense, but the overall responsibility for project planning and management would remain with the project manager and the rest of the project manager's team.

This approach worked extremely well within the Engineering department, and highly successful interaction with the Finance department led to some joint and separate developments involving my input in several financial operations management areas. After three years NP had a successful centre of prototype systematic simplicity based project uncertainty management planning in place for all projects under the auspices of the Engineering Director, plus a growing level of decision making in the Finance department using a prototype systematic simplicity uncertainty management processes based planning toolset.

However, as far as I am aware, the planning approaches developed were adopted and embedded as ongoing practice in these departments without spreading further. Long-term ongoing evolution of a systematic simplicity approach as a NP corporate goal was never achieved so far as I know, probably because as far as I know it was never on the NP agenda. It was certainly never on my agenda.

Three decades later, with the hindsight triggered and synthesised by writing *Enlightened Planning*, I would suggest several significant changes in approach for NP, for any other broadly comparable organisations, and for any consultants that offer support for a systematic simplicity based approach. These suggested changes are briefly outlined below, using NP* to indicate we are discussing an NP equivalent 30 years on, designated NP* for convenience.

One significant change is formally and explicitly recognising the value of beginning at the outset with the goal of creating an ongoing, in-house, organisation-wide uncertainty management processes *group*, referred to in this book as simply the '*processes group*'. The role of this processes group would be to initially support, then continually improve and generalise, the *project* uncertainty management frameworks and processes used by project managers reporting to the Engineering Director, to initially act as a 'project processes team' in the original NP project processes team sense, perhaps employing that label, but with a clear ongoing organisation-wide longer-term agenda in mind. This organisation-wide '*processes group*' would perhaps ultimately involve three *teams*: a *project* processes *team*, an *operations* processes *team*, and a *corporate* processes *team*. The multiple process team structure should certainly cover project management, operations management and corporate management concerns, but the decomposition structure could reflect the particular organisation's structure, and these three suggested teams are simply one possibility. The long-term goal would be one or more of these multiple teams within the processes group being used by all NP* staff reporting to all directors, not just the Engineering Director.

With this ongoing long-term objective in mind, I would base the opening NP* seminar on systematic simplicity as described in this book plus *Enlightened Planning*, make attendance compulsory for staff reporting to the Engineering

Director, and invite any other NP* staff who would like to come. Leadership in terms of opening remarks for this seminar by the CEO could be sought, to follow the IBM Forum 2 programme example, but although CEO support from the outset would be extremely valuable it would not be essential. A useful directly related step might be encouraging any senior staff outside the Engineering department who might be early converts, including key directors, to contribute in a modest but positive manner.

I would also recommend making the first new appointment a 'project processes team leader' who would explicitly see their initial role as 90% meeting the immediate needs of the Engineering Director, 10% as serving as the first of the team leader appointments within a new 'processes group'. Over time, as he or she acquired more project process team members who could look after ongoing Engineering Director concerns, and the other team leaders were appointed, the 10% might grow. This might be in part because projects beyond the Engineering department ought to become a growing concern, in part because addressing the interests of the processes group as a whole ought to become more of a concern.

A second significant change would be making a formal corporate strategy formation framework as addressed in Chapter 9 of this book, using the framework of Figure 9.1, an immediate target demonstration area. The aim would be building on all of the ideas outlined in *Enlightened Planning* chapter 8 (Corporate Strategy Formation). As quickly as possible the 'processes group' needs to ensure that the corporate systematic simplicity approach embraces corporate planning in a manner integrated with some of the organisation's key project planning concerns plus some of the organisation's key operations planning concerns. Given NP* involves a catalyst initiating a '*project* processes team' first, the second priority is a '*corporate* processes team' with a leader and supporting members.

A third significant change would be systematically targeting particular areas of operations management until a success leads to the establishment of an '*operations* processes team' with a leader and supporting members. This would then be immediately followed by systematically targeting all of the remaining operations and project management areas of activity. Priorities in both the operations and project management areas might be determined by intuitively driven heuristics, like 'pick the low hanging fruit first', or more formal assessments of benefits and costs. However, from the outset a clear long-term goal ought to be eventually providing support to all of an organisation's areas of activity that might benefit from this support – the organisation needs strategic clarity from the outset despite massive ongoing ambiguity about the best tactics.

A fourth significant change would be making sure that enough of the staff recruited for the processes group to work in the corporate, operations or project processes teams could be relied upon to work in other processes teams, to maintain flexibility in terms of staff capability and ensure effective ongoing integration of all project, operations and corporate planning processes, avoiding the development of inappropriate silo structure characteristics.

A fifth significant change would be making sure the processes group maintains an ongoing continuous improvement role, constructively challenging and encouraging all of the corporate, operations and project management staff they support as well as responding to requests for assistance. Avoiding a loss of corporate memory can be seen as a very important component of continuous improvement. Some processes group staff might move into line management roles within former 'client' groups the processes group were supporting. Indeed, the processes group might play a very important staff development role, with this given explicit senior management attention. But the processes group should maintain a clearly defined and separate ongoing challenging as well as supporting role, avoiding becoming fully embedded in line management functions.

The first of the processes team leaders appointed, the project processes team leader in the NP* context, should report to the CEO as well as the Engineering Director from the outset, to clearly signal and manage the broad project remit of their team (all NP* projects) plus the even broader general remit of the 'processes group' initiated by the 'project processes team'. The corporate processes team leader might report to the Corporate Strategic Planning Director as well as the CEO with the same rationale in mind. Which director in addition to the CEO the initial operations processes team leader reported to would depend on the area addressed, and one possible reason for more than three teams is decomposition of the 'operations processes team' when very different kinds of operations management are involved.

Initially the three or more team leaders might serve as joint leaders of the processes group. At some point, if not at the outset, it might become important to appoint a processes group leader who was not one of the team leaders. However, it would be important to grow a processes group embracing corporate, operations and project processes teams in a highly collaborative and flexible manner. One way to do this might be using a group leader with a very different perspective and role than the team leaders. For example, the group leader might be an older and more experienced management consulting senior manager who had a broader background than the team leaders and would see his or her role as selling the services of all of the team leaders, plus ensuring that they were all properly resourced to deliver in terms of staff numbers, training and skillsets, and perhaps providing mentoring plus external consulting support where and when it was needed. Eventually, perhaps after many years, but perhaps as soon as possible, the processes group leader might report directly to the board, with a role designation like 'Processes Director'.

Making extensive use of consultants with the right skills and experience might be very important initially, but developing or hiring in-house staff with the right skills, motivation and flexibility in a systematic manner from the outset would be crucial.

Where the evolutionary path would lie between the ultimate goal of a strong central systematic simplicity process expertise group and a highly decentralised approach with a central coordinating point of contact as discussed briefly at the end of Chapter 10 is a key early strategic clarity concern. However, it may not be possible to choose early on, and a change of mind may prove important.

A wide variety of variants of all these ideas are clearly possible, and organisations and contexts which are very different to the NP* example may require significantly different variants. If evolving a corporate commitment to systematic simplicity is a central concern for you, then reading *Enlightened Planning* after finishing this book would probably be a useful next step. Chapters 10 and 11 of *Enlightened Planning* elaborate the discussion of the last few pages in the context of all of the preceding chapters of *Enlightened Planning*.

Concluding comments for Part 2

In terms of how you might approach the evolution of your own use of systematic simplicity approaches, a range of possibilities might be beginning to suggest themselves at this point, depending upon your interests and your current and planned future roles. However, trying to explore them here using a single example like NP* would not serve a useful purpose. This is in part because readers who are senior managers at board level may have some very different immediate concerns to those of intermediate level managers in functional areas. Internal and external consultants, students of management who may be working at this on their own or following short courses or university courses, and others interested in the implications of systematic simplicity for issues like regulation, public safety or environmental concerns, may have very different concerns again. However, if you associate yourself with any one or more of these target reader groups, I hope you will carry on evolving your current understanding of a systematic simplicity approach in terms of any aspects of potential interest with an initial focus on the opening chapters of Part 3 of this book. I also hope some of the later Part 3 chapters will be of interest. The first Part 3 chapter illustrates the importance of a systematic simplicity approach to discounted cash flow analysis. It addresses misconceptions and misuses associated with Net Present Value (NPV) approaches which matter to all of us because of their implications for government decision making as well as for both private and public sector corporate decision making, not to mention personal and family decision making.

You may not be inclined to read *Enlightened Planning*, but I hope this book providing an overview introduction to what systematic simplicity implies will encourage you to engage with the details of some of the central ideas, support those who are directly engaged in adopting and evolving a systematic simplicity approach, and appreciate the full range of benefits portrayed by Figure 11.1 as well as the more direct implications of an opportunity efficiency basis for the pursuit of best practice.

Part 3
Key areas of focus for further enhancement of understanding and capability

Part 3, Chapters 12 to 15, might be seen by some readers as a distraction from the core set of foundation systematic simplicity concerns which are addressed in Parts 1 and 2. That is part of the rationale for having them in a separate Part 3 structure. However, each Part 3 chapter addresses important systematic simplicity concerns which are arguably basic and essential at a different level, and each is worth reading to clarify the generality of the messages that this book tries to convey. Further, each adds to the case for you developing an ongoing interest in a systematic simplicity approach for important reasons which I personally believe most people should at least be aware of, even if the details are not of immediate interest. You may of course choose to disagree. However, try Chapters 12 and 13 before you decide.

Chapter 12
Discounted cash flow analysis

The starting point for this chapter

A key driver of decisions about which projects and other investments organisations choose to undertake as part of their strategy formulation processes is the discount rates that they use for discounted cash flow analysis. Interdependent decision-making concerns include the way funds are raised to finance investments projects and the way projects are shaped from the beginning of their concept strategy stage. Associated implications generally not fully understood include the need for decision making processes which explicitly address expected outcomes in terms of what is assumed to be the primary attribute of interest, usually money, *separate* consideration of associated risk and trade-offs, *plus further separate* consideration of any further attributes, associated risk and trade-offs.

These concerns are discussed in *Enlightened Planning* chapter 7 primarily in 'what needs to be done' terms in the context of project planning for a private sector water and sewage utility, drawing on an earlier discussion of the same context in Chapman and Ward (2011). This book explores them in a very different manner. The discussion uses the historical evolution of my understanding of what is involved in all discounted cash flow analysis contexts relevant to all target readers for this book. It uses several case-based examples selected and discussed in a way designed to convey why the associated uncertainty decomposition issues are not generally understood from a systematic simplicity perspective, and why persuading people to adopt a systematic simplicity perspective may be crucial in contexts of interest to you. The explanation provided assumes no prior knowledge of the relevant literature and avoids technical details as far as possible.

During 1970 I spent a considerable amount of time discussing Net Present Value (NPV) based approaches to discounted cash flow analysis with two economist colleagues who were also very good friends, Chris Hawkins and David Pearce. They were drafting the book *Capital Investment Appraisal* (Hawkins and Pearce, 1971), and debating the controversies of the day about a wide range of basic issues that interested me in a general way. I had no specific applications in mind at that time. While I occasionally joined in the discussion, I was largely in listening and learning mode, building on what I had learned from introductory courses as a university student.

The first lesson that I took away from their often vigorous debates was their unequivocal agreement that the NPV concept is itself a completely meaningless concept unless the 'correct' discount rate is used.

The second lesson that I took away was the considerable confusion about what issues should and should not be embedded in the discount rate estimate used to make capital investment decisions, clearly the basis of what determines the 'correct' discount rate, and the extent of the associated controversy. The expected cost of the capital employed to fund an investment in terms of bond or loan funding was clearly central from most perspectives. But other components with various degrees of support included an opportunity cost associated with return on alternative investments, a risk premium to reflect the risk associated with this particular investment or investment area, and the rate of return on the shares of a private sector company making an investment to reflect the return on investment expectations and associated risk for shareholders. Many experts in this area will now argue that 50 years later all of these issues have been fully resolved. This chapter indicates this is not the case, and argues that the ongoing lack of a single coherent resolution of the full set of issues is not an acceptable situation. It suggests that everyone directly involved in or simply affected by decisions driven by discount rate choices and interdependent decision processes needs more clarity about the implications, and *that effectively means every one of us*. Like many other contentious issues discussed in this book, what is involved is far too important to leave it to experts who are making a wide range of explicit or implicit assumptions which in some circumstances are seriously misleading with consequences that directly impact us all.

The third lesson that I took away was the value of an Internal Rate of Return (IRR) approach as a useful parametric analysis tool for addressing discounted cash flow analysis parameter estimation uncertainty, *provided* decisions were *never* made by simply choosing the investments with the highest IRR, and provided the more general limitations of the IRR concept were clearly understood. IRR is defined as the discount rate which makes the NPV = 0, a flip point value. The basic rationale for using an IRR approach as I understood it at that time was if people involved in making a decision cannot agree on a single 'correct' discount rate, but they can agree that it is lower than the lowest positive IRR for one particular investment possibility when asking the question 'is NPV positive?', then they should be able to agree that particular investment is worth making, because all of their potentially 'correct' discount rate estimates will yield a positive NPV. The 'lowest positive IRR' proviso arose because solving the equation NPV = 0 to obtain the IRR value to be used can involve multiple IRR solution values including negative values. Multiple possible positive 'correct' values simply did not make sense in terms of NPV interpretation, but if all positive possibilities yielded the same answer, what was 'correct' arguably did not matter, and a negative discount rate value was held to be implausible. As I understood it this was seen at that time as a simple but useful demonstration that NPV is a meaningless concept if a 'correct' discount rate is not involved. However, it clearly fails to resolve the argument about what 'correct' actually means.

For reasons to be explored in this chapter, my reading of the situation as of 2021 is we can no longer fail to reach agreement about what the NPV concept itself should mean, or what should be included in the discount rate, or what this should imply about the 'correct' discount rate. Further, in all contexts we have to clearly and firmly reject a traditional single hurdle rate test approach to using the NPV concept – just asking the question 'is the NPV positive?' is never appropriate. We need an effective and efficient multiple test approach. This approach must be based on an underlying goal programming framework to address a possible portfolio of available investment possibilities and a potential choice of funding sources for those investments. This framework *may* have to cope with multiple criteria (expected outcomes and risk) for any attribute. It *may* have to cope with multiple attributes and all associated attribute trade-offs. It *must* employ a *very* careful approach to interpreting *exactly* what we mean by NPV for both public and private sector decisions in a holistic conceptual framework that makes sense of differences in private and public sector approaches, and in both public and private sector decisions we need to restrict the interpretation of NPV to a measure of the surplus or deficit associated with the cash flow net of the cost of the capital used, associated with a test of whether or not we expect to get our money back, as just one of a set of tests which may be relevant. And in all contexts, we need a systematically simple overall approach to an appropriate set of multiple tests, tailored to the features of different contexts, so that simple common contexts can use very user-friendly approaches that are as simple as possible, but more complex contexts do not suffer inappropriately simplistic approaches.

The relevance of all of these statements started to become clear to me during the drafting of Chapman, Ward and Klein (2006), in response to HM Treasury (2003a). Prior to 2003, the crucial conceptual leap to a formal multiple test framework with an underlying goal programming conceptual framework for opportunity efficiency implemented via the general and specific process approach to clarity efficiency did not occur to me, and I was not aware of anyone else adopting a formal multiple test framework approach prior to HM Treasury (2003a). What follows outlines the journey to my current view, with the goal of getting you to the same destination in terms of a broad initial understanding with a minimum of difficulty on your part.

The Alaskan Susitna Falls and insulating a house in the UK examples

In the early 1980s, Gavin Warnock, at that time a Vice President of Acres Consulting Services based in Canada, asked me to apply the thinking behind the SCERT (Chapman, 1979) approach to BP's offshore North Sea projects to the concept strategy stage approval of a proposed hydroelectric project at Susitna Falls in Alaska. The proposed Susitna Falls project would meet most of Alaska's electricity needs for the foreseeable future, but it involved very large capital costs associated with new infrastructure, including new road systems as well as the dams and turbine halls. Gavin was concerned that the NPV evaluations being employed were inappropriately biasing the analysis against proceeding.

I could not see an effective way to decompose the sources of uncertainty the

Susitna decision involved in the SCERT sense underlying the BP approach as outlined earlier in this book. However, I did generalise the parametric analysis ideas underlying the IRR approach, and produced an analysis which argued that the single most important source of uncertainty associated with NPV evaluation was the value of the Susitna Falls investment at the assumed planning horizon, designated the Terminal Value (TV), and:

1. this TV needed formal parametric analysis treatment;
2. this TV was not likely to be zero as currently implicitly assumed because of the high discount rate employed;
3. there was a strong case for suggesting that the proposed Susitna Falls investment could and probably should be viewed as an appreciating asset, on average becoming more valuable in 'real' (net of inflation) terms every year for the foreseeable future.

It was obviously important to recognise that the turbines and generators would need replacing in about 50 years, but the value of all of the moving machinery requiring replacement like turbines and generators was less than 10% of the overall investment value. Provided the dams and roads and other infrastructure were maintained, a reasonable assumption was they would be more valuable than their initial cost after 50 years. The reasons included the differential escalation of energy costs (increases above general inflation) plus the implications associated with capital investment in infrastructure which might be expected as fossil fuels were used up and became more expensive.

With hindsight, I should have questioned the high discount rates being used much more vigorously, and explicitly argued that the currently assumed values were highly uncertain. However, although I had been tutored by economists who had authored a textbook on NPV analysis, and had some further relevant economics background, I did not feel equipped to make a convincing case for lower discount rates, and a direct estimate of the uncertainty associated with the 'wrong economics' was a concept that at that time did not occur to me.

With hindsight, fossil fuel costs have risen less than most people expected in the early 1980s, but growing global warming concerns are now raising comparable issues.

However, accepting these shortcomings, I did in my view correctly identify the central question at the time this analysis was undertaken as making appropriate allowances for *all* potential uncertainty when estimating parameter expected values, looking at the TV given other unbiased expected value parameter assumptions, and *beginning* the analysis by asking the *first of several questions*: 'did this value suggest an *expected* net benefit if the Susitna Falls project proceeded?'.

If proceeding with the Susitna Falls project involved a higher expected cost as currently measured than the fossil fuel alternative, then a *second key question* of crucial importance needed asking: 'was proceeding with the Susitna Falls project a prudent choice given *all relevant uncertainty* and the risk-return trade-offs involved'. If a higher expected cost was involved, the downside risk associated with proceeding would be marginally more expensive electricity in a potential low energy cost future, but the downside risk associated with not proceeding was rising energy costs in conjunction with much of Alaska's fossil fuels being consumed, making not having this hydroelectric capability 50 years hence much more serious than having it in a low energy cost economic situation. An issue of crucial importance was whether or not hydroelectric power was a prudent choice in this context even if it was not the lowest expected cost choice. This issue arose because the downside and upside risk of the two alternative choices was not symmetric.

The basis of the case that I made at the time was that a risk efficient choice involving a minimum expected cost was probably involved if the Susitna Falls project proceeded *if* an appropriate discount rate was used, arguably a significantly lower discount rate than that currently employed. Further, even if the Susitna option had a marginally higher expected cost than the fossil fuel alternative, arguably the case *if* a very high discount rate was appropriate, proceeding with Susitna might be a prudent choice in terms of the risk associated with choosing the fossil fuel option if a high energy cost future was realised.

In the terms developed earlier in this book in the 1990s IBM context using Figures 4.1 and 5.1, *not proceeding* with the Susitna Falls project might be a *very* imprudent gamble, worth avoiding *even* if it was a risk efficient gamble.

Two published papers followed (Chapman and Cooper, 1983 and 1985), but the Susitna Falls project remains unbuilt, with a live website discussing it. The impression I got in the 1980s was that a high discount rate making the value of Susitna Falls fully developed for hydroelectric power provision 50 years hence of negligible consequence drove the thinking, and the argued need for prudence was not persuasive enough. I am now convinced that the Susitna Falls decision makers' failure to appreciate the imprudent gamble issue was arguably just as serious as using discount rates that were too high, and it is important for everybody that both these issues become widely understood in all relevant comparable contexts.

Although I was intuitively deeply suspicious of the validity of the high discount rates employed at the time, I was not aware of a sound conceptual basis for building an argument that a high discount rate was inappropriate in this context. I would now argue that a high discount rate in this context can and should be interpreted as incorporating a 'risk premium' in the discount rate, which is demonstrably biased against a low risk, long time horizon, 'safe' project – in favour of high risk, 'quick buck' alternative proposal – the exact opposite of what a 'risk premium' ought to be doing, and a very clear symptom of the 'wrong economics'. I would now argue this is not a matter of uncertainty in the usual sense. It can be viewed as a kind of ambiguity uncertainty – but it is a matter of misconceptions which require correction on a widespread basis to stop the damage being done.

The 1983 Chapman and Cooper paper uses the insulation of the walls in a UK home as an initial illustrative framework to simplify the discussion before turning its attention to the Susitna case, arguing that the appreciation of the value of the insulation installed in a UK home over time plus the increasing value of the fuel cost savings over time means some of the economic issues are directly comparable to the Susitna case – including the crucial asymmetric risk concern. However, in the house insulation case, parametric analysis made it clear that the biggest source of uncertainty was how long you might live in the house. If you insulated the walls of a UK house in the early 1980s and then decided to move within a year or two, you would lose a small amount of money. But if you did not insulate, and did not move for ten or more years, you would lose a very large amount of money. This was particularly straightforward to demonstrate with a fairly low real discount rate associated with my family investment decisions at the time, using a decision I actually made at that time as a basis for the published example. The home insulation example also illustrates the relevance of secondary attributes. If you did insulate your house, you and your family would enjoy a lower marginal cost of being warmer, and you would probably choose to be warmer some of the time. You would also be more environmentally friendly. However, while a very useful simple parametric analysis procedure was recommended, it did not emphasise the need to consider additional attributes formally, even in the 'smiles' and 'frowns' test sense, and it failed to suggest formal systematic testing for overall portfolio level investment decision implications which needed testing for robustness, now viewed as an oversight on my part.

One very important general lesson from the Susitna Falls member of this pair of cases was that *whenever* a discount rate is used that is too high, this *always* results in a severe bias against relatively safe long-term investments, *systematically* favouring 'quick buck' alternatives as noted above. However, how best to persuade people to avoid using discount rates which were inappropriately high was not clear. My colleagues Chris Hawkins and David Pearce had been very clear about the need to deal with issues associated with inappropriate discount rates a decade earlier, but the Susitna Falls proposal and the fossil fuel electric power alternative proposal seemed a very clear and important example of a failure to find an appropriate way to do so.

A second important general lesson from this pair of cases was that the risk of making an investment may have to be considered in conjunction with the risk of not making it, which begins to clarify why putting a 'risk premium' in the discount rate directly or indirectly used to assess the hydroelectric project was clearly inappropriate, because hydroelectric and alternative fossil fuel electric power projects clearly involve very different kinds and levels of risk. I now see this second lesson as directly linked to the first, and both as symptoms of a large set of interdependent issues which are inherent in a single hurdle rate test approach.

A third important general lesson was recognising the need to decompose the analysis into uncertainty about the discount rate in 'economic desirability' terms using a 'real discount rate' (net of inflation) and a separate set of 'financial feasibility' concerns which had to address inflation and timing issues. In the Susitna case, timing concerns included important electricity tariff issues driven by US law plus related intergenerational equity concerns, to ensure that current consumers did not suffer financially for low cost electricity benefits which future generations would enjoy, addressed in financial feasibility terms in the 1985 Chapman and Cooper paper.

In retrospect, I should have recognised a potential need to formally address further attributes of importance in the Susitna case, like the immediate environmental impacts of the dam as well as potentially complex long-term environmental impacts, within the same discount rate driven decision-making process, but outside the discount rate itself. And in retrospect I should have generalised these lessons to recognise that the basic 'single hurdle rate test' framing assumption nature of NPV-based decision-making approaches being employed was actually fundamentally flawed, because the need to deal with multiple objectives inherently implies that a single test approach is inappropriate. Until very recently I remained somewhat perplexed by how long it took me, and everybody else whose work I have been aware of, to see what the basis of the problems really was. For reasons developed over the next few pages, it is now very clear from a current systematic simplicity perspective that we *always need* a multiple test *framing* assumption approach to decision making involving discounted cash flow analysis, because we *always need* clarity about possible multiple attributes plus expected outcomes and possible associated risk, including possible portfolio level strategy implications, whether or not multiple attributes and risk are actually involved. We may be able to employ very simple working assumptions, but not without testing their robustness. Multiple attribute issues demanding attention and complex risk issues clearly needing attention make this situation more obvious, and certainly helped to trigger the insight which finally made 'the penny drop' for me.

Within this multiple test framework, we also need clarity about the different views of what should and should not be in the discount rate. I am now firmly convinced that the *only* determinant of the basic NPV discount rate ought to be the *expected* cost of the capital used, with associated downside and upside risk captured outside the discount rate, and all further relevant attributes also addressed *outside the discount rate* used for the cost of capital. However, for some people in some contexts this view is highly contentious; it involves an area of contention which needs separation from the basic multiple test debate, and we are dealing with a very complex mess of interconnected problems, not a single straightforward issue.

The UK Nirex example, and subsequent developments

In the 1990s I spent several years advising UK Nirex on the risk and uncertainty management of a project to permanently dispose of UK intermediate level nuclear waste in deep mines in Cumbria. As part of this I became involved in a review of the whole UK Nirex nuclear waste disposal project concept by the Department of the Environment (DoE). The DoE were looking at postponing disposal for 50 years, continuing the current policy of surface storage in 'ponds'. Our analysis persuaded the DoE to accept our argument that if they postponed the Nirex deep mine disposal project for 50 years, the capital cost in 50 years' time could be expected to escalate by a factor of two in real (net of inflation) terms, because the nuclear industry in Cumbria would probably die, and this would probably make another site location a political imperative. A published paper with a UK Nirex colleague (Chapman and Howden, 1997) addressed this and other relevant kinds of uncertainty in several useful ways, building on my earlier Susitna Falls work. Our paper included parametric analysis of the discount rate, and I was aware at that time HM Treasury already had an extensive track record for changing the economic theory basis for their currently mandated discount rate, implicitly admitting they were prone to getting it wrong. However, we were unable to persuade the DoE or HM Treasury that the 6% real discount rate mandated at that time by HM Treasury might be too high. A 3% expectation based on long term UK government bond funding rates seemed a more reasonable approach in my view, argued at the time, but not accepted by the DoE or HM Treasury officials I spoke to, who were not even prepared to discuss the possibility that 6%

was not correct. The UK government accepted the DoE recommendation (DoE, 1994) of 50 years deferral based on an NPV employing a 6% real discount rate, which inferred a saving of £100 million.

In 2003 HM Treasury published a significantly revised version of *The Green Book: Appraisal and Guidance in Central Government* (HM Treasury, 2003a). A particularly crucial change was moving from a *single* hurdle rate test approach to capital investment appraisal to a *multiple* test approach which decomposed the treatment of different investment attributes and associated criteria and objectives. I believe HM Treasury deserve significant credit for recognising the need to move from a single hurdle rate test framework to a formal multiple test approach, and it was a recommendation of enormous importance. However, I also believe it should have triggered a substantial set of further crucial transformative changes, by HM Treasury and by everybody else using NPV analysis. This has not happened so far. The implications are directly relevant for all private sector investment appraisals as well as all public sector investment appraisals, and they are both important and complex.

In summary form, in my view the key features of a multiple test approach which now need immediate widespread understanding by all affected parties are explicit recognition that:

1. a portfolio of possible investments almost always needs strategy level consideration;
2. more than one attribute *may* be relevant;
3. each attribute involves component criteria (expected outcomes plus associated risk);
4. these attributes and component criteria *may* need assessment as separate objectives;
5. risk-return trade-offs and trade-offs between attributes *may* be relevant;
6. only the expected cost of the capital used should be incorporated in the discount rate;
7. it may be very important to choose the source of finance for specific investment categories in an optimal manner as part of the overall approach.

An immediate demonstration of the importance of this generalised conceptual framework in terms of changing decision outcomes was the implications for the Nirex project deferral. The HM Treasury recommended real discount rate was revised from 6% to about 3%, and simply making this change alone meant that the £100 million 'saved' by deferring the Nirex project for 50 years became about £2000 million 'lost', 'other things being equal'.

Other things very clearly should not have been treated as if they were equal. Arguably even more serious errors were associated with past failures to appropriately consider everything else that really does matter in an appropriate manner because a single test approach was used, and two decades later there is still no evidence that past errors may be corrected via revised analysis or avoided in future decisions.

In effect what the DoE were looking at in the 1990s they got wrong because of HM Treasury mandated advice, and using a 6% real discount rate that should have been 3% led the DoE to a £2 billion error in the NPV, *but the DoE also failed to look effectively at a substantial range of further issues which arguably mattered even more*. That was the starting point for a paper (Chapman, Ward and Klein, 2006) which built on these 2003 Green Book revisions.

One important further concern is while HM Treasury (2003a) advocates a real discount rate of about 3%, arguably appropriate for the 1990s Nirex decision, the economic theory basis used by HM Treasury in 2003 to define the discount rate was entirely inappropriate in my view, and that basis is still in use and currently yielding inappropriate values. HM Treasury (2020a) sustains the Treasury's 2003 economic theory position. It is based on a 'social time preference for money' analysis approach. In my view this is not an appropriate starting position, a view stated relatively gently in my 2006 paper with Ward and Klein because I was so pleased that they had moved to a multiple test approach and admitted that the 6% used earlier should be closer to 3%. In retrospect a much stronger challenge to the social time preference basis for a discount rate would have been more appropriate in 2006. In my current view the economists advocating this approach should have been challenged to much greater effect by a wide range of interested parties some time ago, including other economists, and the ongoing lack of an effective challenge is in itself a source of growing concern.

A second important set of concerns is HM Treasury (2020a) is clearly still committed to an event-based view of risk which fails to embrace risk efficiency or any effective way of coping with possible outcomes beyond expected value provisions. As of January 2021, if you use this book's References section to access *Management of Risk in Government: Framework* (Cabinet Office, 2017), you can use Annex D to access a copy of the HM Treasury (2020b) Orange Book as well as the HM Treasury (2020a) Green Book, and presumably further updates will be available via this route.

A third important concern is the importance of an underlying goal programming framework to assess the most appropriate simple multiple test approach, as explored in the Chapman, Ward and Klein 2006 paper. In the terminology of this book, we need to use a formal systematic simplicity approach to 'plan the planning', drawing upon the universal process (UP) and specific process (SP) concepts to develop suitably simple processes for routine use which employ underlying goal programming ideas to address possible multiple attribute and possible risk concerns, plus all associated trade-offs, in a simplicity efficient manner.

I am now convinced that a much more broadly based and systematic approach to forcefully challenging HM Treasury on their whole approach to decision making is clearly required. It needs to address discounting *and risk plus underlying uncertainty and associated opportunity.*

The concerns which a 'social time preference for money' approach ought to address do need to be confronted, but in a very different manner, beginning by addressing the ethical concerns associated with intergenerational issues involving all relevant attributes at a portfolio of government projects level, and always limiting the discount rate to the expected cost of the most appropriate funding for this particular investment. HM Treasury assuming since 2003 that the preference most people have for consumption today rather than saving for consumption tomorrow is a sound basis for a government systematically deferring long-term capital expenditure, is arguably lacking requisite ethics as well as being the 'wrong economics' in a general sense. Compounding this by assuming for most applications that we are all going to keep getting richer at the same rate as we have in the recent past with an inadequate grasp of risk is certainly not acceptable, and it is the 'wrong decision science', not just the 'wrong economics'. The Green Book approach to exceptions is itself a very clear symptom of underlying theory problems of considerable complexity, and these problems need direct holistic treatment in a general framework.

Further, a systematic simplicity approach to all relevant attributes which generalises to accommodate private sector projects in one coherent overall framework is crucial. The reasons are complex and the arguments controversial. Some of them are discussed in more detail in Chapman and Ward (2011) and *Enlightened Planning* chapter 7, but not all. In brief, the starting point is the expected cost of *the most appropriate source of capital available* to fund the investment should be the *only* criteria used to define the discount rate, and using that rate to compute the NPV should *always* be the basis of a first test in a multiple test sequence, for public or private sector decisions, otherwise choices will be biased away from investments that could be funded inexpensively towards investments which are relatively expensive to fund, a generalisation of the Susitna Falls issue.

In a public or private sector context, a first test positive NPV means the potential investment passes a test which says 'you can *expect* to get your money back', with a surplus measured by NPV. In a public sector context this might be called the 'bond test', using an appropriate government bond funding rate expected value. In a private sector context if and when corporate bonds are relevant (as in the private sector water and sewage utility example explored in *Enlightened Planning* chapter 7), 'bond test' is also appropriate terminology.

A second and further following tests might address return over and above 'getting your money back' in relation to other portfolio possibilities, bearing in mind the timescales of those returns with rate of return net of cost of capital and duration of return implications, and all relevant risk. Relevant risk may be specific to the proposed investment, but it may also involve the wider context of overall risk at a portfolio level. Relatively simple risk tests might suffice in some contexts, but in other contexts extremely complex risk tests might be required.

As an example of one kind of complexity, it is now very clear that risk associated with deferring (or not) the disposal of UK nuclear waste was far from simple, and it was clearly not assessed appropriately. The collapse of the UK nuclear industry anticipated in the 1990s if a solution to the nuclear waste issue was deferred had very wide implications that should have received much greater formal public scrutiny than seems to have taken place. These issues needed attention alongside risks associated with ongoing temporary surface storage of the waste, with both accident and malicious attack security implications as well as cost risk associated with expected cost per annum. They also needed comparison to risks associated with proceeding with deep mine disposal and then discovering seismic event and groundwater related concerns which had not been fully anticipated and resolved. These risks mattered, and they still matter, even if the UK decides to stop using nuclear power – the existing nuclear waste was, and still is, an ongoing legacy issue. Further, whether or not the UK might need nuclear power in the future, and whether or not UK nuclear power domestic capability was an asset worth preserving, clearly ought to have been formally assessed as part of an energy planning process undertaken by the government. The 'risk premium' component in the 1990s mandated 6% real discount rate which HM Treasury removed in 2003 was obviously not the way to address these risks. Nor was it a defensible approach to assume that the markets would take care of the very complex and important issues involved.

In a public sector context, there are further complex issues which an example like the Nirex project has to confront, like intergenerational transfer concerns (our grandchildren paying to clear up our nuclear liabilities as well as those of our parents, for example, perhaps at a time in the future when the resources to do so will not be available). This kind of issue needs consideration at a portfolio of all government projects level, in conjunction with a wide range of other relevant interdependent concerns and constraints.

In a sense the Susitna Falls project evaluation probably used the wrong discount rate and seriously underestimated the value of an appreciating asset plus ongoing fuel cost savings of increasing importance, because an effective portfolio perspective in a suitable framework would have lent itself to appropriate lower interest rate funding. In a roughly mirror image situation, the Nirex project evaluation very certainly used the wrong discount rate and seriously underestimated the value of an appreciating liability which will have to be dealt with sometime and has a cost estimate which will continue to grow, plus ongoing annual costs which will continue to increase, and ongoing risks. However, in both cases complex issues beyond financial expected return or cost and associated financial risk are crucial. For example, there are serious ethical concerns associated with intergenerational transfer issues in both situations, serious potential catastrophic incidents associated with nuclear waste whatever is done with it, and major dams also pose potential catastrophic risk concerns.

In most private sector contexts, the issues are arguably very much simpler, and certainly they are very different. The focus of concern in chapter 7 of *Enlightened Planning* discussion is a private sector water and sewage utility, addressing project planning as a whole, beginning with the concept strategy stage. The key discount rate driven decision-making process issue in this context was using an expected corporate bond rate to assess new water mains and sewage works projects, explicitly assuming that the bonds would be secured using the assets they fund in a manner comparable to a mortgage, instead of using higher discount rates reflecting shareholder rate of return expectations, and considering the investment choice implications of this lower cost of capital. This change should lead to some capital investment projects with a significantly higher initial capital cost which are worthwhile because they deliver a longer expected asset life, a more reliable facility, and lower maintenance costs. For example, water mains might be designed for a 100-year life expectancy instead of 50 years. Different, higher quality versions of projects would be pursued as well as making different decisions about whether or not to undertake projects. The issues involved are not particularly complex to deal with, but they are of very great importance. Current very low interest rates strengthen this argument for low-cost bond-funded investment in all private sector contexts provided the way the bonds are secured means that associated risk is low, and comparable arguments ought to apply if public sector ownership of utilities and other organisations is involved. Important portfolio of investment issues needing consideration in a multiple test process sense include avoiding too many projects taking place in the same area at the same time, disrupting traffic or sewage and water services, or a lack of smooth flow of work for preferred sets of trusted contractors.

In the somewhat different context of a private sector pharmaceutical company, building on the corporate strategy formation example briefly explored in Chapter 9, if the investments being considered involved a portfolio of very basic research projects, another portfolio of near-to-market final development projects, and a variety of intermediate development level portfolios of projects, the focus might be unbiased estimates of all the *individual* project expected returns followed by *portfolio* consideration of associated risk plus any other relevant attributes. In this case the efficient diversification of risk concerns addressed by an effective portfolio approach might be the crucial risk management aspect needing attention, and discounting might not even be directly relevant in a portfolio context. Risk in financial terms in this context involves 'hedging' effects which need to be taken advantage of by exploiting any available negative dependence in addition to minimising positive dependence between all of the options selected, an example of the classic portfolio analysis problems confronted directly by Markowitz (1959). Assuming the cost of capital for all these investment possibilities is the expected rate of return for shareholders and this would define the discount rate might be appropriate if discounting is used because of different time horizons. However, governments and charities might influence investment strategies by making funds available for specific areas for a range of reasons with a variety of linked incentive strategies, adding to the complexities involved. As a somewhat different kind of complication, funding for less risky portfolios of corporate assets like buildings and computers might be funded in very different ways to exploit lower expected costs of capital.

In the relatively simple context of a private sector manufacturing company of modest size, the issue remains correctly identifying the expected cost of the money used to fund a possible capital investment as the first test, and then assessing all the criteria other than 'an expectation of getting your money back' in a practical systematically simple manner. But suppliers of assets might be prepared to lease or rent the assets needed instead of selling them, comparable to providing a special kind of mortgage, an important asset financing complication. And criteria like 'establishing a presence in a new market which looks attractive as part of a product market diversification strategy' may need explicit formal attention. The relevant risk might be being in the wrong set of markets because risk efficient diversification was not addressed effectively, or the wrong kind of funding for certain kinds of investments.

In effect in all of these private sector example cases we are just talking about the strategy formation concerns addressed in Chapter 9 of this book, having factored in consideration of the cost of capital and the options available to raise that capital whenever that is directly relevant to sets of decisions that may need consideration in portfolio terms. This chapter treats the Nirex case as addressed by the DoE in conjunction with HM Treasury in the same framework with some especially complex concerns to address, which Chapter 9 did not consider, and this chapter will not explore further either. Doing so is beyond the scope of this book, but the way all governments address national investment strategy structuring plus processes for related strategy development is clearly a topic needing attention, as is its relationship to the way other organisations approach their investment strategy, and the rationale for differences.

Concluding reflections

While I believe HM Treasury (2020a) persists with very serious flaws in the 2003 Green Book which need urgent attention, the need for a multiple test approach identified in 2003, in conjunction with my conviction that the way the 1990s decision to postpone disposal of UK nuclear waste had been made, was the trigger for me to finally start to develop a systematic simplicity perspective on discounted cash flow analysis.

Why drafting the 2006 paper in response to HM Treasury (2003a) was necessary for the overall approach required to begin to clarify itself is still not entirely clear to me. However, I think like most people I was probably trying to hang on to simpler conceptual frameworks which seemed to have worked so far, and linking the Treasury's move to a multiple test approach to formal use of a goal programming conceptual basis for opportunity efficiency was certainly the key trigger. Whatever the exact reason, I am glad I got there eventually, and I hope this chapter's outline story of the long journey I had to take may help you to get there more quickly.

Three closely coupled general lessons you might take from this chapter are:
1. opportunity efficiency always requires consideration of both expected outcomes and associated risk in terms of all relevant option attributes for all aspects of our plans and associated management decision making, this has to include contexts involving discounted cash flows, and it is extremely important to avoid letting the discounting framework confuse the way all relevant objectives and associated trade-offs are assessed;
2. this means a complex set of trade-offs needs careful consideration within a general framework which lets us test simplifying assumptions for robustness, made as simple as possible in practice via effective use of iterative processes like the one outlined by Chapman, Ward and Klein (2006) for public sector decisions as an alternative to that outlined by HM Treasury (2003a);
3. most private sector versions of this approach will be much simpler to apply in practice than the public sector version addressed in Chapman, Ward and Klein (2006), like the water and sewage utility context example explored in *Enlightened Planning*, and some will be very simple, but some could be quite complex in very different sorts of ways, depending on the context.

The most suitable general *conceptual* framework for testing these kinds of simplifying assumptions in my view is 'goal programming'. As mentioned earlier, for an introductory review paper you might look at Tamiz, Jones and Romero (1998). However, following on from this chapter's discussion of the need for a multiple test approach to discounting, with a view to wider implications as well, in my view the basic ideas behind a goal programming framework are worth understanding at the level of the next few paragraphs even if you are not mathematically inclined and you are not particularly interested in discounted cash flow analysis.

Goal programming is an approach to optimising when more than one objective is involved. One objective is the *nominal* 'primary' objective, treated as 'the objective function'. The choice of a 'primary' objective may be nominal in the sense that is driven by ease of measurement or convenience for some other reason. Money is the usual choice, in terms of expected outcome as measured for cost or reward (profit or contribution to profit). All of the other objectives are 'secondary' objectives, treated as constraints, initially associated with 'best guess' levels of achievement feasibility statements. The primary objective is maximised if it is a 'reward' (positive) measure, minimised if it is a 'cost' (negative) measure. Shadow prices (or costs) for all of the secondary objectives are then observed, which indicate how much the reward could be further increased (or the cost could be further decreased) if that constraint could be relaxed by one unit, providing a direct measure of the trade-off between that secondary objective and the primary objective at the current optimal solution. After an initial optimisation iteration, goal programming requires its users to relax or tighten the constraints for another iteration, continuing until a set of shadow price/cost trade-offs are achieved which are judged appropriate.

Direct *operational* use of goal programming is rarely a feasible practical proposition, but goal programming is always a useful *conceptual* basis for thinking about suitably simple systematic approaches to opportunity efficiency as an operational definition of what 'best practice' *ought* to be.

As a very simple example, if return over and above the cost of capital is the only attribute of interest, all investments provide return over the same time horizon, and risk is irrelevant, the optimal portfolio involves ordering the options by return over and above the cost of capital, and allocating funds in that order until some stopping points are reached for each successive option and then the portfolio as a whole.

As a more complex classical portfolio analysis example, if measuring return over and above the expected cost of capital in terms of expected return for each possibility plus a matrix of associated variances and covariances was appropriate, a Markowitz mean-variance quadratic programming approach could be used. However, if a more general financial portfolio planning approach which did not require variance measurement of risk or mathematical programming was of interest, then the chapter 10 approach in Chapman and Ward (2002) could be employed instead.

As a more complex example directly addressing multiple attributes, if we think we have an appropriate plan, developed using a simple intuitively driven search within an iterative procedure like the one outlined by Chapman, Ward and Klein (2006), a useful final robustness test is to ask two questions:

1. 'Are there any other attributes of interest (aspects of reward or cost) which need assessing in terms of shadow price or shadow cost estimates of trade-offs associated with expected outcomes?'
2. 'In terms of any additional attributes or any attributes addressed earlier, are there any other criteria (risk associated with expected outcome for example) which need assessing in terms of shadow price or shadow cost estimates of trade-offs?'

The shadow price or shadow cost values *always* exist – whether or not those making decisions know that they exist and can estimate an appropriate value. The issues are *always*:

1. 'is it worth having estimates of what the shadow prices or costs are;
2. and is it worth considering potential plan revisions as a consequence?'

The uncertainty decomposition addressed in the BP SCERT discussions in Chapters 3 and 4 involved decomposing sources of uncertainty within a given attribute like duration or cost, treating expected outcome and associated downside risk as two separate criteria when appropriate, with a focus on decomposed sources of uncertainty like 'weather' and 'wet buckles'. The rationale for this kind of uncertainty decomposition was seeking opportunity efficiency in terms of contingency planning, with unbiased cost and duration estimates as important by-products.

The uncertainty decomposition addressed in this chapter has to be able to address multiple attributes which all need consideration within the same discount rate driven decision-making process, including risk associated with implications which are not just financial, and certainly not just financial in a short-term sense. The concerns are significantly different, and very different sorts of issues are raised. Looking back 40 years to when Gavin Warnock asked me to apply the thinking behind the BP SCERT approach to discounting in the Susitna Falls project context, it is not surprising I did not see a connection. But you may find it useful to see there is a link, in terms of a different rationale for decomposing sources of uncertainty to those addressed earlier in this book, adding to the portfolio of reasons for directly addressing complexity using decomposition of uncertainty in a manner which is clarity efficient.

The multiple test process approach to NPV analysis advocated by HM Treasury back in 2003 as discussed in Chapman, Ward and Klein (2006) fits into direct use of the goal programming framework – for me an instructive introductory example of its very effective use as a general conceptual framework tool. HM Treasury (2003a and 2020a) do not make this connection, but that is by no means the only problem with their position.

Looking forward, Chapter 13 addresses another somewhat different kind of uncertainty decomposition, building on the same goal programming framing assumption basis for opportunity efficiency driven best practice as this Chapter 12 discussion.

Looking backwards, Chapter 2 employed the same underlying goal programming framework to treat photocopier expected contract cost as the 'primary' criteria, with speed, reliability and non-measurable concerns like colour as secondary attributes. The blue to red light (smiles to frowns) approach discussed in Chapter 11 also rests on the same foundations.

Once you become fully aware of the ubiquitous nature of its application at a range of levels of formality, a goal programming conceptual framework becomes an integral part of the toolset needed to seek opportunity efficiency at a 'deciding how to decide' framing assumption level.

Chapter 13
Addressing important trade-off clarifications involving ethical concerns

The 'value of an avoided fatality' as a starting point

Clarity efficient consideration of trade-offs involving multiple attributes as well as trade-offs between expected values and associated risk within any given attribute is a central feature of a systematic simplicity approach.

Chapter 2 explored the use of a simple linear decision diagram to consider photocopier options in terms of the qualitative analysis of trade-offs between contract cost and secondary attributes like copying speed and reliability, as well as quantitative risk-reward trade-offs for the contract cost primary attribute. The focus of Chapters 4 and 5 was a single monetary attribute like cost, using higher clarity decision diagrams to address BP offshore North Sea projects and related IBM UK bidding decisions when risk-reward trade-offs in terms of enlightened and unenlightened gambles and prudence were important. Sometimes important ethical concerns can be addressed at a fairly high level of clarity using qualitative analysis approaches like the 'red face' and 'halo' tests versions of 'frown' and 'smile' tests, using a red-green-blue traffic light approach, discussed in relation to IBM's specific process for bidding and Figure 11.1. However, sometimes ethical issues require systematic quantification which should be subject to public scrutiny, a concern this chapter addresses. Examples include public and private sector decisions involving trade-offs between lives lost in accidents and money spent avoiding them. Further examples involve injuries or ill health caused by avoidable practices, and environmental damage which could have been avoided or reduced by better practices.

The initial focus of this chapter is a concept usually referred to as 'the value of an avoided fatality'. This concept is extensively used on a worldwide basis, but it is widely misunderstood and sometimes seriously misused. It is a trade-off concept which addresses quantifying a planned trade-off between money and lives. Generalising to money and lives plus injuries follows, then money and further issues like environmental pollution.

This chapter begins with a brief discussion focussed on the issue of trade-offs between money and lives using an analysis example which was widely discussed 50 years ago but remains a useful directly relevant illustration. As reported in the book *The Gift* (Hyde, 2006), around 1970 the US National Highway Traffic Safety Administration (NHTSA) was using a value of an avoided fatality of $200,000. It was based on a published cost-benefit analysis which included itemised provisions of: $10,000 for 'victim's pain and suffering', $900 for 'funeral', and $173,000 for 'future productivity losses'. The US automobile manufacturer Ford used this value when deciding not to fit an $11 safety device to their new Pinto model in 1971 to reduce the risk of fires caused by low speed rear-end collisions associated with a basic design fault. By 1977 at least 500 people had burned to death in Pinto crashes, and the US press had exposed Ford's wilful manufacturing and sale of a car they knew was unsafe and their rationale for not spending $11 per car to make it safer. Hyde's book observes this involved 'a classic example of both cost-benefit analysis and the confusion between "value" as calculated by economists and "worth" as understood in broader frameworks which recognise the importance of "gifts" and other non-market-based concepts'.

Enlightened Planning chapter 9 explains why the NHTSA were not being unreasonable using $200,000 as a value of an avoided fatality, but they would have avoided criticism and perhaps prevented Ford's wholly inappropriate use of this value if they had *formally and explicitly* defined the 'transformation factor' from avoided fatalities to money as T, where:

$$T = V_1 \times E,$$

V_1 = $200,000 was a 'base value starting point using cost-benefit analysis for a single fatality',

$E = 1$ was an initial NHTSA assumption for the 'everything else factor' defined by E, and the NHTSA had made it clear that the E = 1 initial assumption was only suitable for use given three conditions:

1. It should only be used by the NHTSA – it should not be used by other parties like Ford.
2. It should only be used by the NHTSA until feedback from those directly involved in using and funding the roads in question suggested that no change was currently required, or a higher or lower figure was more appropriate.
3. Consideration of possible adjustments must involve accountable decision makers using processes that all relevant parties could trust.

When clarifying why this approach was being used, it would be important to explain that T was a shadow cost concept for planning national roads in terms of the trade-off between the expected additional annual cost of any potential improvements for safety reasons (assuming there are no other benefits) and the expected reduction in fatalities per annum as a consequence. Obvious application areas include decisions to introduce the use of more expensive but more effective crash barriers and other measures separating traffic moving in opposite directions.

Further, when explaining why this approach was being used, it would also be important to explain that once a value of T was agreed, it was a 'revealed preference' value. It was unlikely to coincide with what any given individual person might think was the most appropriate value, but it would reflect the judgement of those who decided what value should be used, they were accountable for that decision in ethical terms, and the value used should reflect the views of those paying for the roads and using the roads in an appropriate manner. The cost-benefit starting point used in this case had no ethical or moral content. Initial confirmation or adjustment would be essential to acquire the endorsement which an appropriate ethical content required. And updates would be necessary as circumstances changed and public opinions changed as a consequence.

Everyone involved wants to minimise fatalities. Everyone involved also wants to minimise cost. This implies a shadow cost for an avoided fatality, *whether or not people wish to recognise the fact.* Employing this shadow cost role for a 'value of an avoided fatality' concept, and using one value consistently for all decisions involving safety concerns relevant to their remit, is the only way the NHTSA can minimise the overall level of expected fatalities for whatever level of cost people want. This approach involves being 'fatality efficient', a form of 'opportunity efficiency', and ensuring that the overall approach as well as the parameter values employed are subjected to appropriate public scrutiny is what gives the approach ethical credibility.

There are very reasonable explanations for why NHTSA did not make all of this clear around 1970. Arguably they were ahead of most other organisations with comparable concerns, very open about their approach, and reasonably generous in the shadow cost used. However, there are no reasonable explanations or excuses for Ford's serious misuse of the NHTSA approach. Ford should have made the Pinto much safer or scrapped it completely.

All organisations should avoid 'a Ford Pinto experience', and any organisations still using approaches with some features of the 1970s NHTSA or Ford approach may be able to significantly improve their management decision making by applying a fully updated systematic simplicity approach with features designed to suit their particular context as soon as possible. This chapter will now use a synthesis of analysis from two contexts to explain some of the key issues that may have to be addressed at an overview level.

A railway system example

In the 1990s I was asked to undertake a review of Railtrack's strategic approach to railway safety. At this point Railtrack was the private sector operator of UK railway tracks and stations, following privatisation of British Rail. A central aspect of my recommendations was a need to *formally and explicitly* define the transformation from fatalities avoided to money using the 'transformation factor' T_S, where:

S = the expected number of fatalities for a set of scenarios spanning zero to the maximum feasible,

$$T_S = V_1 \times E_S,$$

V_1 = a 'base value starting point value in £ for a single fatality',

E_S = an 'everything else factor for each fatality in a situation when there are S fatalities'.

An S = 1 scenario could use an initial assumption that E_S =1, but
1. an S = n scenario associated with the expected number of fatalities in a 'maximum fatalities' scenario might require an initial E_S value which was significantly greater than 1;
2. a set of intermediate E_S scenario values might be required to define a suitable S value profile over the range between S = 1 and S = n;
3. whether or not an S dependent E_S was deemed worth using, Railtrack needed to think about 'risk' associated with fatalities in terms of explicitly considered departures from expectations as well as expected value estimates.

Several interdependent concerns about working assumptions in current use by Railtrack were being addressed which need elaboration to explain the rationale of these three numbered points.

First, several hundred fatalities every year was the average experienced on the UK railway system. Most of these fatalities involved individual suicides or accidents when fewer than 5 people were killed in a single incident. However, 50 people killed in a single incident was a plausible expectation in a 'very serious incident' scenario, and 500 people killed in a single incident was a feasible expectation in a 'catastrophic incident' scenario. For example, if two very high speed trains collided head-on, 500 fatalities could be exceeded by a factor of two or more. It was not plausible to stick to the current Railtrack assumption that 5 or 50 or 500 people killed one at a time in separate incidents was the same as one incident killing this number simultaneously without even asking those directly affected, despite the fact this was prevailing industry practice. It was important to employ an analysis framework which allowed for the possibility that relevant people would like E_S values to increase as S increases. There were observable differences in safety levels demanded by the public in contexts when large numbers of people might be killed at one time. For example, air travel accidents and road travel accidents were perceived very differently, and this was widely understood and accepted. Major aircraft accident levels of fatalities being exceeded in train crashes suggested a different level of public concern than the usual train incident fatalities levels.

Second, prevailing railway safety practice measured 'risk' in expected value terms – what should happen on average – *without addressing variability relative to expected values*. This was not a defensible position in a railway context. Railway safety needed to address 'risk' in terms of expected outcomes *and* associated variability. The chance of a 50 or 500 fatality scenario mattered greatly, not just the expected number of fatalities per annum.

Third, the first two points taken together meant that the chance of a catastrophic scenario and its implications needed urgent explicit attention, in conjunction with the full range of intermediate scenarios. And it needed attention at board level, as an integral part of the railway's overall strategy. Safety risk was not just an issue of what should happen on average, and it was not an issue which could be left to 'add-on analysis' by the 'risk management department experts' given other aspects of corporate strategy. It had to be addressed via an 'add-in analysis' which was part of the overall corporate strategy determination process. It had to involve decisions made and fully understood at board level, with the board accountable for the decision-making process. Further, all key board level decisions had to be made using values and concepts which could be communicated to all railway employees and contractors, and explained to the satisfaction of passengers and regulators in terms of both prior expectations and realised experience, even when things went seriously wrong.

I failed to make a convincing case for addressing these three concerns in the manner proposed. A few years later two serious incidents within two years led to the bankruptcy of Railtrack, which was replaced by the public sector Network Rail organisation. A range of explanations for the bankruptcy of

Railtrack were provided, but not adopting my proposed approach based on the three points explained above is one serious contender, and certainly part of the story.

During the period 2010-13 I provided advice to the UK MoD on how to justify high levels of expenditure on protecting troops against attacks which employed non-conventional weapons in terms of preventative and mitigating measures. My understanding is the proposed approach has since received ongoing attention, but I am not aware of the outcomes. The starting point for my MoD analysis framework was generalising the previously proposed Railtrack approach outlined above.

When writing chapter 9 of *Enlightened Planning*, which addresses a strategic approach to railway safety and security in relation to incidents resulting from malicious attacks as well as accidents for a fictious private sector European railway, referred to as Northern European Railways (NER), I synthesised what both the Railtrack and the MoD experience had taught me, to develop an approach for railways which had greater clarity efficiency plus greater portability, in the sense that it would be easier to use *effectively* in any context. The new features included using an expanded E_S concept to address fatalities *plus* injuries, *plus* physical damage to the railway system facilities, *plus* some aspects of 'enlightened prudence' concerns embedded in an explicit residual component designed to avoid double counting and avoid leaving anything out which should not be overlooked.

Initially this might look like significant additional unwelcome complexity. It certainly resulted in a lengthy tale in chapter 9 of *Enlightened Planning*, and the complexity involved is an important part of the case for discussing these issues in this Part 3 chapter instead of earlier. However, the approach advocated actually facilitates crucial simplifications in terms of both the execution of the analysis and the interpretation of that analysis by all interested parties.

The NER chapter 9 approach used the Railtrack notation discussed above to assume:

$S = 0, 1, 5, 20, 70$ and 350 was the expected number of fatalities for a set of scenarios spanning zero to the maximum feasible,

$T_S = V_1 \times E_S$, and

V_1 = a 'base value starting point value in \$ for a single fatality', using dollars to avoid associating NER with any specific European country.

Using \$ was a purely cosmetic change, but an important further change was expanding the E_S concept proposed for Railtrack as described above to use an NER four-part decomposition structure of the form:

$E_S = A_S + I_S + D_S + R_S$

where the four E_S component factors embrace the use of a V_1 defined as the revealed preference implications of an avoided fatality on the road system in NER's country, directly comparable to an updated NHTSA value for the country in question, and:

1. A_S was the 'avoided fatalities factor' associated with adjusting V_1 for the revealed preference implications of avoided fatalities on the NER railway system as S varies over a range from $S = 1$ to $S = 350$, with 350 being the assumed expected number of fatalities associated with a catastrophic scenario involving from 200 fatalities to the maximum feasible number, representative intermediate scenarios at $S = 5, 20$ and 70.

2. I_S was the 'injuries factor' associated with further adjusting V_1 in order to make a provision for avoided injuries on a per fatality basis assuming that injuries in a number of different categories of seriousness are correlated with fatalities, and assuming that exploiting this correlation was not just useful, it was crucial for clarity efficiency.

3. D_S was the 'damage factor' associated with further adjusting V_1 in order to make a provision for avoided damage to the physical railway system plus all associated knock-on direct cost and an opportunity cost portrayal of lost revenue assumed to be correlated with fatalities, and assuming exploiting this correlation was clarity efficient.

4. R_S was the 'residual factor' associated with a residual provision for any concerns not fully captured by the other three factors which rounded up the $T_S = V_1 \times E_S$ relationship appropriately to capture an NER board view of all issues relevant to well-founded trust for their revealed preferences by all other interested parties, also crucial for clarity efficiency.

Trust in NER board level decisions involving safety and security should be seen as directly dependent upon the R_S values given the other three E_S factor values and the V_1 value. *But trust in board level decisions should also be seen as conditional upon the rest of the NER approach to safety and security, including implementation as well as planning, and communication.*

The choices of numerical values for A_S, I_S, D_S and R_S which might be preferred by each board member could be very different. All board members needed a reasonable degree of collective agreement about plausible working assumptions for individual values for external discussion purposes. But what was crucially important was collective agreement about the board's preferred overall T_S values, because it was the overall T_S values which defined the revealed preferences of *the board implied by decisions taken.*

All board members needed board agreed T_S values they could live with. Currently NER did not address the trade-offs involved using a T_S framework and a set of explicitly approved T_S values. However, implicit T_S values associated with current implicit A_S, I_S, D_S and R_S values (independent of S) could be computed for comparison to new S dependent values proposed by the NER safety and security team. The T_S values used, be they explicitly approved or just implicitly determined by each decision, were a board approved revealed preference statement by NER about how much NER was prepared to spend to reduce by one the number of fatalities associated with each possible S value associated directly with A_S, together with all the correlated issues addressed via I_S, D_S and R_S values. T_S values were shadow costs given ethical content based on a revealed preference interpretation. R_S was a useful focal point for board level agreement about T_S values, given assumed values of V_1, A_S, I_S and D_S subjected to earlier scrutiny.

But different board members could have different views about RS values and other TS components, so long as they agreed the TS values, and the broad nature of the case for the underlying four component values. And if they failed to understand this, they would be making inconsistent decisions, with more fatalities and injuries on average for any given level of cost.

The additive E_S components relationship was 'nominal' for two reasons, both worth understanding. One reason was that a multiplicative alternative to the additive form used above might be preferred, and this choice was a technical matter open to debate. The major reason, of *much* more importance, was the relationship defining T_S in terms of any four-parameter structure was a 'nominal' relationship because if somebody believed the T_S values were about right overall, but one of these component factors should be much bigger, while any of the other components should be much smaller, with no net overall change in T_S, *it was crucial that they and everyone else understood this would make no overall difference to NER decision outcomes.* NER board revealed preferences were defined by the choices the board made as a collective group of people acting as a group, with no direct relationship to the underlying preferences of individual board members. This second reason meant that it might not be worth arguing about the details of different component values, although discussing the rationale of the component structure and the nature of the values used was in general very important, and presentation issues would also need careful attention.

Trust depended upon understanding in broad terms the practical implications of the T_S values used to make choices, plus the nature and motives of alternative perspectives and values, which need not be common, but have to be judged reasonable or not reasonable, given due accommodations for other people's different concerns and perspectives.

The board needed to agree on the net effect of the E_S values given V_1 without any *compulsory* need for agreement about the details of the component contributions within this E_S structure. *However, while agreement about the component values was NOT compulsory, it was highly desirable, and consideration of these values should be addressed in an effective manner.*

Further, and perhaps even more crucially, *NER needed to make it clear to all other interested parties why they could take a comparable view about the need for agreement about TS values, with less concern about consistent views about components.*

Some substantive differences in the component values preferred by different interested parties might suggest differences in perspectives which do need extensive clarifying discussion and reconciliation, and where these differences of opinion really mattered, they might need resolution. But when differences of opinion did not matter, or did not matter very much, everybody needed clarity about why this was the case. That is part of the reason why discussion needed to take place within a commonly understood and accepted framework, so that reaching agreement could focus on what mattered, using shared framing assumptions to clearly articulate alternative perspectives on what mattered most. *Shared framing assumptions were important because without shared framing assumptions effective dialogue would not be feasible.*

A key aspect of the rationale for the use of the $T_S = V_1 \times E_S$ structure defined in terms of four components of E_S was recognising the value of a holistic approach to separate treatment of industry benchmarks, other relevant good practice approaches based on shadow cost and revealed preference interpretations, and common practice values which were relevant over a bad or debatable practice to best practice range, plus the underlying role of legal settlements, out-of-court settlements and fines. There were several alternative options for distributing these different concerns between the four components, and more than one option could be used to clarify different approaches which different groups of interested parties might prefer.

The key was board level judgements and agreements with other interested parties about each of these categories of concern in an integrated framework without the need for any more parameters or any more effort or any more agreement about components than necessary.

The R_S component always formally addressed testing for completeness without double counting. As part of this it was useful to formally recognise the very ambiguous nature of revealed preferences, the further complexity introduced by a 'prudence provision', which all parties might want to include to reduce the risk of catastrophic scenarios in a risk efficient manner. Importantly, this approach demonstrates the futility of excessively detailed calculations based on less important issues when the really big issues that matter greatly are not amenable to precise numerical evaluation. If estimating R_S beyond any given level of precision is not feasible, then spending a lot of effort and money estimating A_S, I_S or D_S to a significantly higher level of precision is a serious waste of time and money, and clarity inefficient to a serious extent. In the NER context, this was wasted time and money which could be better spent taking steps NER knew would make the system safer or more attractive for their customers in other ways. Wasted effort on unproductive precision is a serious distraction when other activities would be much more useful, and the opportunity inefficiency implied needs to be avoided.

Part of the rationale for using an S dependent E_S instead of an S independent $T = V_1 \times E$ approach was to allow incidents involving large numbers of fatalities to be weighted more heavily than incidents involving small numbers of fatalities, via the A_S uplift. This issue might have been pursued via an $E_S = A_S$ concept which did not address the other three component factors. However, *overall* clarity efficiency was enhanced by the simpler four component E_S approach, considering S dependence only once, and allowing the board and other key interested parties to focus on agreed T_S values without necessarily reaching full agreement on component uplifts. As an illustrative example, one NER director might see NER corporate reputation concerns as the really central issue, a second director might see the ethics of fatalities as the key, a third might see the full implications of life-changing injuries as the key – but it is the combined effect that actually matters and requires their collective agreement. They could agree to differ on their individual views about component parameter values, and even the nature of an appropriate V_1 and some of the underlying relationships, but if they disagree about the total implied by T_S, they are going to have to confront the implications and resolve their differences in a way they can all live with in the face of scrutiny by other interested parties.

Further, other parties including shareholders, passengers, staff, regulators, the courts and the general public needed to judge the board's decisions at a T_S level, no doubt with significant interest in exactly how they arrived at whatever numbers they used, but recognising the nominal nature of the components. Different terminology could be used by different parties, but it is crucially important to avoid confusing different terminology and different opinions on values, and comparisons which might become crucial in terms of disputes involving differences of opinion might be complex. For example, the *Enlightened Planning* NER tale cites a report to the UK Rail Safety and Standards Board, *T430: The Definition of VPF and the Impact of Societal Concerns* by Oxford Risk Research and Analysis (Rail Safety and Standards Board, 2006). This report used the term 'value of a prevented fatality' (VPF), a very limited view of 'revealed preference' approaches that explicitly rejected an S dependent approach to the A_S component, did not address an I_S or D_S component, did not explicitly address ethics and trust concerns, and omitted all other aspects of a R_S component. The discussion suggested this approach was consistent with current NER practice and most common practice, the reason it was cited.

In contexts other than railways, replacing the common practice S independent value of an avoided fatality approach with the more general S dependent $T_S = V_1$ x E_S approach using four component factors for E_S might not always be useful in direct operational terms. But the associated robustness tests are important in all contexts, and in my view the very wide range of potential fatalities involved in a single railway incident makes it essential for NER and any comparable railway. Even if S dependence for A_S was not useful in some contexts (when only a very narrow range of fatalities was feasible for example), distinguishing T_S, V_1 and E_S concepts together with the four component factors for E_S is important *in all contexts* for several reasons. Acknowledging trust and underlying ethical concerns is particularly crucial, linked to the shadow cost and revealed preference basis for the T_S transformation and the potential importance of complex issues like 'enlightened prudence'.

Given this holistic approach to T_S, the sensitivity diagrams and decision diagrams discussed earlier in this book can be used (illustrative numerical examples are provided in *Enlightened Planning*).

Significant further generalisation

Further generalisation to address concerns like environmental pollution is feasible within the same framework, as encountered by BP in their Deepwater Horizon incident in 2010. In this incident the blowout of the Macondo offshore oil well in the Gulf of Mexico involved 11 fatalities, which clearly mattered a great deal, and any injuries had there been any survivors would have mattered, but the more than $60 billion in costs to date for BP have been largely driven by the resulting oil pollution. What is clear is that another E_S component related to oil pollution, which is a function of the size of the oil spill, would be needed to expand the framework, and it might need to address oil pollution volumes which are not correlated with lives lost and injuries. In any context, when an incident might lead to significant environmental pollution, the 'risk' cannot just be measured by expected outcomes – the consequences of a plausible catastrophic scenario need attention, along with the relevant range of less serious scenarios.

Other kinds of plausible catastrophic scenarios might be even more complex to address, like nuclear power station catastrophes. However, the same basic systematic simplicity approach would allow much more effective consideration of the wide range of trade-offs which are inherently very difficult but crucially important for all parties affected (as briefly explored in chapter 9 of *Enlightened Planning*).

Whenever the context of interest involves multiple trade-offs, carefully structured composition clearly needs to be addressed as well as prior decomposition. The recommended approach outlined in this chapter provides a powerful way to save effort by making necessarily complex analysis simpler to undertake and simpler to interpret in a systematic manner. It does so by explicitly addressing the importance of recognising that different people will have different views about the very important underlying ethical concerns. Explicitly taking this into account also builds trust and makes the analysis much more credible for all parties. Arguably this is even more important than making the analysis simpler to conduct and interpret. The ethical concerns are central, and differences in views can be crucial, so building and maintaining trust, even when things go badly wrong, is extremely important. Sharing common framing assumptions as a starting point for effective dialogue about appropriate working assumptions has to be a prerequisite for building and maintaining the necessary trust. Delivering this requisite framework is a central systematic simplicity concern.

Chapter 14
Related regulatory, legal and political concerns

The overview nature of this chapter

The focus of both *Enlightened Planning* and this book is management decision making within commercial organisations. 'Commercial organisations' can be defined in very broad terms as 'organisations providing a product or service for a price', without necessarily assuming that the service receiver pays the price. These commercial organisations may be private sector or public sector in terms of ownership, with substantial scope for some 'good' private sector organisations to display the 'good' features of public sector organisations, and some 'good' public sector organisations to display the features of 'good' private sector organisations.

All commercial organisations have to work within the regulatory, legal and taxation frameworks of the country where they are based, plus those of other countries where they operate. Most commercial organisations have a very limited ability to influence the operation of regulatory, legal and taxation frameworks to obtain mutual advantage, but any opportunities which do exist need addressing.

Three of the five tales in part 2 chapters of *Enlightened Planning* illustrate three different kinds of relationships between commercial organisations and their regulators which involve scope for the commercial organisation to influence their regulator to obtain mutual advantage. These three tales also involve scope for a regulator to have a wider useful influence than is often considered by regulators or their responsible governments. This chapter provides an overview and synthesis.

A private sector water and sewage utility example

The chapter 7 tale in *Enlightened Planning* is about Water and Sewage Limited (WSL), a private sector water and sewage utility serving a region in southern England. The tale draws on my six years of experience as a non-executive director of Southern Water, a period which included several changes in ownership and managing directors, beginning a few years after Southern Water was privatised along with the rest of the UK water and sewage industry.

The primary focus of the WSL tale in *Enlightened Planning* chapter 7 was demonstrating the systematic simplicity approach to project management in a broad management of change sense, as discussed in Chapter 8 of this book. A secondary role for this tale in *Enlightened Planning* chapter 7 was exploring the discounted cash flow concerns addressed in Chapter 12 of this book. A feature of the UK water and sewage industry is the use of bond funding for capital investments to gear up the return private sector equity investors can make on their equity investment. A feature of the systematic simplicity approach illustrated in detail in chapter 7 of *Enlightened Planning* and mentioned in Chapter 12 of this book was the recognition that a relatively low cost for bond funding should lead to higher quality (longer life and more reliable) water mains, sewage works, water treatment works and other capital programmes. A tertiary role for this tale was related regulatory concerns, addressed in this chapter.

WSL was assumed to be willing to pass on most of the resulting lower costs of a systematic simplicity understanding of discounting to customers as an integral component of a long-term corporate strategy based on being a model of a 'good' water and sewage utility from a customer and regulator perspective. This long-term strategy included a WSL commitment to doing everything feasible to minimise customer costs for a very high quality of service, adding a profit mark-up for their shareholders which was relatively modest by their industry's standards. The rationale was seeking long-term stable growth in their share value based in part on the possible acquisition of other water and sewage companies in the UK.

WSL planned to set up a separate company to raise and hold all WSL bonds with a focus on attracting investment by people living in the geographic region WSL served. These bonds would in effect be secured against the WSL assets, like a mortgage. These bonds would make a modest but safe rate of return, *and* help to keep water and sewage charges low, *and* give local people a sense of direct control over the amenity use of water reservoirs and associated parks plus sewage works with associated public amenities, a classic 'win-win … win' proposition.

However, for this overall strategy to work for WSL, in competition with a growing number of UK water and sewage companies using offshore funding and avoiding UK taxation as well as operating leaky water mains and unreliable sewage systems, WSL would need strong regulator support for water and sewage utilities adopting this kind of 'good' UK water and sewage utility strategy, including support for appropriate taxation incentives. This strong support would also require reinforcement by strenuous and effective protection from less scrupulous competitors. For example, private individuals investing in WSL bonds and other comparable 'good' UK water and sewage utility company bonds might have these bonds given ISA status, making the return free of income tax, a central government tax law decision not likely to be taken unless the regulator took a very proactive stance on supporting all 'good' utilities. This support for water and sewage industry bond ISA tax status might be reinforced by a forceful campaign to ensure that any company operating in the UK paid the equivalent of full UK taxes via appropriate special levies if they were deemed to be gaining an unfair advantage relative to 'good' UK based companies which paid their taxes. In effect all 'bad' water and sewage utilities *plus* all other 'bad' companies operating in the UK would need to be penalised if they were not playing by the UK tax rules in a fair way. All regulators could take up this challenge, and the water and sewage regulator responsible for pricing and cost issues could champion this cause. It could be sold to the government in conjunction with the water and sewage utility bond ISA tax status issue by the regulator as a form of 'regionalisation' of all of the regional water and sewage companies that were interested in getting closer to their customers in a collaborative sense, as a preferable alternative to 'nationalisation' in the traditional UK sense.

Note that a 'good' water and sewage industry company like WSL may need regulator and government support to survive as a 'good' water and sewage company, and without such support the 'bad' may drive out the 'good' in a classic market failure sense. If all water and sewage utility companies become 'bad' because of this kind of market failure, a market recovery engineered by the regulator and the government will become much more difficult.

The December 2019 UK general election results eliminated the short-term 'nationalisation risk' that all UK private sector water and sewage utilities faced because of what is increasingly perceived as 'bad' utility company strategy by UK water and sewage utility customers, but in the long-term this risk remains and needs to be managed. The politics of the UK water and sewage utility industry are highly controversial. Both *Enlightened Planning* and this book make a point of avoiding any political dogma, but do not avoid the need to resolve the mess political dogmas and market failures have created.

Arguably what all UK water and sewage utility customers need, be they private individuals and families or large corporate users of water and sewage services, is a regulator open to creative thinking about looking after the best interests of all customers by vigorously promoting and protecting all of the 'good' utilities in addition to firmly contesting and constraining all of the 'bad' utilities in the sense WSL was seeking support for. They also need a government willing to appoint and then support such a regulator. It would also help if at least one 'good' utility led the way. If one or more leading 'good' utilities grew, and eventually bought out all the 'bad' utilities, because the regulator made sure that 'bad' utilities could not gain competitive advantage via 'bad' behaviour, only one leading 'good' utility might become a private sector monopoly for the whole country, not just a region. But with an effective regulator this might be avoided, or it might not be a problem. As explored in *Enlightened Planning*, the growth of a leading 'good' utility via a 'regionalisation' might be coupled to the growth of partially separate private sector organisations sharing water resources between regions, with some private sector 'nationalisation' features to complement the 'regionalisation' of the bond ownership approach. There is scope for more than one kind of systematic simplicity thinking in this context, and more than one direction of 'good' development. What is 'good' and 'bad' will remain debatable, with lots of large grey areas, some involving strong opinions grounded on political dogma. However, most people know really 'good' and seriously 'bad' when they see it, political dogma driven arguments need effective direct challenge, and it matters that the system does something imaginative, effective and efficient about important regulation issues in a way that most people could agree makes sense. A degree of agreement about common framing assumptions which are as general as possible, followed by a degree of agreement about suitable working assumptions, is a prerequisite for effective dialogue.

When writing *Enlightened Planning* in 2018 and earlier I did not want this regulation related concern to serve as a distraction, and the current political environment that is driving regulatory policy in the UK does not look particularly promising. But there were some encouraging signs then, and drawing attention to the implications of a possible regulation agenda involving a contribution from systematic simplicity approaches still seems worthwhile. Whether one or two 'good' supplier organisations could help to transform a regulator's agenda without significant leadership from the regulator's senior management and their political masters is certainly debatable. There is a good case for arguing that political leadership from the top down is what is really needed, to ensure that *all* markets operate as 'level playing fields' for all 'good' suppliers and purchasers operating in the UK or any other country you are interested in, with no place for any 'bad' suppliers or purchasers. But all of the parties involved need to do what they can. It is very clear that the issues involved go well beyond water and sewage providers.

A private sector railway company example

The chapter 9 tale in *Enlightened Planning* is about North European Railways (NER), a private sector railway company. This NER tale draws on a review of safety management strategy for Railtrack in the early 1990s plus 2010 to 2013 work for the MoD. The primary role for this tale, as discussed in Chapter 13 of this book, was exploring how a systematic simplicity approach to trade-offs could deal in a sufficiently high clarity manner with complex ethical concerns. A central issue was the trade-offs that have to be made between money in terms of the cost of rail travel and lives lost plus injuries sustained which might have been avoided if more money was spent making the railway safer, funded via railway ticket prices plus government subsidies or tax concessions.

What was not developed in Chapter 13 of this book was the implications for NER and everyone else if NER had a catastrophic level of incident without appropriate insurance facilitated by the regulator. *Enlightened Planning* chapter 9 treats this issue as a second order concern, but it is one of the main messages of that chapter, and it needs brief attention in this chapter. The reason is 'keeping it simple' in many railway safety contexts assumes that 'risk' is measured in expected outcome terms. A systematic simplicity approach demands consideration of possible departures from expectations, including potential catastrophic outcomes and associated enlightened prudence. This requires both NER and the regulator to recognise that implicit 'insurer of last resort' status for the government if NER became bankrupt following an uninsured catastrophic incident is not just bad for the government, it is bad for most of the other parties involved.

The discussion in chapter 9 of *Enlightened Planning* assumed that NER was a 'national treasure', a 'good' organisation in almost all respects, the only serious weakness being the conceptual and operational tools used to consider safety. When Sophie, the new Head of Safety for NER, had explained to the NER board how a systematic simplicity approach would work, towards the end of her overall explanation she pointed out the implications of a catastrophic incident *if it occurred.*

A catastrophic NER incident had a very low probability of occurring, which meant that 'risk' as currently measured for safety analysis purposes in expected outcome terms was modest. However, 'risk' as it ought to be perceived in possible departure from expectation terms was not modest. A catastrophic incident would bankrupt NER. This meant that the national government would be forced to act as an insurer of last resort for some purposes, but very heavy uninsured losses would still be inflicted on a wide range of people, including shareholders which were largely pension funds, train passengers and their families, and onboard railway staff and their families. Sophie suggested that the NER board, the government and the regulator *should* all be held to be negligent for allowing this to have happened, if it happened. Sophie also suggested that the most effective and efficient way for everyone to avoid this was the regulator providing government underwritten insurance, with premiums to cover the full cost geared to the risk involved as measured by the regulator, as part of a regulator remit to ensure that risk levels were appropriate from the perspective of the passengers and onboard NER staff plus all the other relevant parties. That was the case made in chapter 9 of *Enlightened Planning.*

Note that even a 'good' organisation like NER needs this insurance plus the associated scrutiny of their safety practices with built in insurance cost rewards for safety practice improvements and corresponding insurance cost penalties for safety practice shortcomings. A feature of 'bad' organisations is they may be prepared to knowingly operate in an irresponsible uninsured manner, perhaps with their assets offshored, so they can escape their liabilities if a catastrophic incident occurs without even actually going bankrupt. A government allowing this to happen is comparable to a government allowing uninsured car drivers on the road. But it is a much more serious failure in their duty of care in very important respects.

The general relevance of this discussion to this chapter in broad terms is that regulation has a very important role to play over and above 'level playing fields' in the WSL sense, whenever and wherever potential catastrophic incidents are involved. An explicit insurance broker role, coupled to a directly related role as an explicit enforcer of appropriate responses to the true costs of risks being taken, ought to be a key part of the roles of a wide variety of regulators. This includes regulators involved with issues like nuclear power station safety and offshore oil well developments that could lead to catastrophic oil spills. This is an extremely important issue which requires government leadership, although other interested parties may need to take direct action as well as providing lobby pressure.

A public sector electricity utility example

Enlightened Planning chapter 8 uses a tale about Canpower, a public sector Canadian electricity utility owned by its province. This tale is based on my review of Ontario Hydro's approach to corporate strategy formation, as discussed in Chapter 9 of this book.

The primary role for this tale as discussed in Chapter 9 of this book was exploring how a systematic simplicity approach to corporate strategy formation could be developed using the framework portrayed by Figure 9.1.

What was not developed in Chapter 9 of this book was the implications for

Canpower and everyone else if Canpower did not respond effectively to the risk of privatisation posed by the current board level indifference to genuine concerns about the way the board's goal planning reflected the best interests of the citizens of the province. The citizens of the province who owned Canpower were seriously questioning the value of their public sector ownership of Canpower. *Enlightened Planning* chapter 8 treats this issue as a second order concern in terms of giving it limited attention, but the general implications are an important aspect of the main messages of that chapter, and the regulation plus public/private ownership issues are worthy of attention here.

Enlightened Planning chapter 8 assumes that Canpower is a 'good' organisation in many respects, but there are some serious weaknesses which need urgent attention beyond those associated with Figure 9.1 in the Chapter 9 discussion earlier in this book. When Carl, the corporate strategy formation consultant outlining all the implications of Figure 9.1 for Canpower in *Enlightened Planning*, finally addressed the role of goal planning, three points worth making here began emerging.

First, if the best interests of Canpower's owners were carefully aligned with Canpower's corporate goals, many of the current public sector electricity utility capability-culture characteristics would probably change radically. For example, Canpower might preserve their responsibility for customer facing activities like customer billing, connections to the grid and overall system reliability. They might also preserve their responsibility for strategic planning of the portfolio of power types (nuclear, hydro, fossil fuelled, and so on), the ownership and operation of nuclear power stations, the ownership of existing large hydroelectric and fossil fuelled power stations. However, they might immediately start to outsource the provision of a lot of new electricity generation in partnership with local interests addressing complementary concerns, including issues like urban waste incineration and small scale renewable sources of electric power. They might support rather than resist a lot of new small scale regionally based incentives involving electricity generation. Further, they might gradually begin to outsource some of the activities currently undertaken in-house to seek value for money in a way which would strengthen their company-customer-employee and local community relationships in a balanced manner. This might include approaches like using small local firms to undertake electricity power line maintenance in conjunction with in-house staff.

Second, the provincial government might empower the regulator to ensure that this kind of transformation took place quickly and continued to evolve smoothly in a manner which has been optimised from the perspective of Canpower's owners, even if that directly challenged the Canpower board. This might involve taking a highly proactive approach to all aspects of promoting and protecting the 'good' and contesting and constraining the 'bad' in terms of the characteristics of both public and private ownership of this particular electricity utility. This might be seen as a carefully designed alternative to any conventional form of privatisation as well as a much-needed transformation of a conventional public sector commercial organisation, perhaps initiated by the utility itself, but supported by an effective regulator appointed by a government determined to avoid a controversial confrontation over political dogma. If the utility did not initiate it, a suitably empowered regulator supported by the responsible government might do so directly.

Third, both the provincial and the federal governments might work jointly to empower the regulator to undertake the insurance of all nuclear power safety and security concerns. They would need to address national government sponsored and competing foreign government sponsored nuclear technology. It would also be important to ensure that electricity charges and decisions about the mix of source types to be provided over the long-term planning horizon reflected the full long-term expected costs plus associated safety and security risks involved.

Concluding reflections

A key message for you to take away from this chapter is that all of the regulatory, legal, taxation and further political concerns touched on in this chapter are highly controversial and complex, and while this book and *Enlightened Planning* cannot offer any silver bullets, the issues involved are far too important to ignore. *Enlightened Planning* chapters 7, 8, 9 plus a synthesis in chapter 10 suggest a systematic simplicity approach may help. There is already some evidence of regulators achieving a measure of success with approaches involving some of the ideas discussed, but a huge amount remains to be done.

Some readers may be interested in helping to address what is needed. Encouraging you to consider doing so using some of the ideas addressed in this chapter is one of the roles of this chapter, and the development of related ideas in *Enlightened Planning.*

Many people believe in minimal government, including minimal legal constraint, minimal government regulation, minimal public services, and minimal taxation. However, many others believe that important practical social system complexities associated with a 21st century democracy which wants to serve the best interests of all its citizens do require significant levels of enlightened intervention. Wherever your views put you on this range of perspectives, a key set of concerns is what *exactly* should regulation address, what goals ought to be pursued by what means, and how should achieving what is required be funded, bearing in mind the resistance which change of any kind will undoubtedly generate, not to mention the wide range of differences in opinions needing reconciliation. A systematic simplicity mindset and toolset should help to clarify some of these issues, and more clarity is clearly needed.

Chapter 15
Concluding reflections

The focus of concluding reflections in each individual chapter has been the content of that chapter, with limited use of links backwards and forwards. The focus of this chapter is a few key themes and concepts which underlie this book as a whole, *Enlightened Planning*, as an elaboration of the overall approach underlying the systematic simplicity concept this book builds on, and the literature which both build upon.

One of the central issues this book emphasises as strongly as possible is the need to make it very clear *to **everyone affected**, whether or not they are directly involved*, that an approach to managing decisions involving uncertainty, risk and opportunity which does not address risk efficiency in *any* management context does not provide a sufficiently general and capable approach to managing decisions, and this is not just a common practice *project* management issue – it is a concern in operations management and corporate management contexts too. A second is the need to make it clear to everyone affected that the uncertainty underlying the risk concept used has to embrace *all* uncertainty relevant to the context. A third is the need to make it clear to this very general audience that the management of opportunity in an 'opportunity efficiency' sense is the real goal, and trade-offs between relevant attributes as well as expected outcomes and associated departures from expectations in terms of relevant attributes are a crucial part of this. A fourth is the need to make it clear that achieving clarity efficiency at an appropriate level of clarity is always a core goal, and having appropriate processes, a core concern in Part 2 of this book, is central to this.

Drawing on all relevant theory plus associated best practice from a wide range of disciplines and professions is an essential part of the systematic simplicity approach, as is reflective practice based upon relevant experience. No single profession can stake a legitimate 'ownership' claim for systematic simplicity, although they may want to develop their own brand and flavour, and this book encourages them to do so. Each profession needs its own approaches and methods to adapt to its context and traditions, but it also needs to avoid an isolated or siloed perspective, sharing common ground. Systematic simplicity adopts my favourite definition of engineering – 'creative synthesis of ends and means' – as a central mantra, and the evolution of systematic simplicity has itself been driven by this mantra drawing upon several disciplines.

The key messages that I took away from the fairly generalised MS/OR perspective that started my career was the importance of systematic processes to make decisions, the role in those systematic processes of creativity as well as rigorous testing of assumptions, the value and the limitations of quantitative analysis, and the need to make use of knowledge and skills from a wide range of sources.

In terms of Figure 7.1, whatever basic perspective you use, you need some variant of a universal process (UP) concept at a personal level, implicitly if not explicitly. Further, I believe there is a very strong case for any organisation to try to define an operational form of corporate UP so there is a shared basis of understanding to discuss the specific processes needed for all corporate decision making. Using this universal and specific process framework, there are a number of further basic framing assumptions which need clarification. For example, does the organisation buy into the idea that 'risk efficiency' in the fully generalised form explored in this book is essential; or does a widely used common practice, event-based perspective of risk still dominate; or is some other alternative preferred, like an 'expected utility' approach in a multiple attribute form drawn from decision analysis, following Keeney and Raiffa (1976) for example?

Like many academics, I looked closely at the expected utility theory aspects of the overall decision analysis approaches advocated by Raiffa and others, including later multiple attribute versions (Keeney and Raiffa, 1976). An expected utility theory approach can be shown to be equivalent to a Markowitz mean-variance approach if all probability distributions are Normal (Gaussian). It can also be linked to a penalty cost function approach. I rejected this expected utility theory-based approach for practical applications that I was concerned with because viewed in the generalised risk efficiency framework provided by goal programming it is clarity inefficient in my judgement, and I was not alone in doing so. This is a very technical controversy beyond the scope of this book, in my case grounded on the general understanding of 'utility theory' and associated separability theory of economists like Ivor Pearce (Pearce, 1964) as well as more limited separability concepts, but it may be an issue for some readers, and they need to know it has not been simply overlooked.

To me this background meant that the approaches outlined in Chapters 3 and 4 of this book were the only way to go from about 1980. By the mid-1990s the approaches outlined in Chapters 1, 2 and 5 were equally clearly established in my mind as the best way forward. A lot of knowledgeable people supported this position by the end of the 1990s. But by the early 2000s I was becoming increasingly aware of a growing resistance to key aspects of the ideas set out in Chapters 1-5, with the HA concerns discussed in Chapter 6 bringing them into a useful focus for the concluding Part 1 chapter for this book.

My first direct and really enlightening engagement with risk efficiency in terms of a Markowitz mean-variance portfolio theory perspective was attending a paper by A and S Dasgupta (1966) entitled 'Crop-Planning in a Risky Environment', read to the European Meeting of the Econometric Society in Warsaw.

This paper addressed crop planning in India, comparing:
1. a linear programming 'optimal solution' to maximise the income of Indian farmers using estimates of yields and prices (expected values) which replicated the solutions argued for by Indian agricultural economists currently advising the Indian government;
2. a quadratic programming Markowitz model 'optimal solution' to maximise farmers' income using estimates of yields and prices (expected values and associated variances) which produced the same answer if risk was assumed to be bearable and acceptable, because the linear programming solution was just a special case of the Markowitz model solution;
3. the same quadratic programming Markowitz model which assumed risk was a dominant concern requiring minimisation in risk efficient terms.

The crop pattern produced by the third approach approximated the farmers' current choices, and the expected market value of the crop pattern proposed by the 'experts' approximated by the first two approaches was about twice that of the 'risk minimisation' crop pattern currently used by the farmers, consistent with the experts' claims.

In terms of Figure 2.1, the agricultural experts advising the government were arguing for a move from point 'c' to point 'a' without being aware of the need to consider the risk efficient frontier concept portrayed by Figure 2.1. What the Dasgupta paper made clear was the agricultural experts were ignoring risk associated with yields and market prices which the famers could not afford to ignore – the farmers and their families might starve if they did so. The farmers understood why they could not afford to take this risk, and their traditional crop patterns were a highly diversified risk efficient low risk solution. If the government wanted to increase the market value of the agricultural sector, the government needed to take some of the risk from the farmers via clearly set out insurance schemes addressing crop failures and market disruptions, and they needed to take advice from more enlightened experts. There were a number of lessons to be learned from this illustration of the merits of understanding both 'risk' and 'risk efficiency' which are directly relevant to the basis of a systematic simplicity approach.

One is often the reason 'experts' get it wrong, which is they make unrealistic assumptions, and all of the assumptions decision makers use need a systematically simple process for testing their robustness. A second is that risk efficiency has to deal with uncertainty from multiple sources which can involve an inherently complex mix of variability (as in market prices), events that may not happen (as in crop infestations or droughts), ambiguity (what we do not know or understand, including what people and governments may do), and systemic interdependences (relationships between supply and demand for example). A third is *if* we can use underlying theory or high clarity applicable approaches to understand intuitively what the real issues are, *then* we can ask the right questions, and acquire a well-grounded starting point for evolving significant improvements to real practice using approaches that may be fairly simple in practice.

My next formative engagement with risk and risk efficiency in the Figure 2.1 sense was trying to understand the implications of a particular form of 'separability' in mathematical theory terms. I was undertaking a PhD on consumer behaviour theory, supervised by Professor Ivor Pearce, initially trying to develop an empirical econometric approach to building marketing models for the UK Milk Marketing Board. Ivor had developed what he called 'neutral want association' (Pearce, 1964), what some of the economics literature called 'Pearce separability' (probably because it is significantly different to the 'strong' and 'weak' separability concepts everybody else used in ways which were not entirely clear to anybody as I understood the situation), what I refer to as 'pairwise separability' (because that is its basic defining characteristic). Using a Markowitz mean-variance portfolio theory framework to imagine my 'rational consumer' understood Markowitz and wanted to use pairwise separability to choose an investment portfolio as part of his or her overall optimal consumption and saving and earning income decision making, the question I was asking was 'what minimal assumptions in terms of common covariance patterns would a one-pass approach using pairwise separability require?'. Chapman (1974) was the answer, in the broader context of Chapman (1975), if you are interested. This was directly relevant to the issue of ordering sources of uncertainty to reflect dependence as discussed in Chapter 3, the more general issue of ordering phases in an iterative process as addressed in Part 2, and the really general point that 'separability' does not require 'independence', but the nature of the forms of dependence assumed is not a simple choice, and a systematic understanding of the options available matters. For example, causal dependence portrayals and statistical dependence portrayal are two broad classes of alternatives, with very different characteristics.

The approach developed for BP leading to high clarity decision diagrams to make risk efficient choices and understand enlightened caution, enlightened gambles and enlightened prudence all built on this earlier basis plus a synthesis of a number of earlier experiences, including two key tasks as a fulltime consultant with Acres Consulting Services in Canada during 1974-5. One involved using a Graphical Evaluation and Review Technique (GERT) approach, employing a Markovian process framework to work on a month-by-month basis plus underlying PERT (Program Evaluation and Review Technique) and Generalised

PERT ideas as described in Moder and Philips (1970) to help a team of consulting companies plan a very large pipeline project (never built) to bring Arctic gas to US markets. The second was a study of US safety standards for nuclear power stations in terms of seismic (earthquake) risk using sources like NUREG (1975) with a view to making recommendations about Canadian nuclear safety regulations.

Chapman (1979) was the first published paper discussing these early BP developments in the language which I adopted at that time, referring to the overall approach as Synergistic Contingency Evaluation and Review Technique (SCERT). My rationale for adopting this label was building on the PERT, Generalised PERT and GERT terminology with a contingency planning focus, plus signalling further generalisation in a tradition which embraced all aspects of these approaches, plus a prototype systematic simplicity treatment of further fault tree and event tree concepts used by safety experts, plus risk efficiency concepts. It is worth understanding that this high clarity view of contingency planning is not currently an integral part of a lot of common practice 'project risk management' – it is simply beyond its scope. Further, most common practice 'project risk management' does not address risk efficiency, and it seems to have adopted an 'event' view of 'risks' plus a probability-impact graph (grid) portrayal of risk from an early simplified approach to looking at safety management for dangerous industrial facilities before Markowitz (1958) and before a number of internationally respected authors like Howard Raiffa (Raiffa, 1968) made the use of subjective probabilities both defensible in academic circles and indispensable in best practice.

When Stephen Ward and I distilled our collective synthesis of what we had learned from a wide range of collaboration with others on the development of three separate professional risk management guidelines and standards in addition to extensive consulting experience, research and teaching to write the first edition of *Project Risk Management* (Chapman and Ward, 1997), we did not confront the shortcomings of common practice as we saw them in a direct and vigorous manner. We assumed implicitly that what we saw as a well-grounded better approach might be currently preferred by only a minority of practitioners, but it would soon become a widely used majority preference. We were wrong about this, because despite the very favourable critical reception and international moderate bestseller status of this 1997 book, several widely used professional guides subsequently continued to fall short of dropping common practice that we firmly believe is bad practice.

We started to try to address the issues explicitly and directly by the early 2000s in a number of ways. These included papers like Chapman and Ward (2004) and Chapman (2006) as well as ongoing contributions in APM (1997, 2004) and ICE and IFoA (1998, 2005). There is a good argument for suggesting that we clearly did not make our case vigorously enough or use tactics that were effective enough over the last two decades. We have certainly not succeeded so far. But we have a significant number of well-informed supporters who see our approaches as part of the leading edge of several disciplines, we do not intend to stop trying, and this book involves a change in tactics and primary target audience.

In my view everybody needs at least an outline understanding of all Part 1 chapters, and most people need some understanding of the early Part 2 chapters. Part 3 is about setting out the scope for further evolution of systematic simplicity development, this chapter trying to illuminate aspects of that development which I think needed a mention before finishing.

A paper by Warren Black (Black, 2017), with the title *Originals: How Non-conformists Will Ultimately Disrupt the World of Risk Management*, argues that my work with Stephen Ward on 'uncertainty management' makes us 'risk originals' who will disrupt the world of 'risk management'. Black's paper places us in the same category as the behavioural economist Daniel Kahneman, a Nobel Prize winner and the bestselling author of *Thinking, Fast and Slow* (Kahneman, 2012). This very flattering assessment of my work with Stephen involves a focus on features of our work that Stephen and I would not emphasise as much as alternative features, and any comparison of this kind cannot be taken too far. However, we certainly endorse the idea that introducing a systematic simplicity perspective to the way 'best practice' *should* be pursued as endorsed by *all* guides and standards might be usefully seen as 'disruptive' in a positive sense. This is because the current approach to professional guides and standards requires a significant departure from current practice in terms of a rethinking of how uncertainty, risk and opportunity *should* be approached for effective and efficient treatment which can be trusted by *everyone affected by the decision involved*. Professor Terry Williams, in his endorsement of the *Enlightened Planning* book reproduced in the first backmatter section of this book, supports important underlying aspects of this view, as do many others.

The final overall message is the urgent need to seek a shared understanding of what we mean by key terms like uncertainty, risk and opportunity, plus the value of an agreed shared form of universal process, to facilitate the development of specific processes so that 'managing decisions' can be much easier and much more effective in ways that can be adapted to the context and trusted by everyone involved or affected.

Endorsements from a range of perspectives for the book *Enlightened Planning*

The book *Enlightened Planning: Using Systematic Simplicity to Clarify Opportunity, Risk and Uncertainty for Much Better Management Decision Making* (Chapman, 2019) included a foreword by Stephen Ward and endorsements by eleven other colleagues which you may find helpful when assessing your interest in this book, so they are provided in this section.

Stephen Ward is Emeritus Professor in Management, Southampton Business School, University of Southampton.

We all engage in planning. As individuals much of our planning is of a tacit, informal nature, but for managers there is an expectation, even a requirement, that planning will be a more formalised process, with clear rationale and objectives, requiring the cooperation of various other parties. However, this clarity can be difficult to achieve, not least because complexity, uncertainty and risk must be confronted, whatever the context. Appreciating and planning appropriately for the implications of complexity, uncertainty and risk associated with different possible courses of action is a major challenge.

Whatever the enterprise, some degree of planning is necessary to achieve desired outcomes, and large projects require a great deal of planning. But common experience shows that plans frequently require major modification, become thwarted, or fall short of achieving desired outcomes, usually because of factors that were not considered sufficiently during the process of planning.

In this book, Chris Chapman explains how we can do much better, by adopting an 'enlightened planning' approach that systematically addresses complexity, uncertainty, and risk that really matters, together with a creative search for opportunities. The concept of 'enlightened planning' involves a coherent synthesis of a rich variety of concepts and analytical tools that can be used directly in a wide range of contexts.

As a practical matter, all planning and attendant decision making must make simplifying assumptions about reality. Unfortunately, managers, particularly hard-pressed ones, often seem to be attracted to simplistic approaches that limit the scope of analysis and result in important features of a planning context being ignored.

A very common example is a preference for estimates of key contextual variables that consist of unrealistically narrow ranges of possible values, or even just single value (point) estimates. Simplistic estimates of this kind can seriously compromise the credibility and usefulness of plans.

Another example is the common practice of using probability-impact grids to characterise sources of risk, with attendant simplistic assumptions that all sources of risk are derived only from a set of events that may or may not occur, and that events are assumed to be independent of one another. This practice severely restricts recognition of important aspects of uncertainty that drive risk, including knock-on effects of one event on another.

How to keep things appropriately simple in any planning process requires careful thought. Rather than uncritical use of simplistic approaches, enlightened planning calls for intelligent and critical use of simplifying assumptions in scoping planning effort that facilitates the exploration of key issues and related uncertainty that really matters. What are these key issues? They include: deciding what factors to take into account, the potential for dynamic interactions between factors, understanding the goals of all relevant stakeholders, the ambiguous nature of some goals, potential trade-offs between goals, how far ahead to plan, and how much detail to go into. Uncertainty and risk is associated not only with such features of the planning context, but also with the planning process itself.

A particularly valuable feature of this book is its focus on practice, employing detailed case studies (tales), derived from Professor Chapman's extensive consulting experience in a wide range of planning contexts. Each of the tales in Part 2 illustrates aspects of enlightened planning, describing how recognition and understanding of key issues and what to do about them develops as protagonists progress their analysis and thinking. Each of these tales is set in a particular context, but the approaches described are readily transferrable to other organisation contexts. All the issues addressed are of strategic importance to operations management, project management, and corporate management. Most ought to be of concern at board level to ensure effective governance of planning processes, and leadership of enlightened planning.

This book is the culmination of decades of reflection about what best practice planning and decision making under uncertainty should look like. Potential readers should on no account be deterred by the length of this book, or of individual chapters. For, make no mistake, this book represents a major opportunity for all managers, and their advisors, to substantially enhance organisational performance through enlightened planning.

Matthew Leitch is a consultant, author, business school educator and risk standards committee member whose website is www.WorkingInUncertainty.co.uk

'Enlightened Planning' is not just a book about how to manage risk on projects or in business planning, but if you need a book on those topics then this is an excellent choice. It does two things that are important steps forward. First, it includes a management process explicitly designed to incorporate a wide range of appropriate methods. This is not just a process which boils down to a list of risks and a procedure for doing things with them. Instead it encourages consideration of a much wider range of techniques from operations research modelling down to quick estimates. This kind of flexibility is a frequent aspiration for risk management publications, but in this book Chapman successfully achieves it. Second, the book focuses on how to choose the right management technique at the right time to get the best combination of clarity and economy. It explicitly tackles something most busy managers can feel all the time, which is a drive to know and understand more, frustrated by lack of time and opportunity to do so.

The book is extensively illustrated with detailed practical examples from real life, including calculations and charts. The rich conceptual content and practical detail mean this is not a book you can read over a weekend. But tackled patiently, a section at a time, over a period, it will make most intelligent managers into better managers.

Paul Thornton was a founder and Managing Partner at The French Thornton Partnership. He is a Past President of the Management Consultancies Association and the Operational Research Society.

French Thornton was a programme management consultancy that led numerous well-known initiatives in the financial, transport and retail logistics sectors, and my earlier management consultancy career involved a wide range of clients. As a lifelong management consultant, my career focus has been helping organisations to achieve lasting, beneficial change. Coming from an Operational Research background, my instincts were to adopt a modelling approach to whatever problems we were confronted with. If standard models didn't adequately represent the real-life complexities of the situation, then develop and extend them until they did was the basic idea. This approach risked getting bogged down in endless cycles of model development and redevelopment. However, the main alternative (and the one often favoured by macho managers) was to assert that the problem was really a simple one, and to solve that problem irrespective of how much genuine complexity was being brushed under the carpet.

I first became aware of Chris Chapman's work in the 1980s, and we got to know each other in the early 1990s when he succeeded me as President of the Operational Research Society. Chris was providing long-term support to major corporations and utilities on projects that flew under the 'Risk Management' banner, many of them concerned with huge capital investment programmes.

Drawing on these multi-year consulting engagements, and his extensive research work, Chris has now codified significant subsequent evolution of his approach, which is set out fully for the first time in this new 'Enlightened Planning' book.

A key aspect of this new book's approach is that much of the real-world complexity is addressed by thoughtfully tailoring the overall planning process to accommodate the cultural stresses and strains within the enterprise. This frequently facilitates the use of very simple conceptual and operational tools that build on sophisticated underlying conceptual and operational tools. 'Systematic simplicity' is an excellent description for this approach. For example, as discussed in Chapter 6, simple but effective quantitative probabilistic analysis can be used when assessing competitor behaviour in a bidding context based on work Chris did with IBM UK and earlier work with BP International, but qualitative cultural issues also need attention, like a corporate understanding of the difference between good luck and good management, bad luck and bad management, and why people taking more risk knowing what they are doing can be crucial to organizational survival, explored in detail in Chapter 3.

I also like the 'systematic simplicity' approaches to cultural concerns, including sound ethics. For example, Figure 11.1 in the last chapter uses a 'red face test' notion Chris attributes to me, but what I particularly like is the way this simple ethical test is linked to more general 'frowns test' and 'smiles test' variants, driven by a systematic approach to important concerns which are not amenable to simple metrics but need simple systematic attention. Examples used earlier in the book in the IBM based bidding example in Chapter 6 include staff being needed if the bid is won who are already heavily committed to other crucial contracts (a 'frown') and a bid in a new area of business the company doing the bidding wants to develop expertise for with a view to future business (a 'smile'). Railway safety as addressed in Chapter 9 raises more complex ethical issues involving trade-offs between monetary costs, avoided fatalities and avoided injuries, and these ethical issues are crucial and current in a wide range of important contexts.

Professor Jeffrey K. Pinto, Black Chair in Technology Management, Penn State University, USA.

Creating and managing knowledge as it applies to project management has, at times, taken on the nature of a Sisyphean labour. At an age when project-based work has grown ever more common and projects of the broadest array – infrastructure, information systems, new technology and services development – represent real opportunities to advance the human condition, our understanding of how best to manage them for maximum value often remains mired in misapplication, flawed thinking, and a variety of personal and organizational biases. In short, the dichotomy is real and it is growing: between, on the one hand, the increased need for organizational undertakings best supported by projects and project management and on the other, the seemingly intractable challenges in advancing our knowledge base sufficiently to gain best use from our efforts. The data support this contradiction: the Project Management Institute reports that for every billion USD invested in projects, some 125 million USD is classified 'at risk', a figure that is actually growing at double digits year-on-year. Failure rates in IT projects are high and have remained depressingly stable for well over a decade. The data are clear: the need for projects is at an all-time high while the manner in which practitioners and academics alike deliver on this promise remains mired.

It is against this backdrop: a time for projects that is both highly exciting in its possibilities and rather sterner in its realization, that Professor Chris Chapman's book is so welcome. The underlying premise of his work (and it is a message that is borne out again and again in projects great and small alike) focuses on the nature of project front-end planning and offers a deceptively simple message regarding what we keep getting wrong with these processes – we continue to make the simple difficult while making the difficult seem seductively simple. Professor Chapman has been one of the leading theorists and original, holistic thinkers in the project management discipline for several decades now. In 'Enlightened Planning', he brings his considerable talents to bear in a work that is compelling and powerful. It offers a new way of viewing the project planning process: one that directly considers the ways in which our organizations, culture, and processes can interact to get planning done the right way. Equally welcome is the manner in which Professor Chapman illustrates these ideas, through a series of compelling case examples that show in practice the principles he espouses. I have a strong admiration for this book. Terms like 'strategic clarity', 'enlightened planning' and 'systematic simplicity' are certain to become more than talking points; they offer the means to reorient our thinking. They cut right to the heart of what we need to be doing to put into practice effective project planning approaches. The framework provided also links this thinking directly to planning for operations management and corporate strategy formation concerns which are directly interrelated in important ways. The final result is a thought-provoking and important work for practitioners and scholars alike.

Professor Terry Williams is Director of the Risk Institute, University of Hull, UK.

As Professor and Head of the Management Science Department at Strathclyde University and a Professor and then Director of the Management School of the University of Southampton before coming to Hull, I have been aware of the work Chris was doing for many years. I invited him to be a key speaker at a Nato Science Programme conference in Kiev in 1996, used *Project Risk Management* (Chapman and Ward, 1997) in my book *Modelling Complex Projects* (Williams, 2002), which shares his (and my) 'practitioner who is also an academic' perspective, and invited him to contribute a chapter to my book *Project Governance: Getting Investment Right* (Williams and Samset, 2012). His new 'Enlightened Planning' book provides a reflective synthesis of his earlier work plus a comprehensive set of important new conceptual and operational tools with significant implications.

An irony of the risk management field is that it has become prone to the risk of standardized ways of considering and quantifying risk. The paper *Organising risk: discourse, power, and 'riskification'* (Hardy and Macquire, 2016) in the Academy of Management Review has shown how organisations and 'experts' in risk have developed a dominant discourse which limits the way we think about risk. What the field urgently needs is thinking that takes us to the basics of what risk and uncertainty are, and looks at them in a fresh way. This book is indeed such thinking, introducing important new fundamental concepts such as 'clarity efficiency' and the 'estimation-efficiency spectrum' (although keeping some well-used ideas from previous books such as the 'seven Ws'). Pleasingly, it aims to provide good estimates rather than the simple assumption of bias and the application of standardized contingency factors, often done following Flyvbjerg's work. Having edited a couple of books about planning projects with scant information, this book would have given us a really useful structure on which to consider the ideas with which we had to grapple and I hope its ideas are taken up by practitioners, academics, and also by the various bodies of knowledge.

Stephen Cresswell practises as Into Risk Ltd, London UK, www.intorisk.com

I have been an independent consultant for a decade, building on an earlier decade of experience, initially in business development in the IT and Telecoms industry, then as a project management consultant with Bombardier Transportation and the Sweett Group. My growing interest in risk and uncertainty led me to Chris's publications in the early 2000s and I took part in his 2006 International Project Management Association 'Managing Project Risk & Uncertainty in New Ways' Advanced Training Course in Copenhagen. This course and subsequent reading of his publications have been a key influence in my development as a 'reflective practitioner' – with many of the methodologies and approaches being applied, with success and benefit, in my client assignments. Particularly important was an appreciation of how to get beyond seeing 'risk' in terms of independent events, treat interdependencies effectively, and meet the challenges involved in persuading clients' personnel conditioned by simplistic approaches to change their approaches.

The 'enlightened planning' perspective explored in this new book involves deep thinking about strategy, uncertainty, complexity and implementation, with considerable attention to perspective and some philosophical aspects. However, this new book is also rich in simple tools and practical concepts and mantras that help with the 'how to do it' and 'craftsmanship' associated with planning and analysis in new ways. I fully anticipate using all aspects when faced with challenging problems. My favourite new concept is 'closure with completeness'. The basic underlying ideas have always been there in the approaches Chris has advocated, but they are now brought together, made explicit, and named. Closure with completeness gives a very concise plain English label and rationale for the inclusion of items such as an 'allowance for unidentified risk' in a project cost estimate. It also naturally prompts people to question whether the analysis addresses everything relevant.

This new book builds on a consolidation of an extensive research and consulting career, drawing on both successful applications of new ideas and some lessons learned the hard way. Reading this book from beginning to end was a serious challenge, but I expect to get large return on the time invested.

Mike Annon, PMP, is Owner of I&C Engineering Associates, Waterford CT, USA.

My 45 years of experience with over 50 nuclear energy and fossil fuelled power plant facilities in managerial and management consulting roles has convinced me that most organizations believe they know how to plan. However, too frequently they need to 'rescue' their plans at considerable cost with serious associated delays because their initial planning efforts were incomplete. Since the 1980s I have published, led workshops and managed projects with a focus on the processes, other tools and teamwork needed to 'get started on the right foot' and to rescue projects which failed to do so.

After I attended a 2009 professional training course in Chicago led by Chris based on the second edition of his book *Project Risk Management* (Chapman and Ward, 2003), I started to embed many of his ideas about new ways of looking at 'uncertainty', 'risk' and 'opportunity' in my work with clients. Contributing feedback comments on his book *How to Manage Project Opportunity and Risk* (Chapman and Ward, 2011) helped me to extend and update these ideas. His new 'Enlightened Planning' book has a wide range of further new ideas which will be incorporated into my planning efforts with future clients. I particularly like his new book's approach to visualising what I would term 'beginning with the end in mind', explicitly linking the assumed project lifecycle framework plus the 'seven Ws' framework and a 'goals-plans framework' to the project planning phase structure framework which integrates these four key frameworks. It helps with the front end of project management, and with integrating operations management and corporate management team concerns, to facilitate delivering what both the project owners and the project's ultimate 'customer' actually want by asking them the right questions at the right time and engaging in the right kind of dialogue.

Rodney Turner is now retired. Most recently he was Professor of Project Management at SKEMA Business School, in Lille, France, where he was Scientific Director for the PhD in Project and Program Management. Rodney is Vice President, Honorary Fellow and former Chairman of the UK's Association for Project Management, and Honorary Fellow and former President and Chairman of the International Project Management Association.

Consider a trio of quotations:

No battle plan ever survives first contact with the enemy.
Field Marshal Helmuth von Moltke

In preparing for battle I have always found that plans are useless, but planning is indispensable.
General Dwight D. Eisenhower

The perfect is the enemy of the good. By this I mean that a good plan violently executed now is better than a perfect plan next week. War is a very simple thing, and the determining characteristics are self-confidence, speed, and audacity. None of these things can ever be perfect, but they can be good.
General George S. Patton

The quotation by Field Marshal von Moltke can suggest there is no point planning, because the plans will be wrong. But President Eisenhower, while agreeing that the battle will not evolve as the plans envisage, suggests that the process of planning is essential, because it creates a strategy for the battle, and though the battle will not evolve as the plan envisages, having done the planning, we can understand what the likely scenarios are, and respond to the scenarios that occur. General Patton takes a slightly different approach. He starts by quoting Voltaire, and says we should not aim for the perfect plan, because we will already have lost the battle. But we should aim for a good plan, one of the defining characteristics of what Chris Chapman refers to as 'systematic simplicity'.

Henry Simon, in his concept of bounded rationality, agrees with these sentiments with ideas also supportive of a 'systematic simplicity' approach. We can never make a perfect decision, because we do not have all the information we need, we cannot perfectly analyse all the information we do have, and most importantly of all, we cannot foretell the future, so we do not know precisely how things will evolve. Therefore, we need to make good decisions, ones that satisfice, and not strive for perfect decisions.

Chris Chapman, in this unique book, explores how we can plan effectively in this uncertain environment. In Chapter 2 he introduces a universal planning and complexity management process that outlines how we can be better able to respond as plans unfold. This process is based on 'systematic simplicity', with the aim of providing good plans, based on sound interpretation of the data plus wider possibilities. In Chapter 3 he introduces a range of approaches to uncertainty using this process – the plan will not evolve precisely as envisaged, and we can't predict the future, but we can make forecasts within sensible ranges, and plan effectively for likely scenarios. Chapters 4 to 7 further explain the use of these systematic simplicity ideas in project management areas where Chris has an established international reputation and related operations management areas. Chapter 8 addresses strategy formation and corporate planning, and Chapter 9 expands further when low probability but very high impact scenarios may be involved, on planning for the likely and unlikely scenarios, understanding the possible range of outcomes, and developing robust plans that are appropriately prudent.

This book will be invaluable to anyone involved in strategic planning or corporate decision making as well as those interested in project planning.

Martin Hopkinson is a project risk professional and author based in Winchester, UK.

With the advent of computerised tools, our business and project planning processes have evolved to demand ever increasing levels of breakdown and detail. This book identifies why this approach has become less enlightened than we might think. For example, projects often maintain schedules with thousands of activities, employing a team of planners to keep abreast of the myriad of changes as they occur. Chris Chapman describes how these projects could improve their estimates, make better decisions and foster a progressive planning culture by limiting the number of activities to 75 or fewer. His approach involves understanding activities, interdependencies and the implications of uncertainty in greater depth. It is underpinned by a welcome clarity about the assumptions that we make when planning, often without noticing.

The book is illustrated with practical examples drawn from the author's long experience of working with businesses and government departments in a wide range of different industries and countries. If you deploy only some of the tools and techniques that are described, it is difficult to see how your planning process cannot become more enlightened.

Jesper Schreiner, Managing Director, Danish Project Management Association.

I attended the Copenhagen IPMA advanced training programme on Project Risk Management provided by Chris in 2012, subsequently used his ideas as a practitioner and as a teaching consultant, and contributed a two hour session to his 2017 IPMA programme as a Visiting Speaker, discussing my experience putting his ideas into practice with clients, so I was familiar with his overall approach when reading his new 'Enlightened Planning' book.

What I particularly like about this new book is the way Chapter 1 clarifies key basic concepts like the relationship between opportunity, risk, uncertainty and underlying complexity, and Chapter 3 then clarifies the relationship between all the components of his 'opportunity efficiency' concept, using practical examples based on his work with BP, IBM UK, the UK MoD and other clients.

I also like the Chapter 7 ideas which are new to me – in particular breaking down the current practice silos within project management between risk management, estimating and other aspects of planning.

I find the new 'Enlightened Planning' book – and the embedded mindset of systematic simplicity – a very useful contemporary contribution to a better understanding of the fundamental complexity often encountered in the handling and the clarifying of risk and opportunities for better management decision making.

Dr Dale F Cooper, Director, Broadleaf Capital International, www.Broadleaf.com.au

Chris Chapman has written an important but challenging book. It is important because it addresses matters central to most organisations: how to make important decisions when confronted by significant uncertainty. I shall return to the challenges later.

This book describes two journeys. The first is the one we readers are invited to join, an intellectual exploration as concepts are developed from relatively simple matters through to ideas that seem deceptively simple at first but are embedded in a subtle matrix of nuance that requires profound understanding and interpretation. The second is Chris Chapman's own journey along roughly the same route, but with many of the bumps and wrinkles smoothed out to make the lives of his readers easier. This second journey, interwoven through the first, provides the justification for the steps along the way. It explains the practical circumstances in which the main concepts were developed, with case studies from some of Chris's large clients emphasising the significant practical value and the substantial benefits that can be obtained for modest investments of time and effort.

Here I must declare an interest. I joined Chris at the University of Southampton in 1978. With a background in operational research and mathematical modelling, an understanding of psychology and a fascination with decision-making, I was drawn quickly into risk management with Chris. Our first work together was with Acres, examining the reliability of an LNG facility proposed for the high Arctic, using software Chris had developed with BP and adapted by us for the specific reliability context, combined with semi-Markov analysis that seemed innovative at the time. We went on to work together on other large projects: hydroelectric developments in Alaska and northern Alberta, upstream oil and gas off Newfoundland and oil and gas pipeline transport in Alaska, some of which are described in this book. Although our paths have diverged geographically since then, and we often use slightly different words to describe similar things, the approaches I learned from Chris, and those we developed together, are still central to my own international risk management practice.

In particular, my risk management work has always had a strong focus on practical value, on how risk management can be used to support better decisions, with a clear recognition that analysis by itself is not sufficient. This is echoed strongly in this book: uncertainty must be analysed, but only so far as is necessary to add value and make a sound decision, one that can be explained and justified clearly to stakeholders. Enlightened planning, as described by Chris in this book, provides a window into how this might be achieved.

Some of the core concepts in this book that I still use regularly (albeit sometimes using different words) are risk efficiency and opportunity efficiency, diagrams like histogram and activity trees that explore and explain important uncertainties and their inter-relationships, graphs that demonstrate key sensitivities and their practical implications, and illustrations of the differences between options so decision makers can evaluate outcomes outside the constraints of simplistic one-dimensional metrics.

Another important concept that resonates strongly with me and my colleagues at Broadleaf is that developing an understanding of the structure of uncertainty is an unequivocally necessary precursor to quantification. We have seen far too many examples of quantitative models where understanding was clearly lacking and the outcomes were at best misleading, often technically incorrect and at worst fatally flawed.

A core concept that Chris develops is clarity efficiency. This reflects the notion that there should be a balance between the amount of effort that is devoted to exploring important decisions (with the context and uncertainty that surrounds them) and the understanding that is generated for those who must make those decisions. Making such trade-offs is a critical part of enlightened planning, just as it is of risk management as we practise it.

This brings me back to the challenging aspect of this book – you need to read it carefully and with close attention to detail to form the necessary understanding and to get the most from it. There is no 'magic formula' that you can extract and apply in a few minutes. The answer does not leap off the page, but must be absorbed as concepts are developed along the path described here. You must follow the path, without shortcuts, to gain the enlightenment that Chris offers. Your understanding will almost certainly be different in detail from Chris's or mine, but the effort you apply will be well worthwhile.

Michael Pidd is Professor Emeritus of Management Science in the Lancaster University Management School. He is a Past President of the Operational Research Society, a Fellow of the British Academy of Management and a Fellow of the Academy of Social Sciences.

Systematic simplicity, via enlightened planning, is the main theme of this welcome book from Chris Chapman. Why is it welcome? Stories of large projects that exceed their initial cost estimates or fail altogether are easy to find in the media. It's easy to criticise, but much harder to show all relevant parties how things could be done better. Introducing significant change in an organisation is never easy. Why is it never easy? Because any major corporate change requires a response that links and integrates operations management, project management and corporate management. Successfully managing such changes is particularly difficult.

Chris addresses this complex challenge using a very broadly grounded 'enlightened planning' approach based on many years as a professor and international consultant. The scope of the material covered, the broad intended audience, and the demonstration of important nuances involved in practice are discussed using case studies, which explore qualitative as well as qualitative concerns.

As Chris Chapman puts it, 'there are no silver bullets, but some approaches are much better than others'. Operational Research and Management Science are sometimes defined as 'The science of better'. This fits well the book's advocacy of a 'systematic simplicity' approach based on rigorous analysis and practical insights.

About the author

The systematic simplicity approach to managing decisions advocated by this book was synthesised from a career based on pursuing a practice-research-teaching-practice cycle for about 50 years. Improving practice was always a central goal in this iterative process. Understanding the way my pursuit of this goal evolved in a chronological order with a kind of detail most authors do not provide may help you to better understand what this book is about and why it takes the form employed – that is the rationale for the approach taken to the next few pages. It should also help to underpin the candid conversational style including discussion of the way my thinking evolved used throughout this book, a style which seemed essential given the nature of the intended messages and some of the controversy.

I was born and brought up in Toronto. A University of Toronto BASc in Industrial Engineering (1962) and a University of Birmingham MSc in Operational Research (1964) provided my initial academic grounding. An Athlone Fellowship funded by the UK Board of Trade gave me the opportunity to spend 1962-4 in the UK.

1964-5 was spent as an IBM computer sales trainee in Toronto. This built on computer systems experience working for IBM in Toronto for three summers during my undergraduate degree, plus a year working in a project planning systems development role with Ferranti in London as the first part of the Athlone Fellowship. Working for IBM Canada initially, and then seeing where that led, was the 'career plan A' adopted while still an undergraduate.

In 1965 an offer of a lectureship (assistant professorship) in econometrics from Gordon Fisher was accepted – the opportunity was unanticipated but too good to miss. Gordon had taught one of my University of Birmingham MSc programme econometrics options, and the following year he founded the Econometrics Department at the University of Southampton as its first Professor of Econometrics. For nine years my career focus was managing a new MSc programme in Economics, Econometrics and Operational Research (OR), designing and teaching the OR content, and completing a PhD in consumer behaviour theory as a staff candidate supervised by the economist Professor Ivor Pearce. The PhD shaped my view of 'separability' and several closely coupled concepts which underlie the foundations of this book as a whole, building on Pearce (1964). It also provided a deep understanding of the foundations of risk management central to this book, building on Markowitz (1959). During this period, I developed a passion for research into the issues exposed by practice, initially centred on the development of consumer behaviour theory to support marketing decision making for the UK Milk Marketing Board. I also started to acquire a passion for consulting. One key client was Buckinghamshire County Council. On Gordon Fisher's recommendation they hired me as an expert witness to help stop a 'Third London Airport' being built at Cublington. The economists David Pearce and John Wise were recruited to help, working as a fully integrated partnership. The Cublington recommendation was scrapped. We obviously cannot take full credit, but I believe we were on the right side of a complex cost-benefit analysis based argument, and some of the issues and approaches are directly related to the overall shape of a systematic simplicity approach. During this period I became a senior lecturer (associate professor) and served as the assistant dean of my faculty (Social Sciences). Taken as a whole, this period was a central part of an extensive apprenticeship which significantly shaped my perspective and career choices. I had not seriously considered an academic career or living in England until Gordon's offer, but never regretted my 1965 largely intuitive change of mind, despite ongoing uncertainty about the permanence of these decisions for 20 years.

For 15 months in 1974-5 I worked full-time with Acres Consulting Services in Canada. This opportunity was initiated by a three-month consultancy assignment invitation from Oskar Sigvaldason. Oskar was then head of Acres Special Services Department, later president of Acres. I learned a lot about consulting, including key teamworking and client management concerns. One key study relevant to this book was leading the risk and uncertainty analysis of a proposal to reduce by one year the construction duration of a pipeline to bring high Arctic gas to US markets. Another was a comparison of Canadian and US design regulations for nuclear power stations in relation to seismic (earthquake) risk. I built a lasting relationship with Acres. However, the offer of a permanent full-time role with Acres in Canada was declined. I returned to the Department of Economics in the University of Southampton, which had absorbed Econometrics while I was away. Working for Acres was immensely stimulating, and my wife Jean and I and our two young sons greatly enjoyed living in Niagara-on-the-Lake. However, with a young family I was not prepared to accommodate commuting to clients in Calgary, Edmonton, Ottawa and similar locations for a week at a time for a significant proportion of the year, and for a complex set of reasons on balance an academic career base in the UK seemed the best feasible choice.

For the next decade one focal area of my career was consulting to help clients build processes and embedded model sets which addressed problem areas with no available off-the-shelf approaches. Through Robin Charlwood, an Acres colleague, I established an eight-year relationship with BP International in London. I helped BP to develop planning and costing approaches for their North Sea operations, adopted by BP for worldwide use on all large or sensitive projects for more than a decade. In this period BP projects using the approaches I helped to develop were generally within time and cost commitments, with no surprises which could not be accommodated. Through Oskar Sigvaldason, Robin Charlwood, Gavin Warnock and several other Acres colleagues I also worked with Acres teams for other clients in Canada and the USA, building on the BP work, with any lengthy assignments scheduled so that my family could accompany me. Illustrative key clients included: Gulf Canada (Beaufort Sea and Grand Banks oil and gas project design studies, including the Hibernia oil production platform project off the east coast of Canada, where icebergs were a key concern, and platform cost uncertainty coupled to oil reserve volume uncertainty plus oil price uncertainty proved critical); Petro-Canada (a design strategy study for a pilot liquefied natural gas (LNG) project on Melville Island in the high Arctic); Fluor Engineers and Contractors Inc (a design study addressing how best to get a proposed 48 inch gas pipeline across the Yukon River in close proximity to an existing 48 inch oil line, with a wide range of relevant threats and interested parties); Potomac Electric Power Company and the US Department of Energy (comparison of energy storage via pumped hydro or compressed air in deep mines). Research driven by my consulting interests was published and I became a Reader in Management Science. The other focal area of my career during this period was helping Professor Ken Hilton develop the Department of Accounting and Management Science, which he extracted from the Department of Economics with my support. As well as teaching, I managed new MSc programmes and undertook various other academic roles. This period put into practice the maturing practice-research-teaching-practice basis of this book, initiating and shaping some of the basic ideas.

For nearly a decade the focus of my career then shifted significantly. I had become a Professor of Management Science with a personal chair, and Head of the Department of Accounting and Management Science. I now made a full commitment to maintaining an academic career base. Ken Hilton had increased the size of our department by 50%. I increased it by a further 100%, adding two new groups with professorial leadership: Finance & Banking and Information Systems. My consultancy became more UK focussed. I started accepting invitations to work through UK-based consultants, including work with Sir William Halcrow and Partners which had a significant impact on my thinking about important sources of risk that were difficult to quantify. Some consultancy was undertaken through the university. Examples central to this book include several studies helping National Power to develop BP-type approaches to building electricity generation stations, and a series of studies over the period 1993-5 helping UK Nirex to plan a repository for nuclear waste disposal and deal with Department of the Environment (DoE) arguments about deferring the project. The DoE adopted an HM Treasury mandated real discount rate of 6% when 3% would have been more appropriate in terms of my arguments at the time. HM Treasury's own post-2003 advice is consistent with my 3%, for directly related but different reasons. These issues are important in private as well as public sector contexts, and the reasons are explored briefly in Chapter 12. I pursued research conventionally funded by research councils and professional bodies as well as the MoD and other organisations, some directly relevant to this book. Involvement with professional bodies began, including accepting an invitation to act as founding chair for the Association for Project Management (APM) Specific Interest Group on Project Risk Management. I started to spend more time teaching experienced managers, including a significant culture change programme for IBM UK, their 'Forum 2' programme. This was a two-day in-house event run about 40 times, introduced by their CEO on each occasion, built around my input, central to this book's Part 1 discussion. This wider set of activities and concerns reduced the time available for consultancy, but it did not weaken the practice-research-teaching-practice basis of my career, and prototype variants of many of the key ideas in this book matured during this period.

A five-year break from university management roles then involved a different shift in focus, centred around two years as President of the Operational Research Society.

Three years as Director of the Southampton University Management School (SUMS) then involved a new university management role. I was appointed Director with a transformation mandate by a new Vice-Chancellor. While I had been Head of the Department of Accounting and Management Science the University had established SUMS as a separate Management School to provide MBAs and other post-experience courses. My advice to avoid making these activities separate was rejected, but SUMS had my support once that decision had been made. The new Vice-Chancellor wanted SUMS fully integrated with the University, located on campus, made profitable, and made reputable in research terms. These objectives were achieved in the planning horizon which I eventually set myself. My successful exit strategy from my role as director involved recommending that the current Head of the Department of Accounting and Management Science took over as director of a new Management School created by a full merger of SUMS plus the department, with me in supporting roles to help complete the transition. Outcomes included doubling MSc and MBA student numbers, an RAE (Research Assessment Exercise) rating of five (the top rating on the scale used for UK research assessment at that time) for the new Management School, and strengthened relationships with the faculties of Engineering and Mathematics. The latter was facilitated by founding the Centre for Operational Research, Management Science and Information Systems (CORMSIS), with the director's post alternating every two years between Management and Mathematics, initially held by the Professor of OR in Mathematics, Paul Williams. The new School of Management has continued to evolve, becoming the Southampton Business School (SBS) in 2014. CORMSIS has thrived with a series of directors focussed on collaboration within and beyond the university, the sustained efforts of the directors, industrial liaison officers and members working as a team being particularly important. A separate but overlapping Centre for Risk Research (CRR), founded in 1990 by Johnnie Johnson (Management/SBS), which he led with great success until retiring at the end of 2018, also thrives and continues to evolve, with Ian Dawson's very able leadership at present. Both centres embrace an emphasis on practice and a broadly defined perspective.

From 1991 until 1993 I served as an expert witness providing a critical review of Ontario Hydro's strategic plans for the next 25 years, central to Chapter 9 in this book.

In 1992 and 1996 I served as a Business and Management Studies panel member for the Research Assessment Exercise (RAE). The judgements of these panels determined the distribution of the research funding component of the UK government's university funding for business and management for two four-year periods. At the invitation of the panel's chair as his 'quantitative analysis expert' I unobtrusively but explicitly confronted the management and governance implications of different people arguing for different weightings when using quantitative measures of attributes which do not lend themselves to simple metrics plus important non-measurable concerns when important decisions have to be made by a group of people with very different perspectives and agendas, and the need to use available measures coherently as far as possible, issues which are central to this book as a whole.

In 1999 I was elected an Honorary Fellow of The Institute of Actuaries. My work on their joint working parties with the Institution of Civil Engineers on risk management guides addressing projects, then whole enterprises, then operations, shaped the three-component separability structure for all management decision making adopted by this book.

From 1997 to 2003 I served as a non-executive director of Southern Water, with three different chairmen of the board and three different ownership structures, useful in terms of direct governance experience and more general background experience.

There are a number of relevant differences between advising other organisations and taking your own advice when directly engaged in management and governance functions. My operations, project and corporate management experience as a head of an academic department, my change management experience as a management school director, a variety of other academic and professional roles, and my board level governance experience as a Southern Water non-executive director, all reinforced my consultancy experience in a manner relevant to the overall 'practice basis' for this book. They were all modest roles in corporate terms, and you may not see universities as 'commercial organisations', but each helped to shape and let me directly test some of the concepts and other tools discussed in this book, and they all influenced my views on requisite skillsets and mindsets in ways directly relevant to this book. They were an integral part of the education and practical experience basis that underlies my current perspective. That is the primary reason for mentioning them here, as part of explaining 'where I am coming from' to help you see where this book might take you.

In 2004 I retired from my full-time academic post. I was made an Emeritus Professor, with a part-time contract for teaching and research, and accepted an invitation from Mike Nichols to become a Senior Associate of the Nichols Group. Three subsequent consultancy studies are relevant to this book.

In 2005 I worked in Venice with Gavin Warnock and Robin Charlwood, renewing our Acres connections begun in 1974. Both had been Acres vice-presidents, but now had their own consultancy companies, Gavin based in Edinburgh, Robin in Seattle. We worked through Gavin's Monitor (International) Ltd. Our client was Consorzio Venezia Nuova, the contractor for the MOSE flood protection scheme for Venice. We were successful in persuading the government that the cost estimates had to be significantly increased because earlier risk provisions based on conventional 'received wisdom' estimation methodologies were biased on the optimistic side. The MOSE project proceeded, with construction completed and the results tested for the first time in 2020. This study helped to shape Part 1 ideas.

In 2006 and 2007 I worked with Mike Nichols and a small team to help him write a report for the Secretary of State for Transport which explained why UK Highways Agency cost estimates were consistently optimistically biased, despite following HM Treasury guidelines on these issues, and what to do about it. I then supported a team of Nichols consultants help the Highways Agency start to implement our recommendations, initially revising all current cost estimates in a manner approved and supported by HM Treasury. At that time Mike Nichols was Chairman of the Association for Project Management. We met when he chaired the joint working party of the Institution of Civil Engineers and the Institute and Faculty of Actuaries that I served on which produced the *RAMP Risk Analysis and Management of Projects* (1998 and 2005) guides. These Highways Agency studies and the RAMP guides also helped to shape Part 1, especially Chapter 6.

From 2010 until 2013 I provided advice to the UK Ministry of Defence (MoD) on appropriate frameworks for justifying high levels of expenditure on preventative and mitigating measures for low probability non-conventional weapon attacks on troops, a form of analysis also relevant to terrorist activities. A generalisation of the framework developed underpins Chapter 13, along with earlier work on strategic approaches to safety for Railtrack.

The book *How to Manage Project Opportunity and Risk: Why Uncertainty Management Can Be a Much Better Approach than Risk Management* (Chapman and Ward, 2011) was the extensively rewritten and retitled third edition of *Project Risk Management: Processes, Techniques and Insights* (Chapman and Ward, 1997 and 2003). The 1997 first edition was a critically acclaimed modest bestseller, with roughly a third of its sales in Europe, a third in North America, a third in the rest of the world. Significant evolution in perspective was involved in the 2003 and 2011 editions.

The *Enlightened Planning* book continued the evolution outlined by Chapman and Ward (2011), developing it from a much broader perspective. Its evolution was the focus of my professional activities until 2019. I used it to teach the 2020 version of my Project Risk Management MSc course, attended by 250 students from about ten MSc programmes.

Promoting the use of the underlying systematic simplicity approach in the ways outlined by this book is central to my current and future professional goals.

Acknowledgements

Stephen Ward reviewed several drafts of this book and made significant contributions to its final form. Since the 1980s Stephen has always brought a highly constructive and candid critical perspective to everything I have written or we have written jointly. In addition, many of the underlying concepts in this book were originally created directly by Stephen or they were inspired by his original ideas. For example, Stephen's redefinition of the well-known 'keep it simple, stupid' acronym KISS as 'keep it simple systematically', which we adopted in the 1990s as a basic mantra, was the inspiration for the term 'systematic simplicity', building on his earlier notion of 'constructive simplicity' (Ward, 1989).

I am grateful to all of the colleagues whose endorsements for the book *Enlightened Planning* are reproduced in the first backmatter section of this book – for that contributed to this book, but also for their earlier contributions to this book's underlying ideas. The nature of those earlier contributions varies greatly, and elaboration here would not be appropriate, but they were all much appreciated.

Many other colleagues and friends have also contributed key concepts, ideas and support over many years, and I would like to thank them all without attempting a list of names that would inevitably fall short even if it was unbearably lengthy.

Ruth Lunn, the Lead Editor at UK Book Publishing, has been very helpful, and I am very grateful for an excellent start to what I hope will be a productive partnership with all of her colleagues.

Taylor and Francis Group, LLC, a division of informa plc, have kindly granted permission to reproduce variants of diagrams used in their Routledge imprint book *Enlightened Planning*, the source of all this book's figures.

I have a very supportive family, who have helped with this book directly and indirectly in various ways. Carol Chapman, one of my two greatly cherished daughters-in-law, has recently discovered a rapidly developing talent as an artist. Her pastel drawing of an owl is reproduced on the front cover, and I am very grateful for her permission to use it. To me the very striking eye looking at us captures the wisdom traditionally symbolised by owls which we all seek whatever our approach to managing the way we make decisions, and I hope you see this symbology as appropriate for this book.

References

APM (1997) *PRAM Project Risk Analysis and Management Guide*. Association for Project Management (APM), Norwich.

APM (2004) *PRAM Project Risk Analysis and Management Guide*, second edition. Association for Project Management (APM), Norwich.

Black, W. (2017) *Originals: How non-conformists will ultimately disrupt the world of Risk Management*. Downloaded from www.linkedin.com/pulse/orginals-how-non-conformists-ultimately-disrupt-world-warren-black , 12 May 2017.

Cabinet Office (2017) *Management of Risk in Government: Framework*. Downloaded from www.gov.uk/government/publications/management-of-risk-in-government-framework to use to access Annex D documents, 18 January 2021.

Chapman, C.B. (1974) Modular portfolio selection: an introduction, in Dickinson, J.P. (editor), *Portfolio Analysis: Book of Readings*. Saxon House/Lexington Books, Farnborough.

Chapman, C.B. (1975) *Modular Demand Analysis: An Introduction in the Context of a Theoretical Basis for Consumer Demand Analysis*. Saxon House/Lexington Books, Farnborough.

Chapman, C.B. (1979) Large engineering project risk analysis. *IEEE Transactions on Engineering Management*, EM-26, 78–86.

Chapman, C.B. (1992a) My two cents' worth on how OR should develop. *Journal of the Operational Research Society*, 43(7), 647-664.

Chapman, C.B. (1992b) *Risk Management: Predicting and Dealing with an Uncertain Future*. Exhibit #748, Province of Ontario Environmental Assessment Board Hearings on Ontario Hydro's Demand/Supply Plan, submitted by the Independent Power Producers Society of Ontario, 30 September.

Chapman, C.B. (2006) Key points of contention in framing assumptions for risk and uncertainty management. *International Journal of Project Management*, 24, 303-313.

Chapman, C.B. (2019) *Enlightened Planning: Using Systematic Simplicity to Clarify Opportunity, Risk and Uncertainty for **Much Better** Management Decision Making*. Routledge, Abingdon and New York. (Copyright date 2020)

Chapman, C.B. and Cooper, D.F. (1983) Parametric discounting. *Omega— International Journal of Management Science*, 11(3), 303–310.

Chapman, C.B. and Cooper, D.F. (1985) A programmed equity redemption approach to the finance of public projects. *Managerial and Decision Economics*, 6(2), 112-18.

Chapman, C.B. and Howden, M. (1997) Two phase parametric and probabilistic NPV calculations, with possible deferral of disposal of UK Nuclear Waste as an example. *Omega, International Journal of Management Science*, 25(6), 707-14.

Chapman, C.B. and Ward, S.C. (1997) *Project Risk Management: Processes, Techniques and Insights*. John Wiley and Sons, Chichester.

Chapman, C.B. and Ward, S.C. (2002) *Managing Project Risk and Uncertainty: A Constructively Simple Approach to Decision Making*. John Wiley and Sons, Chichester.

Chapman, C.B. and Ward, S.C. (2003) *Project Risk Management: Processes, Techniques and Insights*, second edition. John Wiley and Sons, Chichester.

Chapman, C.B. and Ward, S.C. (2004) Why risk efficiency is a key aspect of best practice projects, *International Journal of Project Management*, 22(8), 1050-1058.

Chapman, C.B. and Ward, S.C. (2011) *How to Manage Project Opportunity and*

*Risk: Why **Uncertainty** Management Can Be a **Much** Better Approach than **Risk** Management*, retitled third edition of 'Project Risk Management' 1997 and 2003. John Wiley and Sons, Chichester.

Chapman, C.B., Ward, S.C. and Klein, J.H. (2006) An optimized multiple test framework for project selection in the public sector, with a nuclear waste disposal case-based example. *International Journal of Project Management*, 24, 373-384.

DoE (1994) *Review of Radioactive Waste Management Policy Preliminary Conclusions: A Consultative Document, Radioactive Substances Division*. Department of the Environment (DoE), Room A523, Romney House, 43 Marsham Street, London SW1P 3P4.

Flyvbjerg, B., Bruzelius, N. and Rothengatter, W. (2003) *Megaprojects and Risk: An Anatomy of Ambition*. Cambridge University Press, Cambridge.

Gawande, A. (2011) *The Checklist Approach: How to Get Things Right*. Profile Books Ltd, London.

Hardy, C. and Macquire, S. (2016) Organising risk: discourse, power and "riskification". *Academy of Management Review*, 41(1), 80-108.

Hawkins, C.J. and Pearce, D.W. (1971) *Capital Investment Appraisal*. Macmillan Studies in Economics, Macmillan, London.

HM Treasury (2003a) *The Green Book: Appraisal and Evaluation in Central Government*. HM Treasury, 1 Horse Guards Road, London SW1A 2HQ.

HM Treasury (2003b) *The Green Book Supplementary Guidance – Optimism Bias*. Downloaded from www.hm-treasury.gov.uk , November 2010.

HM Treasury (2014) *Improving Infrastructure Delivery: Project Initiation Routemap Handbook*. Downloaded from www.gov.uk/government/organisations/ infrastucture-uk , February 2015.

HM Treasury (2020a) *The Green Book: Appraisal and Evaluation in Central Government.* Downloaded from Annex D of Cabinet Office (2017).

HM Treasury (2020b) *The Orange Book: Management of Risk – Principles and Concepts.* Downloaded from Annex D of Cabinet Office (2017).

Hopkinson, M., Close, P., Hillson, D. and Ward, S. (2008) *Prioritising Project Risks: A Short Guide to Useful Techniques.* Association for Project Management (APM), Princes Risborough, Bucks.

Hyde, L. (2007) *The Gift: How the Creative Spirit Transforms the World.* Cannongate, Edinburgh. First published in the US and Canada in 1983 by Random House.

ICE and IFoA (1998) *RAMP Risk Analysis and Management for Projects.* Institution of Civil Engineers (ICE) and the Institute and Faculty of Actuaries (IFoA). Thomas Telford, London.

ICE and IFoA (2005) *RAMP Risk Analysis and Management for Projects – A Strategic Framework for Managing Project Risk and its Financial Implications,* second edition. Institution of Civil Engineers (ICE) and the Institute and Faculty of Actuaries (IFoA). Thomas Telford, London.

Kahneman, D. (2012). *Thinking, Fast and Slow.* Penguin Books, London.

Keeney, R.L. and Raiffa, H. (1976) *Decisions with Multiple Objectives.* John Wiley and Sons, New York.

Markowitz, H. (1959) *Portfolio Selection: Efficient Diversification of Investments.* John Wiley and Sons, New York.

Nichols, M. (2007) *Review of Highways Agency's Major Roads Programme: Report to the Secretary of State for Transport.* Nichols Group London. Available on the Department for Transport (UK) website at www.dft.gov.uk/pgr/roads/nicholsreport/ .

Pearce, I.F. (1964) *A Contribution to Demand Analysis*. Oxford University Press, Oxford.

Rail Safety & Standards Board (2006) RSSB T430 – *Definition of VPF & the Impact of Societal Concerns – Final* 30/1/2006. Oxford Risk Research and Analysis, Clarendon Enterprise Centre, Oxford.

Tamiz, M., Jones, D. and Romero, C. (1998) Goal programming for decision making: An overview of the current state-of-the-art. *European Journal of Operational Research*, 111, 569-81.

Ward, S.C. (1989) Arguments for constructively simple models. *Journal of the Operational Research Society*, 40(2), 141–153.

Williams, T.M. (2002) *Modelling Complex Projects*. John Wiley and Sons, Chichester.

Williams T.M. and Samset, K.J. (2012) *Project Governance: Getting Investments Right*. Palgrave Macmillan, Basingstoke.

Website information

A website for the book *Enlightened Planning* (Chapman, 2019) may be accessed currently using www.enlightenedplanning.uk . It was established in July 2019.

When this website also becomes accessible using the address www.systematicsimplicity.uk after this book is published, the website's role will be updated and extended to promote the systematic simplicity ideas underlying both books to a wider audience and support those who want to use this book as well as *Enlightened Planning* or other related books when leading courses and workshops designed for people interested in any areas, aspects and levels of management decision making. An important focus of this website will be supporting professional courses for practitioners and their managers at all levels, including board level managers. University courses will also continue to be addressed in a central manner. The website will concentrate on perspectives and areas of application where I have relevant experience to share in terms of slides, case studies and other material which might be useful.

How this website will evolve in the longer-term has not yet been determined, but my intention is to indicate websites with relevant papers and other material created by others that I am aware of with a view to drawing on related experience by others and contributing to a wider discussion of systematic simplicity approaches.

Printed in Great Britain
by Amazon